"My Hideous Progeny"

"My Hideous Progeny"

Mary Shelley, William Godwin, and the Father-Daughter Relationship

Katherine C. Hill-Miller

DELAWARE

Newark: University of Delaware Press
London: Associated University Presses

Associated University Presses
440 Forsgate Drive
Cranbury, NJ 08512

Associated University Presses
25 Sicilian Avenue
London WC1A 2QH, England

Associated University Presses
P.O. Box 338, Port Credit
Mississauga, Ontario
Canada L5G 4L8

The paper used in this publication meets the requirements of the American National Standard for Permanence of Paper for Printed Library Materials Z39.48–1984.

Library of Congress Cataloging-in-Publication Data

Hill-Miller, Katherine.
    "My hideous progeny" : Mary Shelley, William Godwin, and the father-daughter relationship / Katherine C. Hill-Miller.
        p. cm.
    Includes bibliographical references (p.) and index.
    ISBN 0-87413-535-4 (alk. paper)
    1. Shelley, Mary Wollstonecraft, 1797–1851—Criticism and interpretation. 2. Godwin, William, 1756–1836—Influence. 3. Shelley, Mary Wollstonecraft, 1797–1851—Family. 4. Fathers and daughters—Great Britain—History. 5. Fathers and daughters in literature. I. Title.
    PR5398.H5   1995   94-18535
    823'.7—dc20   CIP

PRINTED IN THE UNITED STATES OF AMERICA

Contents

Acknowledgments

Among the many writers and scholars who helped me during the preparation of this book, I owe special thanks to Carl Woodring and Nigel Nicolson for their support and encouragement. Thanks are also due to Donald Reiman, to Betty Bennett for information about the Godwin-Shelley correspondence, and to Charles Robinson, who read the manuscript with great care and sympathy. I am grateful to Bruce Barker-Benfield for his invaluable introduction to the Abinger papers at the Bodleian Library.

Friends and colleagues have been generous with their time and knowledge. I am especially indebted to Barry Nass, who read early versions of the manuscript. Thanks are also due to Susan Miller, Ann Landi, Margaret Schiller, Marge Hallissy, Norbert Krapf, Maithili Schmidt-Raghavan, Natascha Würzbach of the Universität zu Köln, Sally Ellis, and Mary Van Pala. My Eng 510 class read and responded to the manuscript when it was close to completion; thanks for this generosity to Christine Byron, Jeff Cox, Yuko Domo, David Fritz, Dale LaRocca, Liz Ranellone, Beth Shevell, and Gilbert Tippy.

The C. W. Post Research Committee funded this project over several years; I am deeply appreciative for the support of Geoffrey Berresford and Eric Walther. Walter Jones granted the academic leave that allowed me to put the finishing touches to the manuscript. I was aided often and skillfully by the staffs of the New York Public Library, the Columbia University Library, the Duke University Library, the London Library, and the British Library. Special thanks to Doucet Fischer at the Carl H. Pforzheimer Library; to Jo Bianco at the C. W. Post Library; and to Louis Pisha, who can find anything on a database.

For permission to quote from unpublished papers in the Abinger collection, I am deeply indebted to Lord Abinger. I am also grateful to the Johns Hopkins University Press for use of material from *The Letters of Mary Wollstonecraft Shelley* and *Daughters and Fathers;* to Oxford University Press for use of material from *The Journals of Mary Wollstonecraft Shelley* and *The*

Letters of Percy Bysshe Shelley; and to the University of North Carolina Press for use of material from *Mathilda.*

On a more personal note, I owe thanks to Pelly Ambata, Veronique Liethaert, and especially Denise Keyes, who always said, "Why doesn't Chris come to play with P. J.?" The deepest thanks must go to the people closest to me, who lived with this project for such a long time. Thanks to my son, Chris, who never complained when I couldn't be the den mother. Thanks to my husband, Fred, a brilliant editor and true feminist. I dedicate this book with love and gratitude to my mother, Genevieve Bytner Hill, who taught me how to combine work and motherhood, and to my father, M. Joseph Hill, who has edited my prose for as long as I can remember.

Introduction

This book examines a slice of Mary Wollstonecraft Shelley's life and work. Specifically, it analyzes the psychological and literary influence of William Godwin, Mary Shelley's father, on Shelley's choice of profession and her subsequent literary career.

"My Hideous Progeny": Mary Shelley, William Godwin, and the Father-Daughter Relationship began as a study of the more general question of literary daughters and their fathers—that is, as an examination of the various ways in which fathers who were writers trained their daughters to follow in their intellectual footsteps and the impact of this training on the daughter's life and ideas. History affords many examples of daughters who take up their fathers' work: Artemisia Gentileschi, the Renaissance painter; Elizabeth I, queen of England; Anna Freud, psychoanalyst. Because writing was for such a long time one of the few professions open to women, literary history provides even more examples of fathers who encouraged their daughters to make their living by their pens: Maria Edgeworth, Margaret Fuller, Anne Thackeray, Virginia Woolf. It was from this perspective that I first approached Mary Shelley and William Godwin with the idea of writing a single chapter for a more general book. But the case of Mary Shelley and William Godwin quickly demanded more space. While much had been written about the literary influence of Percy Bysshe Shelley on his wife, there was little available about the specific influence of Mary Shelley's earlier, and much longer-lasting, literary relationship to her father.[1] Further, while commentators had analyzed Shelley's *Frankenstein* from almost every conceivable viewpoint, little was written about Shelley's lesser-known novels, in which father-daughter relationships play a key role.[2] And the tie between Mary Shelley and her famous father provides such an idiosyncratic, yet oddly paradigmatic, example of a father-daughter relationship. Mary Shelley adored her father; she also felt deep hostility toward him, and expressed this combination of passionate attachment and anger in the pages of her novels. While Shelley's latent anger at her father was, of course, generated

9

by the specific circumstances of her upbringing, the development of their relationship follows one recognizable pattern in the relations between fathers and achieving daughters—a pattern that both suggests why some daughters write, and why, when they do, they take their fathers so much to task.

This study, then, has three major purposes. First, it seeks to illuminate the nature of William Godwin's influence on Mary Shelley. In her afterword to *Daughters and Fathers*, Carolyn Heilbrun describes three major ways in which fathers influence achieving daughters. In the first, the daughter's ambition is driven by the father's preference for sons and his apparent disappointment in the fact of the daughter's sex. In the second, the daughter hungers after the father's more exciting and attractive life, in comparison with that of any woman she knows. And in the third, the daughter develops ambition as a result of her father's support for her talents and intelligence, but then finds herself propelled into a world for which she is not fit, and in which she has no place.[3] This last pattern best describes the influence of William Godwin on Mary Shelley, with the refinement that it was Godwin himself who intermittently made his daughter feel unfit for the world to which he had trained her. Godwin fostered his daughter's literary ambitions and gave her the education she needed to be a writer. But as she entered adolescence, Godwin's response to his adoring daughter seemed to shift radically, and as she became a woman and mother, it shifted yet again.

These shifts in Godwin's attitude toward his talented daughter, and in Mary Shelley's subsequent attitude toward her father, provide the material for pursuing the second purpose of this book: using the relationship between Mary Shelley and William Godwin to illustrate both a typical pattern of female development and a typical course followed by father-daughter relationships over a lifetime. From one perspective, of course, the Godwins and the Shelleys are anything but typical. Their joint family history contains enough premarital affairs, illegitimate births, premature deaths, shocking elopements, and suicides to fit the requirements of a contemporary soap opera. But if one looks beneath the dramatic and romantic elements in the relationship between Mary Shelley and William Godwin—beyond Mary's brilliant dead mother, beyond Mary's apparently wicked stepmother, beyond Mary's adolescent elopement with a married poet—one can locate what is, in fact, one common pattern that characterizes the shifting relations between fathers and their talented daughters. During Mary Godwin's childhood, William Godwin gave his daughter much more than the usual female aspirations and education: he gave his daughter a "masculine" education and taught her, as his intellectual heir, to expect to inherit the prerogatives of literary sonship. Mary Godwin embraced her father's expectations passionately, but as Mary Godwin grew into adolescence and began to develop into a woman, her age, combined with the sexual dynamics of the father-daughter relationship, demanded that William Godwin alter his behavior. He withdrew his affection; he withdrew his professional support and encouragement. This apparent paternal rejection, set in the landscape of Mary Godwin's emergent womanhood, created a reservoir of hostility toward her father and catapulted her into female adulthood, a state that Gilbert and Gubar have described as being associated with "filthy materiality." Godwin appeared to reject his daughter as she became a woman; in Mary Godwin's eyes, this rejection robbed her of the prerogatives of sonship and pushed her, instead, into monstrous daughterhood.

After Mary Shelley became a wife and mother, William Godwin's attitude toward his daughter moved to a third stage. Having treated her as a son during her childhood, and having rejected her in the climate of her developing sexuality during her adolescence, Godwin expected maternal support and consolation from his daughter as he grew older. Mary Shelley responded to her father's expectations and cared for him, financially and emotionally, until the day he died. She became, apparently, the embodiment of the dutiful daughter. In fact, her lingering hostility toward her father was deflected and muted, and it expresses itself in the pages of her last novels. Ironically, Godwin's early "masculine" training made Mary Shelley as good a daughter as a son: as time passed, she earned enough by her pen to support herself, her son, and her aging father.

Since this book examines the development of a father-daughter relationship and, in that context, the growth of a girl from childhood to womanhood, it follows contemporary feminist revisions of psychoanalysis and discusses the fact of father-daughter incest. This is not to suggest that the relation between Mary Shelley and William Godwin was incestuous in any literal sense of the word—it most assuredly was not. But recent scholarship has paid increasing attention to what has been termed the father's "seduction" of his daughter, and to the incestuous patterns of emotion that structure the young girl's socialization into adult womanhood.[4] These incestuous patterns of emotion are certainly at work in the relationship between Mary Shelley and William Godwin. They play themselves out in the behavior of both father and daughter; they are central to most of the novels written by the daughter and to at least one novel written by the father. To assert that a young girl's upbringing is based on incestuous patterns of father-daughter behavior seems shocking initially. But in fact, such an assertion only affirms the obvious—at least if one believes in Freud's ideas about the fundamentally sexual nature of human drives and development. The term "incest," as used in this book, generally refers not to a physically intimate act but instead to the sexual, and therefore taboo, emotions that naturally and universally exist between fathers and daughters. From this perspective, the use of the term "incest" merely recognizes that parenthood is sexually charged; that children develop their gender identities and personalities by complicated, fundamentally sexual, responses to parents of both sexes; and that children and parents participate collectively in a "family romance" in which children mature by passionately attaching themselves to the parent of the opposite sex, and then giving up this attachment in favor of identification with the parent of the same sex.[5] In this sense, the little boy's development is as "incestuous" as the little girl's, since he matures by first wanting to marry his mother and kill his father—the traditional Freudian description of the male oedipal complex—and then giving up his passion for his mother in favor of identification with his father. But though incestuous emotions are part of the very fabric of the nuclear family as we know it, they also form the ground for the most widespread taboo in human culture. This study also takes as a given that sexually charged feelings between fathers and daughters, while normal and pervasive, are nonetheless associated with powerful taboos, and, as a result, the discovery of these emotions by parent or child leads to an unavoidable sense of guilt.

This book has a third, more fundamental purpose: analyzing Mary Shelley's response to her father's influence by studying how she portrays the figure of the father in the pages of her novels. The fact of daughterhood is the key to Mary Shelley's fiction, as it was to her life. All her novels examine daughterhood in some way; her first two and her last two focus on the condition of the daughter quite explicitly. And, as critics have often observed, mothers are absent or hidden in Mary Shelley's fiction. As a result, Shelley repeatedly defines daughterhood as the act of relating to a father or father-figure. From a biographical perspective, this definition is not surprising. Shelley's own mother, Mary Wollstonecraft, died shortly after her birth; Shelley subsequently fastened all her emotional energy on her father, her only remaining parent. Throughout her entire life, being a daughter meant relating to William Godwin in the real world and to her mother by an act of imagination. But Shelley's definition of daughterhood is compelling from a second perspective. In her insistence that being a daughter means relating to a father rather than a mother, Shelley focuses attention on the way women relate to the culture at large. That is, Shelley grasps the fact that fathers, not mothers, dominate and control the culture and the daughter's access to it; that fathers are more powerful than mothers in framing the way society sees and shapes its women. Therefore, in the realm of Mary Shelley's fiction, literal fathers also represent cultural fathers, and Shelley uses her stories about daughters, with all their autobiographical resonance, to explore and portray the nature of daughterhood itself. In this context, her fictional fathers, who are often patterned in some way on William Godwin, become emblematic of fatherhood itself and of the role of paternal power, authority, and sexuality in the daughter's life. Mary Shelley concludes that the father's influence makes daughterhood a disappointing and precarious state, a characterization that can be extended to the female condition itself.

To the extent this book examines the sexual dynamics of the "family romance," it also participates in the recent discourse concerning Mary Shelley's attitudes toward the institution of the nuclear family. The issue of "family" is an important matter for the woman writer generally. In Mary Shelley's case, it was a concern that often organized and dominated her life, impinging upon and informing her career as an author. Anne Mellor has concluded that Mary Shelley was committed to the institution of the bourgeois nuclear family and idealized it in her novels, even while acknowledging its flaws; Kate Ellis argues, to the contrary, that Shelley calls into question the very viability of the nuclear family as the nexus of domestic affections and as an instrument for human socialization.[6] It seems to me that Mary Shelley accepts the nuclear family as an unavoidable given, and therefore as the originating locus of human identity. In this context, she uses her novels to express and explore the nuclear family's sexual dynamics, especially from the point of view of the daughter. Since daughterhood is the universal female experience—a woman might not be a mother, sister, or lover, but a woman is always someone's daughter—Shelley's exploration of the "family romance" rings with particular resonance.

This book is organized into five chapters. The first chapter consists of a biographical essay that tells the story of the relationship between Mary Shelley and William Godwin, emphasizing Godwin's alternating encouragement and rejection of his daughter. Chapters 2 and 3 deal with *Frankenstein* and *Mathilda*, respectively, but read Mary Shelley's first two novels as a response to and reformulation of her adolescent experience. In a sense, Shelley uses her first two novels to define her position as a daughter, just as women writers define their position as authors. As Gilbert and Gubar put it, the woman writer in order to define herself as an author . . . must redefine the terms of her socialization. Her revisionary struggle, therefore, often becomes a struggle for what Adrienne Rich has called "Revision—the act of looking back, of seeing with fresh eyes, of entering an old text from a new critical direction . . . an act of survival." (*Madwoman in the Attic*, 49)

This same line of reasoning may be applied to Shelley's portrayal of the daughter's situation in *Frankenstein* and *Mathilda*. Shelley uses *Frankenstein* and *Mathilda* to tell the story of the daughter's socialization at the father's hands in a new way and thus redefines and controls that socialization's terms. To use Rich's language, Shelley sees her adolescent past with fresh eyes; she reenters the text of her own history—and, in the case of *Frankenstein*, the literal text of William Godwin's novels—from a new critical direction, for the purpose of rewriting. The result is a revisionary account of the genesis of womanhood, an explanation for the sources of the daughter's disappointed, and baffled, sense of guilt. Not surprisingly, the adored father appears at the center as both lover and villain.

Chapters 4 and 5 examine *Lodore* and *Falkner,* Mary Shelley's last two novels. Though very different in tone and apparent intent from her first two novels, *Lodore* and *Falkner* reexamine the daughter's relation to the father and draw many of the same conclusions. *Lodore* and *Falkner* were written against the backdrop of Shelley's maturity as she raised a son alone and struggled to cheer and support her aging father. *Lodore* and *Falkner* retrace some of the same ground as *Frankenstein* and *Mathilda:* the intense sexuality of the father-daughter tie, the role of the father in the daughter's socialization, the ability of the father to direct the daughter's destiny. But *Lodore* and *Falkner*, unlike *Frankenstein* and *Mathilda*, give the daughter some measure of ascendancy over the father. In Shelley's last two novels, the daughter paradoxically eludes the father's control by apparently becoming precisely what he asks: a conventional, supportive, maternal figure. Unlike Shelley's first two novels, which are filled with dead and powerless mothers, her last two novels explore and exalt the subversive power of maternity—a power that inevitably, if intermittently, gives the daughter a satisfying measure of control over the figure of the father.

This study makes little mention of the influence of Percy Bysshe Shelley on Mary Shelley. While that influence was considerable, it is not the subject of this book, and Percy Shelley is treated here mainly as another father figure whom Mary Shelley adored and sometimes battled. This erasure of Percy Shelley is deliberate: it is another attempt, among several recent ones by other authors,[7] to read Mary Shelley as an author in her own right, rather than as an adjunct to her husband, or as her husband's student, collaborator, and editor. In the final analysis, after all, Mary Shelley was more her father's student than her husband's; and, in this light, it is even more to Mary Shelley's credit that she turned her father's teaching to such good account and used it to move beyond him.

৵✗৵

A note on names: Mary Shelley's given name was "Mary Wollstonecraft Godwin"; after her marriage, she used the name "Mary Wollstonecraft Shelley." Those sections of this book that discuss Mary Shelley before her marriage in 1816 refer to her as "Mary Godwin"; subsequently, she is called "Mary Shelley."

"My Hideous Progeny"

1

William Godwin
and Mary Shelley

Mrs Godwin had discovered long before my excessive & romantic
attachment to my Father.
—Mary Shelley to Maria Gisborne, 1834

I have been alone—& worse—I had my father's fate for many a year a
burthen pressing me to the earth.
—Mary Shelley to Edward Trelawny, 1837

For Mary Shelley, more than for most daughters, literary heritage meant
destiny. Born in 1797 to Mary Wollstonecraft and William Godwin, two of
the most celebrated writers of the age, Mary Shelley spent much of her life
contending with the ghosts of both her mother and her father. Though
Mary Wollstonecraft died giving birth to Mary Wollstonecraft Godwin,
the great feminist writer remained a potent presence for her daughter. The
young Mary Godwin carried her mother's books with her wherever she
traveled, reading and rereading them in times of stress. As an adolescent,
Mary Godwin made communing with her mother's spirit an act of literary
and social revolt: she fled to Mary Wollstonecraft's grave during long after-
noons of discord with her hated stepmother, and, under the branches of the
willow tree at the graveside, she read voraciously and entangled herself in
intimacies with a socially most unsuitable partner, the married and atheistic
Percy Bysshe Shelley. Mary Godwin Shelley always remained convinced
that whatever happiness came to her was delivered through the office of
people's admiration for her mother.[1] And she admitted in her middle years
that "the memory of my Mother has been always . . . the pride & delight of
my life" (MWS *Letters*, 2:3–4)—a striking statement for a woman who
could not remember her mother in any real sense.

But if Mary Wollstonecraft cast a long shadow over her daughter from the grave, William Godwin cast an even longer one from his home in Skinner Street. Godwin died when his daughter was thirty-eight years old. From the time of Wollstonecraft's death, Godwin became a primary focus for his daughter's emotional energy—a figure to be emulated, propitiated, undermined, and consoled. Mary Shelley knew her father's work intimately: she read and reread Godwin's novels before she sat down to write her own, most notably in the case of *Frankenstein*. Shelley loved her father passionately, harboring what she herself described as an "excessive & romantic attachment" (MWS *Letters*, 2:215) to him. Shelley was encouraged in her literary career by her father, and sought to model herself after him. Yet Shelley was frustrated and limited by her father in almost equal measure. Godwin was instrumental in creating the conditions for Mary Shelley's genius; he was equally central to the formation of Mary Shelley's vision of the perplexing and precarious nature of daughterhood. William Godwin exercised a formidable intellectual and psychological influence over Mary Shelley—an influence portrayed, battled, and eventually laid to rest in the pages of her novels.

I.

When Mary Wollstonecraft died after childbirth, on 10 September 1797, she left William Godwin with two small girls: Fanny Imlay, three years old, her illegitimate daughter by the American adventurer Gilbert Imlay; and Mary Godwin, eleven days old, conceived four months before Wollstonecraft's marriage to William Godwin and eagerly anticipated as their son "William."[2] William Godwin was so distraught at Mary Wollstonecraft's death that he could not bring himself to put the event into words in his journal. The entry for the day Wollstonecraft died—of a puerperal fever brought on by a piece of placenta left in her womb after Mary Godwin's birth—reads "20 minutes before 8," followed by three blank heavily scored lines.[3] Godwin was too prostrate to attend Wollstonecraft's funeral; in the days that followed her burial, he began to grapple with his grief by immersing himself in writing Wollstonecraft's biography and editing her works. By 24 September, two weeks after her death, he noted that he had completed the "Life of Wt., p.2."[4]

Bereft of his beloved wife, William Godwin was badly equipped to raise two small girls alone. Though he had made himself a prominent political theorist when he published *An Enquiry Concerning Political Justice and Its*

Influence on General Virtue and Happiness in 1793, his financial means were slender. Already forty-one years old when Mary Godwin was born, Godwin was entrenched in solitary habits—even during his courtship and marriage to Mary Wollstonecraft, the two authors maintained separate residences. And Godwin's temperament did not easily lend itself to fatherhood. Godwin described himself as "often cold, uninviting, and unconciliating"—and admitted that he possessed an inextinguishable love for fame and admiration (Paul, *William Godwin*, 1:358–59). Mary Shelley wrote that her father had a quick temper and could be "somewhat despotic on occasions" (1:47). Godwin was vain and ambitious; he was proud, sensitive, and shy. But determined to provide for his daughter and stepdaughter, Godwin found that parenthood, coupled with the experience of having enjoyed and then lost domestic happiness with Mary Wollstonecraft, expanded his emotional horizons vastly.

At first, Godwin entrusted the daily care of his two daughters to a succession of female friends, relatives, and servants who moved into and out of the Godwin home. The most long-lived of these was Louisa Jones, a housekeeper who doted on Fanny and Mary with a solicitude approaching that of a real mother. Godwin struggled to write and make money, while his attachment to his children blossomed. He once defended himself against what he viewed as a character slur by pointing to his paternal affections. "Am I, or am I not, a lover of children?" Godwin wrote. "My own domestic scene is planned and conducted solely with a view to the gratification and improvement of children. . . . Are not my children my favourite companions and most chosen friends?" (2:74). At about the same time, when Godwin was forced to travel to Dublin for ten weeks just before Mary's third birthday, he filled his letters home with concern and affection for his daughters. "And now what shall I say for my poor little girls?" Godwin wrote. "I hope they have not forgot me. I think of them every day, and should be glad, if the wind was more favourable, to blow them a kiss a-piece from Dublin to the Polygon" (1:370).

Little Mary Godwin, for her part, fastened all her emotional energy on her only living parent. As an adult, Mary Shelley looked back to her early days and described her love for a father as "the first and the most religious tie."[5] She openly acknowledged that "Until I knew Shelley I may justly say that [my father] was my God—& I remember many childish instances of the excess of attachment I bore for him" (MWS *Letters*, 1:295). Such passionate attachment bred an equally intense fear of her father's rejection. Mary Godwin adored her father and always worried about being supplanted in his affections. During Godwin's Dublin trip she even feared he might abandon her entirely, and Godwin had to write home with clear assurances to the contrary: "Tell Mary I will not give her away, and she shall be nobody's little girl but papa's" (Paul, *William Godwin*, 1:365).

The loving "papa" quickly realized he had to make more regular arrangements for the care of his daughters. And, having tasted the joys of domesticity with Mary Wollstonecraft, Godwin himself craved a stable and loving household. Just after Wollstonecraft's death, Godwin had proposed to two women in quick succession: Harriet Lee, the author, and Maria Reveley, the future Mrs. John Gisborne. In 1801, Godwin's search for a marriageable woman finally focused on his neighbor, Mary Jane Clairmont. Or, perhaps more accurately, Clairmont's hunt for an available husband focused on Godwin. Tradition has it that Godwin was sitting and reading on his balcony when a woman appeared at a neighboring window and exclaimed rapturously, "Is it possible that I behold the immortal Godwin?"[6] It was a greeting calculated to appeal perfectly to Godwin's vanity. Mrs. Clairmont was an adept manager and a good cook; they were married within seven months, on 21 December 1801.

Many of Godwin's acquaintances saw an irony in his decision to marry a second time. Godwin was, after all, the philosopher who had called marriage "a monopoly, and the worst of monopolies."[7] He and Wollstonecraft had made themselves notorious by writing in favor of women's rights, against eighteenth-century patterns of marriage and courtship, and by openly consorting without the benefit of marriage until a few months before Mary Godwin was born. Percy Bysshe Shelley was attracted to William Godwin in part because of what he called the "Godwinian anti-matrimonial system"; by the end of the eighteenth century, William Godwin represented to the popular mind everything politically radical, morally suspect, and potentially injurious to domestic virtue and established family structures. He was even accused of advocating infanticide (Paul, *William Godwin*, 2:72). In this context, remarriage seemed an abandonment of Godwin's most celebrated theoretical principles. Had "The Professor," as Charles Lamb called him, undergone a revolution in thought?

Part of the skepticism about Godwin's second marriage also grew from his friends' objections to the personality of his second wife. Mary Jane Clairmont certainly did not possess the grace and gifts of Mary Wollstonecraft. Robert Southey, for one, thought it utterly sacrilegious to replace Mary Wollstonecraft with Mary Jane Clairmont: "To take another wife with the picture of Mary Wollstonecraft in his house," he fumed, "Agh!"[8]

Charles Lamb, who had become a regular visitor to Godwin's house, was made to feel unwelcome by the new wife, whom he speedily labeled "That Bitch."[9] He then went on to describe her at more length: "The Professor's Rib has come out to be a damn'd disagreeable woman.... If a man will keep *Snakes* in his House, he must not wonder if People are shy of coming to see him *because of the Snakes*."[10] James Marshall, one of Godwin's oldest friends, probably described Mary Jane Godwin most fairly as "a clever, bustling, second-rate woman, glib of tongue and pen, with a temper undisciplined and uncontrolled; not bad-hearted, but with a complete absence of all the finer sensibilities."[11]

Godwin, of course, saw his new wife in a very different light. "We are both of us," he wrote to her, "persons of no common stamp, and we should accustom ourselves perpetually so to regard each other, and to persuade ourselves, without hesitation, without jealousy, and with undoubted confidence, that we are so regarded by each other" (Paul, *William Godwin*, 2:190). Equally important, Godwin recognized that Mary Jane Clairmont filled many of his deep emotional needs. Shortly after Mary Wollstonecraft's death, Godwin had reflected upon the kind of domestic companion he most desired, using these words: "No domestic connection is fit for me but that of a person who should habitually study my gratification and happiness" (1:360). To a great extent, Mary Jane Godwin strove to foster precisely this sort of connection: she comforted and supported Godwin, and she insulated him from distractions that interfered with his writing. Further, she seemed to provide Godwin with a species of maternal support that, for all the philosopher's emotional aloofness and devotion to rationality, he still very much required. On the occasion of his own mother's death, Godwin even went so far as to inform his wife that, with his real mother gone, he expected Mary Jane Godwin to assume the role of replacement mother:

> I was brought up in great tenderness, and though my mind was proud to independence, I was never led to much independence of feeling. While my mother lived, I always felt to a certain degree as if I had somebody who was my superior, and who exercised a mysterious protection over me. I belonged to something—I hung to something—there is nothing that has so much reverence and religion in it as affection to parents. That knot is now severed, and I am, for the first time, at more than fifty years of age, alone. You shall now be my mother; you have in many instances been my protector and my guide, and I fondly trust will be more so, as I shall come to stand more in need of assistance. (2:180)

In asking his wife to behave as a mother figure, Godwin betrayed an expectation that recurred in later years with other female family members, especially his two oldest daughters. And in cherishing his second wife's role as "protector and guide," Godwin both repeated the pattern of his relationship to Mary Wollstonecraft and demonstrated the extent to which Wollstonecraft had awakened in him a new reverence for emotion and for domestic affection of a particular brand.

As Mary Shelley points out in her notes for a projected biography of her father, the experience of marriage to Mary Wollstonecraft had, indeed, altered William Godwin. Where he had previously guarded himself against love, he later threw himself into it.[12] Where he had previously allowed no place for the play of feeling in his philosophical system, he later recognized and even celebrated its force. This revolution in emotion, which translated itself into a revolution in thought for William Godwin, can be traced in his *Memoirs of the Author of a Vindication of the Rights of Woman* and in his autobiographical novel *St. Leon*. In both works, Godwin idealizes and transforms Mary Wollstonecraft, and he simultaneously glorifies the domestic affections—the latter a startling departure for a man who established his philosophical reputation by condemning marriage on principle. Godwin's idealized literary portrayal of Mary Wollstonecraft is important for understanding Godwin's desire for maternal nurturance and its impact on Mary Shelley.

But if Godwin's marriage to Mary Jane Clairmont answered his own emotional needs, it did little to comfort and support Fanny Imlay and little Mary Godwin. Though Godwin had hoped to give his two daughters a more secure and predictable home, he unwittingly did just the opposite. When Godwin remarried, Fanny was seven and Mary was four. Godwin's second wife brought two children of her own by previous liaisons: Charles Gaulis Clairmont, also seven, and Jane Clairmont, eight months younger than Mary. Another son, William Jr., was born a year and a half later, bringing the size of the brood to five. Godwin's two daughters no longer shared their adored father's exclusive attentions; as they saw it, their new stepmother favored her own children and ignored or denigrated them. Fanny eventually grew to tolerate Godwin's second wife, but Mary always despised her. As Mary Shelley's first biographer bluntly puts it, from young Mary Godwin's point of view, "Mrs. Godwin was repellent, uncongenial, and very jealous of her."[13] Mary hated what she saw as Mrs. Godwin's unnatural preeminence in the Godwin household—the second Mrs. Godwin was, it seemed to her, so inferior to the real Mrs. Godwin, her mother, Mary

Wollstonecraft. And the presence of a second, living wife threatened Mary's own preeminence in her father's affections. Young Mary Godwin grew to think of her stepmother as that "odious woman" (MWS *Letters*, 1:34) and asserted that "as to Mrs G. som[e]thing very analogous to disgust arises whenever I mention her" (1:43). In this climate, Mary Godwin fastened all the force of her emotional attachment even more powerfully on her father and on the haunting idea of her lost, loving mother.

As Betty Bennett has pointed out, William Godwin gave Mary Godwin access to a far richer intellectual experience than most women of her period.[14] In the years leading up to her adolescence, Mary Godwin emerged as her father's potential intellectual heir, the child most suited to carry on his work as a writer and thinker. His oldest natural child and only offspring by his beloved first wife, Mary Godwin appeared to her father to be both a link to a cherished past and a talented bit of intellectual clay to be molded for the future. He entertained great hopes for her. He proudly described her to a correspondent as "singularly bold, somewhat imperious, and active of mind. Her desire of knowledge is great, and her perseverance in everything she undertakes almost invincible. My own daughter is, I believe, very pretty" (Paul, *William Godwin*, 2:214). As Mary Shelley herself put it many years later, speaking of her father's expectations for her, "I was nursed and fed with a love of glory. To be something great and good was the precept given me by my father."[15] Young Mary Godwin took her father's hopes entirely to heart; she learned to measure herself against her parents and to envision herself inheriting their intellectual legacy. As she wrote a correspondent in 1827, "Her greatness of soul [Mary Wollstonecraft's] & my father['s] high talents have perpetually reminded me that I ought to degenerate as little as I could from those from whom I derived my being . . . my chief merit must always be derived, first from the glory these wonderful beings have shed [around] me, & then for the enthusiasm I have for excellence" (MWS *Letters*, 2:4).

Godwin did more than give his oldest daughter high expectations about her role as his literary successor. He also gave her the encouragement and training necessary to meet these expectations. Some biographers have argued that William Godwin gave Mary Godwin no formal education and that whatever education she had before she met Percy Bysshe Shelley was "self-gained."[16] Godwin himself acknowledged that he did not teach Mary Wollstonecraft's daughters in strict accordance with Wollstonecraft's own principles about educating girls. As he wrote a correspondent who inquired about the training given to Fanny and Mary:

They are neither of them brought up with an exclusive attention to the
system and ideas of their mother. I lost her in 1797, and in 1801 I married
a second time. One among the motives which led me to chuse this was the
feeling I had in myself of an incompetence for the education of daughters.
The present Mrs. Godwin has great strength and activity of mind, but is
not exclusively a follower of the notions of their mother; and indeed,
having formed a family establishment without having a previous provision
for the support of a family, neither Mrs. Godwin nor I have leisure enough
for reducing novel theories of education to practice, while we both of us
honestly endeavour, as far as our opportunities will permit, to improve the
mind and characters of the younger branches of our family. (Paul, *William
Godwin*, 2:213–14)

The fact that Wollstonecraft's daughters were not trained "with an
exclusive attention to the system and ideas of their mother" does not mean,
however, that Godwin gave them no systematic education. In *Thoughts on
the Education of Daughters* and *A Vindication of the Rights of Woman*, Wollstonecraft argues for a thorough reform of female education including,
among other things, educating girls alongside boys in national schools,
encouraging girls to engage in regular and unrestrained physical exercise,
eliminating the emphasis on female "accomplishments" from the girls' training, and striving to develop the girls' faculties of reason and understanding.[17] Wollstonecraft's ideas about reshaping female education are wide-
ranging, complex, and concrete—too complex, in fact, to be incorporated in
their entirety into a home education. While Godwin acknowledges his
decision not to adhere to Wollstonecraft's principles in a specific way, he
seems to have followed Wollstonecraft's educational philosophy, and his own,
in the most important of ways: by training his daughters, and Mary Godwin in
particular, in the importance of reason, imagination, literature, and history.

Godwin insisted, above all, that his daughter's education be designed to
sharpen her reasoning and critical faculties. In 1812, he wrote of Mary to his
friend, William Baxter, "I am anxious that she should be brought up . . . like
a philosopher, even like a Cynic."[18] But as a novelist and as an author of
educational books for children, Godwin also recognized the importance of
cultivating his child's imagination. When Mary Godwin was almost five,
her father discussed the "education of female children" in these terms:

You enquire respecting the books I think best adapted for the education
of female children from the age of two to twelve. I can answer you best on
the early part of the subject, because in that I have made the most experiments; and in that part I should make no difference between children male

and female. . . . I think the worst consequences flow from overloading the faculties of children, and a forced maturity . . . the imagination, the faculty for which I declare, if cultivated at all, must be begun with in youth. Without imagination there can be no genuine ardour in any pursuit, or for any acquisition, and without imagination there can be no genuine morality, no profound feeling of other men's sorrow, no ardent and persevering anxiety for their interests. (Paul, *William Godwin*, 2:118–19)

In the same letter, Godwin goes on to list several books well suited to developing a child's imaginative faculties, among them the works of Mrs. Barbauld. Godwin's remarks suggest the extent to which he thought the early education of the sexes should be identical: like Mary Wollstonecraft, Godwin insists that boys and girls should read the same texts. And, according to Godwin, developing the imaginative faculties has a moral as well as an aesthetic end: it leads to an increased sense of social responsibility in both men and women.[19]

As Godwin's children grew older, he introduced them to history and literature. In 1805, Godwin and his second wife began the Juvenile Library, a publishing venture dedicated to producing educational books for middle-class children. Between 1805 and 1811—from the time Mary Godwin was eight until she was fourteen—Godwin wrote and published at least eleven books in this series under various pseudonyms. His children's books reveal educational biases he developed early and maintained throughout his life. When Percy Bysshe Shelley requested advice on a reading program many years later, Godwin recommended that Shelley study Greek, Roman, and English history, as well as the work of the best English prose stylists and poets.[20] These are precisely the subjects Godwin covered in the educational books he wrote and edited for his Juvenile Library series during Mary Godwin's childhood: histories of Greece, Rome, and Great Britain, and collections of classic poetry and prose were to be used as daily reading exercises.[21] Godwin tested his children's books on his own family. As he recounts in the preface to his *History of England*, Godwin was "accustomed to consult my children" about his educational texts: "I put the two or three first sections of this work into their hands as a specimen. Their remark was *How easy this is! Why we learn it by heart, almost as fast as we read it!*"[22]

Along with Godwin's specific educational emphasis on reason, imagination, literature, and history, he gave his children access to something much more singular: an intellectual climate of great diversity and excitement. As Mary Godwin grew up, her father was still visited by the likes of Hazlitt, Lamb, and Coleridge. Tradition has it that Mary and Fanny hid behind the parlor couch to listen to Coleridge recite *The Rime of the Ancient Mariner;* Godwin himself tells us that he took his brood of children to hear Coleridge's lectures on literature at the Royal Institution in 1811–12.[23] Godwin's friends included artists, dramatists and actors; he took his children to the theater, where they might see plays by family friends or by Godwin himself. Many years later, Mary's stepsister Jane—who later changed her name to Claire Clairmont and became the mother of Byron's illegitimate child—recalled the sense of bustling intellectual enterprise that Godwin fostered in his household: "All the family worked hard, learning and studying: we all took the liveliest interest in the great questions of the day— common topics, gossiping, scandal, found no entrance in our circle for we had been brought up by Mr. Godwin to think it was the greatest misfortune to be fond of the world."[24]

Jane also remembered, with some dismay, the emphasis Godwin placed on literary achievement, and the sense of competition this emphasis created among the siblings. As Jane ruefully wrote to Jane Williams, she grew to resent the fact that, in the Godwin household, "if you cannot write an epic poem or novel, that by its originality knocks all other novels on the head, you are a despicable creature, not worth acknowledging."[25]

Though Jane Clairmont found the competitive family atmosphere intimidating, Mary Godwin flourished. She formed work habits, modeled after her father's, that lasted throughout her lifetime: she studied and wrote in the morning, and she devoted the afternoon to exercise or recreation. Godwin gave Mary the run of his extensive library, and she learned from her father to view reading as a serious investigative endeavor. As she wrote Maria Gisborne much later, "Papa is continually saying & writing that to read one book without others beside you to which you may refer is mere childs work" (MWS *Letters*, 1:122). Most important, Mary Godwin began to model herself after William Godwin and Mary Wollstonecraft by writing. In the 1831 introduction to a new edition of *Frankenstein,* Mary Shelley describes her early literary activity in this way:

> It is not singular that, as the daughter of two persons of distinguished literary celebrity, I should very early in life have thought of writing. As a child I scribbled; and my favourite pastime, during the hours given me for recreation, was to "write stories." Still I had a dearer pleasure than this, which was the formation of castles in the air. . . . My dreams were at once more fantastic and agreeable than my writings. In the latter I was a close imitator—rather doing as others had done, than putting down the suggestions of my own mind.[26]

Shelley's fond affection for "the formation of castles in the air" attests to the success of Godwin's early emphasis on imagination. And her account of the origins of her literary aspiration reveals something further: Mary Shelley's awareness of the power of literary parentage in her choice of a career.

Shelley's characterization of herself as a "close imitator" in her juvenile writing certainly describes her practice in the very few examples of her early work that survive. All the manuscripts of Mary Godwin's early writing were lost during her elopement with Shelley to France—though Percy Shelley insisted he wanted to "study those productions of [Mary's] mind that preceded our intercourse" (MWS *Journal*, 1:8). They left her writing box behind in Paris with instructions for forwarding, and never saw the box again. Mary Godwin's first published work survives; entitled *Mounseer Nongtongpaw*, it is an imitation and expansion of Charles Dibdin's song of the same name. Godwin published *Mounseer Nongtongpaw* on 1 January 1808, as number 6 in the Juvenile Library's Copper Plate Series.[27] Mary Godwin was only eleven years old. The poem proved to be remarkably popular: it was pirated in the United States and reissued in England in 1830 in an edition with illustrations by Robert Cruikshank.[28] William Godwin was so proud of his precocious daughter's efforts that he sent her poem to an acquaintance the very next day with this note: "That in small writing is the production of my daughter in her eleventh year, and is strictly modelled, as far as her infant talent would allow, on Dibdin's song."[29]

Mary Godwin also self-consciously imitated her father's works. When Aaron Burr visited the Godwin family in December 1811, he listened to a lecture given by William Godwin, Jr., on a most Godwinian topic: "The Influence of Government on the Character of the People."[30] The author of the lecture was Mary Godwin. Mary Godwin probably also wrote a number of additional titles for the Juvenile Library. As Emily Sunstein concludes, it is possible that Mary composed some or all of the eight stories published under the name of "Mrs. Caroline Barnard" in *The Parent's Offering* of 1812.[31]

In short, when Mary Godwin eloped to the Continent with Percy Bysshe Shelley at the age of sixteen—an event to be considered at more length later—she was already a published writer who had determined to follow in her parents' footsteps by working as an author. Her professional aspirations had been planted by a father who viewed her as his, and Mary Wollstonecraft's, natural literary heir; her father also provided the training and encouragement necessary to launch his daughter as a writer and thinker. Until the beginning of her adolescence, in fact, William Godwin gave Mary

Godwin expectations and education that suggested vast possibility: all the potential horizons of a son, with few of the limits usually imposed on daughters. It was an education and a childhood that in today's vocabulary might be described as "ungendered"—that is, an education that made the least possible differentiation between males and females, that encouraged daughters to develop professional aspirations, and that allowed daughters to envision themselves in many roles, including those usually reserved for sons. It was a childhood that created the conditions for Mary Shelley's achievements as a writer. And it was a childhood that, as we shall see, simultaneously prepared the ground for the development of Mary Shelley's vision of the disturbing, and disappointing, nature of daughterhood.

II.

To say that William Godwin gave his oldest natural daughter the aspiration and training necessary to make her a writer—that is, all the expectations of literary inheritance and sonship—is not to say that their relationship was always warm and affectionate. Quite the contrary: Godwin was emotionally withdrawn and often cold; he knew, and his children saw, that effusive displays of tender feeling were generally beyond his emotional grasp. Godwin felt comfortable showing warm affection to Fanny and Mary when they were very small, but his expressiveness diminished as they grew older. Mary Shelley eventually attributed her father's emotional distance to his shyness and to an inability to grasp his children's feelings quickly. "Often," as Shelley put it, "did quiescence of manner and tardiness in understanding and entering into the feelings of others cause him to chill and stifle those overflowings of mind from those he loved, which he would have received with ardour had he been previously prepared."[32] For his part, Godwin was aware of the impact his temperament had on Mary. On the occasion of sending her off to board with the Baxter family in Scotland, in June 1812, he described the currents of their relationship in this way:

> The old proverb says, "He is a wise father who knows his own child;" &
> I feel the justness of the apothegm on the present occasion. There never
> can be a perfect equality between father & child; & if he has other objects
> & avocations to fill up the greater part of his time, the ordinary resource
> is for him to proclaim his wishes & commands in a way somewhat senten-
> tious & authoritative, & occasionally to utter his censures with seriousness
> & emphasis. It can therefore seldom happen that he is the confidant of his

child, or that the child does not feel some degree of awe & restraint in intercourse with him.[33]

Godwin was certainly correct to observe that Mary stood in awe of him. She adored him at the same time. As Mary Godwin passed through childhood, she satisfied her passionate attachment to William Godwin by living up to his literary expectations, by identifying herself with his hopes for her, and by modeling herself after him.

But as Mary Godwin entered adolescence, William Godwin's aloof demeanor seemed to turn to outright rejection. In fact, the beginning of Mary's adolescence marked a long period of alienation from her father, an alienation that only ended when she married Percy Bysshe Shelley at age nineteen. This paternal rejection is central to Mary Shelley and her career: it haunted her all of her life and became emblematic of the many other types of rejection she encountered. It shaped her response to her burgeoning femininity and gave birth to her vision of the precarious nature of daughterhood; it provided part of the creative impulse for her first two novels—*Frankenstein* and *Mathilda*—both of which tell the story of the daughter's painful induction into adult womanhood.

As Mary Godwin grew older and entered adolescence, her need for emotional support from her father increased. Simultaneously, William Godwin was able to provide it even less successfully. As Nancy Chodorow has pointed out, given the psychic currents of the oedipal nuclear family, fathers are crucial to a daughter's psychological development at two particular junctures: during her negotiation of the oedipal period and during her navigation of the adolescent passage.[34] During adolescence, the girl's attachment tends to turn away from the mother-figure and toward the father. As a girl moves through adolescence, her identification with her father can help her consolidate her "work identity." At the same time, her libidinal attachment to her father allows her to pull away from the weight of dependent feelings associated with symbiotic ties to a mother or mother-figure, to form a sense of herself as a separate individual and a woman. A father will always be a more distant figure than a mother, and a figure to whom an adolescent daughter relates in terms of fantasy and idealization.[35] Yet a successful father makes himself available for identification, allows himself to be a cherished though distant love object, and provides consistent emotional support.

From the father's point of view, however, the daughter's passage through adolescence often creates an anxious—and even threatening—moment. As the daughter passes out of the sexual latency of childhood and begins to develop into a mature woman, the father often rejects her. As Lynda Boose explains, the daughter's new physical maturity invites incestuous desire—the father's response to his daughter's burgeoning sexuality often manifests itself in what the daughter sees as inexplicable rejection:

> For the father, whose unbidden desires no longer hide themselves in an infant's unconscious repression, the assertion of new emotional and physical distance from the daughter serves as a defense against conscious recognition. In trying not to be the incestuous father, he instead becomes the rejecting one who turns away from his daughter precisely at the moment in her psychological maturation when she will begin turning more actively towards him.[36]

As Boose goes on to say, this moment of unexplained paternal rejection is confusing and traumatic for the adolescent girl: it sets her developing sexuality into a scene dominated by the father's inexplicable rejection and thus connects paternal rejection to emblematic rejection by the male world.[37] In fact, the father's rejection is the very mechanism that precipitates the adolescent girl into the full—and disappointing—meaning of adult womanhood and, simultaneously, perpetuates the daughter/woman's association with sex, guilt, and the "filth" of physical existence.

In Mary Godwin's case, her father's rejection meant the end of a childhood full of wide horizons and possibility and the beginnings of her recognition of the limits associated with adult womanhood. Mary Godwin had been brought up expecting to inherit the prerogatives of a son. As she entered adolescence she received, instead, lessons in the guilt and restriction associated with being a daughter. As Margaret Hennig has observed in another context, "for girls, especially for the achievement-oriented among us, adolescence often brings with it a traumatic switch in the definition of competence."[38] William Godwin's rejection began as an apparent banishment of his daughter to Scotland in 1812, when she was almost fifteen, was intensified and protracted by Mary's elopement with Shelley, and did not end until Mary Godwin married Shelley in 1816, when she was nineteen. Godwin's rejection of his daughter can clearly be placed in the context of her developing sexuality.

As Mary Godwin entered her teens, her father entered a period of acute financial embarrassment that consumed his time and later came to color his relation to his daughter quite directly. More significant, as Mary Godwin entered her teens and her passionate attachment to her father naturally increased, the enmity between Mary Godwin and her stepmother reached a crisis. Mary Jane Godwin had always resented Mary Wollstonecraft's two daughters. Her resentment stemmed partially from natural prejudice: she preferred to advance her own children's interests—especially Jane's—and begrudged the resources spent from the family's slender means to educate Mary and Fanny. Mary Jane Godwin was also intensely aware that many of Godwin's famous visitors were more interested in Mary Wollstonecraft's daughters than the second Mrs. Godwin; she knew they thought of the precocious Mary Godwin as, at least in potential, a more fitting successor than she to the place of Mary Wollstonecraft in the Godwin household. As Mary Godwin entered adolescence, Mrs. Godwin's resentment increased. The Godwin marriage was on shaky ground at this time. In 1811, Mrs. Godwin actually moved out of the house for a short time. Mrs. Godwin may have felt she was losing her youth and attractiveness just as Mary Godwin was blossoming into the first flower of womanhood. As Mrs. Godwin complained to her husband in the same year, when Mary Godwin was about to turn fourteen, "in the hardest struggle that ever fell to the lot of woman, I have lost my youth and beauty before the natural time" (Paul, *William Godwin*, 2:187). And it was at precisely this period that Mrs. Godwin discovered, as Mary Shelley later told Maria Gisborne, the young Mary Godwin's "excessive & romantic attachment to my Father" (MWS *Letters*, 2:215).

Mary Jane Godwin no doubt felt threatened by the passionate tie Mary felt to William Godwin, as well as by the literary expectations Godwin had for his daughter. The sense of competition was strong enough to cause discord; it was long-lasting enough that William Godwin had to reassure his wife as late as 1826, when Mrs. Godwin was vacationing on the Continent and Mary Shelley was visiting her father in London, that "You are very wrong in saying I do not want your society, and still more in supposing Mrs. Shelley supplies the deficiency. I see her perhaps twice a week; but I feel myself alone ten times a day" (Paul, *William Godwin*, 2:296–97).

If the second Mrs. Godwin disliked her stepdaughter, Mary Godwin returned the compliment with all the force available to her adolescent constitution. Her dislike was no doubt tinged with jealousy over what she saw as Mrs. Godwin's unnatural place as the preeminent woman in the household—the second Mrs. Godwin was, after all, so inferior to young Mary Godwin's idealized vision of her own mother. Mary Godwin placed all the blame for family turmoil on her stepmother and insisted upon holding her beloved father completely blameless. When her father refused to speak to her several years later, after her elopement with Percy Bysshe Shelley, she was certain Mary Jane Godwin was to blame and lamented to Shelley "I detest M^rs G[odwin] she plagues my father out of his life & then—well no matter—why will not Godwin follow the obvious bent of his affections & be reconciled to us" (MWS *Letters*, 1:3).

For his part, William Godwin seemed alternately distracted by his continuing financial difficulties and irritated by the competing claims of his daughter and his second wife. Mary's adolescence coincided with one of the worst periods of Godwin's life. Largely due to the losses incurred by his Juvenile Library project, Godwin's financial situation was desperate—so much so that he stared at complete strangers at the theater, wondering if they might loan him money (Paul, *William Godwin*, 2:186). In a fit of pique, he told his wife he thought of her as a burden the law would not allow him to be free of (2:187); in a burst of similar exasperation, he told his wife to "Tell Mary that, in spite of unfavourable appearances, I still have faith that she will become a wise and, what is more, a good and a happy woman" (2:184).

Caught in the conflicting currents of her passionate attachment to her father and her rivalry with her stepmother, buffeted by the confusing currents of her emerging sexuality and her father's emotional withdrawal, Mary Godwin became physically ill. She developed an arm ailment which, as Muriel Spark points out, might well have been a psychosomatic response to the emotional pressures of her family situation (Spark, *Mary Shelley*, 14).[39] In the spring of 1811, when she was thirteen and a half years old, she was sent away from the Godwin household to board at Miss Petman's school at Ramsgate, in the hope that the sea air would cure her arm. Though Godwin had good medical reason to send Mary away, and though the separation was intended to calm Mary's feelings as well as preserve the peace of the whole household, Mary could not help but read the separation from her father as an abandonment—and an abandonment directly connected to the fact that she was becoming a woman. Her arm improved, though it is not clear whether the improvement was due to the salt air or the temporary escape from friction with her stepmother. Mary stayed with Miss Petman for nearly eight months; during this period, Godwin wrote to his daughter only four times, and failed to visit her for her fourteenth birthday, though he was vacationing in the area. When Mary returned home to London in December, family conflict resumed with a vengeance. Mary's arm ailment re-emerged, this time affecting the entire arm; she appears to have suffered a depressive crisis, lost her sense of professional purpose, and became so withdrawn she had to be "*excited* to industry."[40] Her father decided to send her away a second time, both to improve her health and to relieve the mounting tension with Mrs. Godwin. Mary faced what she saw as another abandonment, precisely when she needed her father most; again, the abandonment was tied to her developing womanhood. Godwin arranged a long stay with the Baxter family, who lived close to the sea in Scotland. Even the normally inexpressive Godwin confessed worry at sending his young daughter away so far, for so long: "I cannot help feeling a thousand anxieties in parting with her," he wrote William Baxter as Mary sailed north, "for the first time for so great a distance."[41] When Mary Godwin left the Godwin household for Dundee on 7 June 1812, she was just short of fifteen and a very torn adolescent girl.

Mary Godwin's stay in Scotland became the event that marked and engulfed her adolescence. When she wrote a new introduction for the 1831 edition of *Frankenstein*, Mary Shelley reflected that she had "lived principally in the country as a girl, and passed a considerable time in Scotland" (*Frankenstein*, 223). This description of her early years must have come as a surprise to her father, because Mary principally lived in Godwin's home during her childhood, and she spent time in the country and Scotland only when Godwin sent her there to restore her health and the family peace. The point is that Mary's absences from Godwin's house—absences she read as acts of banishment and paternal rejection—became the events that defined her adolescence, overshadowing all else. Mary's banishment to Scotland is crucial to central aspects of *Frankenstein* and *Mathilda*. Mary Shelley even suggests that the "waking dream" that gave birth to *Frankenstein* had its origins in the "waking dreams," or adolescent fantasies, of Scotland, imaginative flights that were her "refuge when annoyed—my dearest pleasure when free" (1831 introduction to *Frankenstein*, 223).

Paradoxically, Mary Godwin's adolescent exile to Scotland became an emblem of great opportunity as well as a symbol of paternal rejection. As Mary Shelley remembered in 1831, Scotland was also "the eyry of freedom, and the pleasant region where unheeded I could commune with the creatures of my fancy" (223). In Scotland, away from family crisis, away from condemnation of her rebelliousness, and away from conflict over her emerging sexuality, Mary conquered depression and wrote. Seeing herself as rejected by her father's house, she made the Baxter house hers and used the resulting imaginative freedom to explore new versions of herself and her situation. As she puts it,

> It was beneath the trees of the grounds belonging to our house, or on the bleak sides of the woodless mountains near, that my true compositions,

the airy flights of my imagination, were born and fostered. . . . I was not confined to my own identity, and I could people the hours with creations far more interesting to me at that age, than my own sensations. (223)

As this passage suggests, Mary Godwin's Scottish exile allowed her to discover and shape the first of her "true compositions," "airy flights of imagination" that did not closely imitate others and that, significantly, permitted her to escape the confines of her identity. In their imaginative reformulation of her circumstances, these "airy flights" may have allowed Mary to come to grips with what she read as paternal rejection and may also have given Mary some relief from her painful "sensations" of adolescent confusion. Further, it may be argued that Mary Godwin's exile to Scotland, associated as it was in her mind with her emerging sexuality and her father's consequent rejection, simultaneously shaped her vision of the precarious nature of daughterhood and began to sow the seeds for her first two novels. And Scotland, with its freedom and opportunity for imaginative flight, did one more thing for the adolescent Mary Godwin: it consolidated her determination to become, like her father and mother, a writer.

III.

When Mary Godwin returned to London from Dundee on 30 March 1814, she was sixteen and a half years old. She had blossomed into a very attractive young woman with an oval face and golden hair and had developed, as her father wrote to Coleridge, the mind of a woman. But her new maturity did not totally prepare her for the chaos and conflict of Godwin's household. As soon as Mary arrived back at Skinner Street, she discovered she still despised her stepmother and her stepmother still despised her. She learned that Godwin was still deep in debt and found that his financial worries and schemes for raising money took all his time. Godwin welcomed Mary home but had little time for her. To escape the carping of Mrs. Godwin and the intrusions of her stepsister Jane, Mary Godwin began to make daily trips to her mother's grave in St. Pancras's cemetery, where she could read, indulge in imagination, and solidify even more her identification with Mary Wollstonecraft, her father's real wife.

During Mary Godwin's absence in Scotland, a new player had appeared on the stage of the Godwinian domestic drama. He was Percy Bysshe Shelley, twenty-one years old, a young aristocrat and heir to a considerable fortune.

Shelley was a poet and radical who had been expelled from Oxford for writing a pamphlet entitled *The Necessity of Atheism;* he had recently married and had one small child and a second on the way. Shelley had become a regular in the Godwin household and, as one of Godwin's ardent disciples, embraced in particular the revolutionary politics and social nonconformity espoused in Godwin's *Political Justice.* He had a fervent respect for the life and work of Mary Wollstonecraft. And he was willing to express his intellectual discipleship in very practical terms: he was engaged in raising large sums of money to pay off Godwin's debts by negotiating post-obit bonds, financial instruments through which Shelley obtained large sums of money by promising to pay back even larger amounts when he came into his inheritance after his father's death.

Shelley and Mary had first met on 11 November 1812, when she was home for a visit from Scotland, and Shelley and his wife Harriet joined the Godwins for dinner. But in 1812 Mary was still an adolescent girl, and Shelley was still infatuated with his wife. When Shelley and Mary met again in the spring of 1814, the situation had changed: she was a lovely and talented young women with intellectual and literary aspirations; he was disenchanted with a wife who had little capacity for the world of literature and philosophy; and he was ready for a passionate and dramatic liaison. Mary Godwin fit all Shelley's romantic taste for a brilliant young woman he could mold intellectually and commune with spiritually, and she was of unimpeachable literary descent. As Thomas Jefferson Hogg tells the story, when Mary Godwin rushed up to him and Shelley in Godwin's Skinner Street shop, he asked Shelley who she was—another daughter? "Yes," replied Shelley tautly. "A daughter of William Godwin?" Shelley devoutly answered, "The daughter of Godwin and Mary."[42]

For her part, Mary Godwin was ready to escape the strains of life at Skinner Street and eager to ally herself with someone who confirmed her in her identification with the accomplishments of her illustrious parents. It did not hurt at all that Shelley was the sort of lover who could remind Mary Godwin that Mary Wollstonecraft's life "clothed thee in the radiance unde-filed / Of its departing glory" or "Thou canst claim / The shelter, from thy Sire, of an immortal name."[43] Shelley was, like Mary herself, a disciple of both her parents. Equally important, laboring as she already did under a sense of paternal rejection and standing on the brink of womanhood, Mary Godwin was eager to test her new sexuality and to fill the emotional void left by Godwin's withdrawal. In many ways, Percy Shelley became a new and competing father figure to Mary Godwin. As Mary Godwin implored

Shelley a few months later, "[P]ress me to you and hug your own Mary to your heart perhaps she will one day have a father till then be everything to me love" (MWS *Letters,* 1:3). And Percy Bysshe Shelley did, for a while, become the pillar of Mary's emotional stability and her literary and intellectual mentor. Like William Godwin, Shelley exhorted Mary to live up to the example of her celebrated parents. As Mary puts it, "To be something great and good was the precept given me by my father: Shelley reiterated it."[44] To Mary's eye, Shelley became, as Godwin had been, her "guide, teacher & interpreter" (MWS *Journal,* 2:461); she was his "pupil—friend—lover—wife."[45] She studied Greek at his suggestion; they kept a joint diary of their lives and literary activities; they read books together; he encouraged her when she wrote her fiction. Later, Mary Shelley wrote novels that conflated the figures of father, lover, and mentor, thereby expressing the passion she felt for both men and her sense that William Godwin and Percy Shelley somehow stood in the same relation to her.

In March 1814, when Mary and Shelley met for the second time, events unfolded quickly. Conscious of the symbolically appropriate location, they met repeatedly at Mary Wollstonecraft's grave. They declared their mutual love and devotion; they may even have consummated their love at the graveside. Following Mary Wollstonecraft's willingness to break social taboos in matters of love and William Godwin's published condemnation of marriage in *Political Justice,* they eloped to France on 28 July 1814.

William Godwin was aghast. The confounded father could not "conceive of an event of more accumulated horror."[46] As Muriel Spark has pointed out, Godwin correctly feared for his sixteen year-old daughter's happiness: notwithstanding Shelley's immense personal attractions, he was in many ways volatile, irresponsible, perhaps unstable.[47] Further, Godwin was only too aware of the opportunities his daughter's elopement afforded his enemies. When Shelley and Mary eloped to the Continent, they took Jane Clairmont with them. Mary's ardent lover left behind in England a furious five-month's-pregnant wife and a year-old daughter. Godwin did not want to be entangled in this sort of scandal. He could be accused yet again of advocating moral licentiousness in his works and in the example of his family—a tack that Harriet Shelley immediately took.[48] Since Godwin had just concluded a large loan from Shelley, he could even be accused of selling his daughters.[49] And at some level, of course, Godwin was simply horrified at losing Mary. He felt robbed of his favorite daughter, cheated of his literary heir, and deprived of the material link to his cherished past with Mary Wollstonecraft—and by a much younger man, who was supposedly his ardent disciple. Though Godwin had withdrawn from close emotional involvement with Mary, he was still shocked and threatened. He felt that Shelley had "play[ed] the traitor to me";[50] as Mary Shelley told Maria Gisborne many years later, "Papa loves not the memory of S[helley]— because he feels he injured him" (MWS *Letters*, 2:247). Godwin continued to have complicated financial dealings with his daughter's lover and even- tual husband over the next years, but the enmity between Godwin and his former pupil never vanished. Shelley was transformed, in Godwin's eyes, into "a disgraceful and flagrant person."[51]

There followed a long period of even more intense estrangement be- tween Godwin and his daughter, an estrangement that formed the specific background against which Mary Shelley conceived and began *Frankenstein*. Although Godwin had advocated free sexual relations between consenting men and women, and had himself lived with Mary Wollstonecraft without the benefit of marriage, Godwin viewed his daughter's elopement with all the horror of Frankenstein contemplating his creature coming to life. As Godwin commented in August 1814, before Mary, Percy, and Jane re- turned from the Continent, "Jane has been guilty of indiscretion only . . . Mary has been guilty of a crime."[52] Godwin cut himself off from his daugh- ter completely. He refused to communicate with Mary at all and forbade Fanny Imlay to see or talk to her half-sister. Godwin did not write or speak to Mary when she lost her first child in February 1815, or when she bore a son, named William in honor of Godwin himself, on 24 January 1816. It was against this background of Godwin's rejection that Mary, then eighteen years old, conceived and began to write her first novel, *Frankenstein*. Shelley confessed to Mary that he was "shocked & staggered by Godwin's cold injustice,"[53] especially since Shelley was working during this entire period to raise money for Godwin, whose finances were worse off than ever. Mary was aware of the hypocritical and self-serving nature of her father's behav- ior—when Godwin threatened never again to speak to Fanny Imlay if she saw Mary, Mary called her exile from Skinner Street "a blessed degree of liberty this" (MWS *Journals*, 1:44). And when Godwin refused to speak about Shelley to anyone but an attorney or to deal with his financial bene- factor in any way except through intermediaries, Mary, who had just fin- ished reading her father's *Political Justice*, exclaimed "Oh! Philosophy" (MWS *Journals*, 1:37).

Generally, however, Mary refused to blame her father for his intransi- gence and worried about his bad debts and reputation. She preferred to blame Mrs. Godwin for the rift, writing in her journal "she is a woman I shudder to think of—my poor father—if—but it will not do" (1:40). She called Harriet Shelley "detestable" for working against a scheme to raise money for Shelley and Godwin (1:40); she continued to find satires of Godwin's works "ineffably stupid" (1:31).

The impasse between father and daughter was broken late in 1816, after nearly two years of Godwin refusing to have anything to do with his daughter, by two calamitous events: the suicide of Fanny Imlay in October 1816 and the suicide of Harriet Shelley two months later. When Fanny Imlay fled Godwin's home and drank laudanum on 9 October 1816—why, it is not clear, but perhaps because she felt herself a burden in a household wracked by debt, where she had no blood relative[54]—Godwin finally broke his silence and answered Mary's letter of condolence. His letter was a cold, self-involved communication, in which Godwin began by telling Mary that her sympathy could be of no use to him, and ended by admonishing her to avoid all publicity and not tell anyone of Fanny's death.[55] Following Godwin's wishes, no one in the family claimed Fanny's body, and she was buried, nameless, in a pauper's grave in Swansea.

Then, on 10 December 1816, Harriet Shelley's body was fished from the Serpentine. In her case the reason for suicide was all too obvious: she was far advanced in pregnancy, and, since Shelley had left her for Mary, the father could not have been her husband. But her death opened the way for the legalization of Shelley's tie to Mary—a decision that Godwin immediately urged and one for which Shelley and Mary were completely prepared. On 29 December 1816, Mary came home to Skinner Street for a formal dinner of reconciliation; she and Shelley were married on 30 December 1816, with Mr. and Mrs. Godwin as witnesses. As Don Locke puts it, Godwin had been eager to bridge "the abyss of dependence and recrimination that had separated him from his daughter, his disciple, and the grandson that bore his name."[56] Less to his credit, Godwin was also happy to see his daughter married to the eldest son of a baronet,[57] who with any luck could be a continuing source of ready cash. With the marriage of Shelley and Mary, Mary's relation to her father entered a new and somewhat unexpected phase.

IV.

With Fanny Imlay's death and Mary Godwin's marriage to Percy Bysshe Shelley in late 1816, the dynamics of Mary Shelley's relation to her father shifted radically. During Mary Godwin's childhood, Godwin stimulated and cultivated his daughter's literary aspirations; during her adolescence, he seemed to reject her as she became a woman. But after Fanny Imlay's death and Mary's marriage to Shelley, Godwin expected something entirely different from Mary Wollstonecraft's daughter—all the comfort, consolation, and emotional support traditionally supplied by an oldest daughter to her aging father.

The shift in Godwin's attitude toward his daughter Mary was occasioned largely by the death of Fanny Imlay. Since she was the oldest girl in the Godwin family, Fanny Imlay had always played the social role traditionally assigned to the eldest daughter: chief assistant to the mother in all domestic matters, substitute mother and domestic manager in the mother's absence, caretaker of the father's emotional needs when his wife was unavailable. Anne Mellor has remarked that "Godwin's favorite child, oddly enough, was Fanny Imlay."[58] And in one sense Mellor is absolutely correct. Until her death, Fanny was the daughter whom Godwin expected to be the family's domestic bulwark, and to whom Godwin turned in domestic matters. Though she was not William Godwin's natural daughter and was related by blood to no one in the Godwin household except her half sister, Mary, Fanny played the feminine role instinctively and found it natural to act as Godwin's domestic prop whenever Mrs. Godwin was away. As Christy Baxter, daughter of the Scottish Baxters, observed, Fanny had "a keen sense of domestic duty, early developed in her by necessity and by her position as the eldest of this somewhat anomalous family."[59] Fanny was by nature compliant, self-effacing, and eager to please; she even defended her stepmother against Mary Godwin's raging criticisms. Fanny Imlay was responsible for the lion's share of household chores and cared for the younger children. When Mary Jane Godwin left or took the other children on holiday, Fanny frequently stayed behind to cook and keep house for her stepfather.[60] From this point of view, Fanny clearly occupied a very important place in Godwin's affections, and Godwin certainly felt a good deal of tenderness for her. This is not to say, however, that Fanny was Godwin's "favorite child" in all respects, since he clearly held such particular ambitions for his only biological daughter, Mary Godwin.

In fact, Fanny's position as oldest daughter—and therefore as the daughter traditionally designated to assume the mantle of domesticity— probably shielded Mary Godwin from these same domestic expectations and therefore heightened even more Godwin's tendency to view Mary as his literary heir. Until Mary Shelley was nearly twenty, William Godwin had little reason to ask traditionally "feminine" behavior from her, and he stressed instead the more "masculine" identifications of writing and intellectual activity, not only because he cherished Mary Godwin's talents, but also because he already had one daughter to play the "feminine" role for him. In this respect, Mary Godwin's family position contributed to her literary aspirations in the same way Virginia Stephen Woolf's did: With an older half-sister present to assume the domestic role, the younger sister became even more likely to profit from her father's tutelage and from her father's "masculine" expectations for her. But for Mary Shelley, unlike Virginia Woolf, the domestic role of oldest daughter and caretaker to her father suddenly, and disconcertingly, fell open. It was a role Mary Shelley embraced immediately and with some pleasure—though with a stronger portion of anxiety and anger.

At roughly the same time Fanny Imlay committed suicide, a second event qualified Mary yet more for the eldest daughter's role as supporter and consoler to her father, that is, her marriage to Percy Bysshe Shelley. With her marriage to the wealthy future baronet, Godwin presumed it would be a simple matter for Mary to relieve him of his deepest anxiety: finding the money to pay his mounting debts and thus finally make his Juvenile Library solvent. This is one of the contexts in which William Godwin's escalating demands for money from his daughter and son-in-law should be read—as an inversion of the parent-child, and specifically the father-daughter relation, a reversal of roles in which the father demands emotional support and financial maintenance from his daughter rather than vice versa. Godwin himself knew there was something "unnatural" about taking money from his daughter. "It is against the course of nature," he wrote Mary, "unless, indeed, you were actually in possession of a fortune."[61] Nevertheless, over the next six years, Godwin's demands for his daughter's emotional support and her husband's money embroiled Mary Shelley in a series of family crises. Simultaneously, the young Mary Shelley faced a string of losses, all associated with her position as a daughter, mother, and wife, that consolidated yet further her sense of the precarious nature of womanhood.

Immediately after the Shelleys' marriage at the end of 1816, all parties were reconciled, after two and a half years of what Mary saw as painful rejection by her beloved father. She was delighted to be treated as an outcast no longer. Both her diaries and Godwin's diaries record frequent meetings in 1817 and early 1818—dinners, visits, evenings at the theater, Mary staying with her father in London or Godwin staying with his daughter at Marlow. Godwin wrote to Shelley of his eagerness to have Mary stay with him in his home, so father and daughter might reestablish old ties, saying, "[S]uch a visit will tend to bring back years that are passed, and to make me young again. It will also operate to render us more familiar and intimate, meeting in this snug and quiet house."[62] Godwin also took an active interest in Mary's literary career again, sending her books and giving her ideas for new writing projects.[63]

But Godwin's mounting debts and his ambiguous relation to his son-in-law haunted the happy reunions. Godwin and Shelley had reestablished amicable relations, but the older man and his former pupil both felt a residue of mistrust and skepticism. The situation was exacerbated by the fact that Mary Shelley was often caught between the conflicting claims of her father and her husband. Godwin's money difficulties loomed larger. In March 1817, three months after the Shelleys' wedding, Percy Shelley sent Godwin "a check to within a few pounds of my possessions."[64] Nevertheless, by the next month, Godwin informed Shelley that he still owed at least £500, "and without clearing this, my mind will never be perfectly free for intellectual occupations."[65] Because of a dispute over the legal ownership of his Skinner street home, Godwin had not paid rent on the premises since 1807; on 13 August 1817, a man named Read established formal title to Godwin's house and shop, and Godwin suddenly realized he might be liable for thousands of pounds in damages and back rent.[66] In September, Shelley began the long process of negotiating yet another post-obit bond to pay both his own debts and Godwin's. Shelley himself was in desperate financial straits at this time: he owed more than £1500, and was actually imprisoned for debt for two days in October 1817 when he made a trip to London.[67] When Godwin visited Shelley and Mary at Marlow from 20 to 22 January 1818, Shelley apparently promised to give Godwin another large sum from the proceeds of the post-obit bond. When the bond was finally negotiated on 31 January 1818, Shelley immediately sent a check to Godwin, but the sum was some £500 short of what Godwin expected. Convinced that Godwin failed to handle his large loans in a way that actually paid off his debts, Shelley "resolved to keep in [his] own hands the power conferred by the difference of the two sums."[68] Godwin felt misled and cheated, and wrote Percy Shelley in a fury

> I acknowledge the receipt of the sum mentioned in your letter. I acknowledge with equal explicitness my complete disappointment. . . . I will never again discuss with you any question of this sort upon paper; but I do not desire the presence of any third person. . . . What I have to say I *must* say,

if I ever stand in your presence again; but I had rather it were without a witness.[69]

This misunderstanding over Shelley's loan to Godwin reopened all the wounds of their earlier estrangement. Godwin and Shelley stopped seeing each other, though Godwin continued to pepper Shelley with letters. Mary, for her part, felt caught between the demands of her father and her husband. Her initial pleasure at being reunited with Godwin gave way to sharp anxiety about Godwin's money problems; she repeatedly implored Shelley to help her father financially.[70] Meanwhile, it became increasingly clear that Shelley and Mary would soon have to leave England for Italy. Shelley's health was deteriorating rapidly and his doctors insisted that only a warm climate could save him. Further, the Shelleys were still deeply in debt and could live much more cheaply abroad. Added to their own worries was a third responsibility: Mary's stepsister Jane, who had changed her name to Claire Clairmont, had borne an illegitimate daughter to Lord Byron. The year-old girl, Allegra, had to be delivered to Byron in Italy, lest he refuse to support her. Confronted with this tangle of difficulties, Mary still hated leaving her father behind in England. Although married and with a family of her own, Mary Shelley quaked at the idea of her father's silent disapproval. As she wrote to her husband:

> The idea of it [moving to Italy] never enters my mind but Godwin enters also & makes it lie heavy at my heart. . . . I assure you that if my Father said—Yes you must go—do what you can for me—I know that you will do all you can—I should far from writing so melancholy a letter prepare every thing with a light heart. . . . I know not whether it is early habit or affection but the idea of his silent quiet disapprobation makes me weep as it did in the days of my childhood. (18 October 1817, MWS *Letters*, 1:57)

Notwithstanding Godwin's utter disapproval, the Shelleys set out for Italy on 11 March 1818. Besides Shelley and Mary, the party included William Shelley, now two years old; Clara Shelley, five months old; Claire Clairmont and her daughter, Allegra, who was now fourteen months old; and two nursemaids.

Once in Italy, Shelley largely stopped communicating with his father-in-law, but Mary and Godwin corresponded frequently.[71] Godwin's long letters about his financial difficulties were clearly intended for Shelley's eye as well as Mary's;[72] in addition to providing news about England, they blamed Mary and her husband for Godwin's money problems and writing blocks. On 1 June 1818, for example, Godwin suggested to Mary that his *Answer to Malthus* had been "fatally interrupted by the events of February last," referring to his argument with Shelley over money and the Shelley family's subsequent decision to leave London.[73] A few weeks after he wrote this letter, Godwin was served notice to move out of his house and shop on Skinner Street. This notice began a long series of legal maneuverings that finally ended in 1825. For the next seven years, Godwin fought in court to retain possession of his home and to avoid payment of back rent. As Godwin sent Mary letters describing his financial and legal battles, her depression over her father's situation, as well as her guilt at being able to help him so little, became acute. She wrote Maria Gisborne early in 1819,

> My father is now engaged in a lawsuit—the event of which will be to him the loss or not of £1500—You may conceive how anxious I am, as well as he; for my part, I am so devoured by ill spirits, that I hardly know what or where I am. (MWS *Letters*, 1:94)

It was during this period and against this background that Mary Shelley fell into a habit that characterized her relation to William Godwin until the day he died: she used her writing to support him financially. As Emily Sunstein has discovered, Mary Shelley may even have helped her father with money during their period of estrangement, when Godwin refused to speak to her. Sunstein argues persuasively that Mary may have written *The Prize; or the Lace-Makers of Missenden*, which Godwin's Juvenile Library published under the name of Mrs. Caroline Barnard in 1816.[74] After their reconciliation, Mary's anxiety about her father's finances and her desire at least to replace the £500 Godwin still insisted Percy Shelley owed him, led her to send Godwin a series of pieces that he could, in one way or another, publish for his benefit. In 1820, eight months after she received Godwin's letter, Mary gave her father *Mathilda*—a novel whose subject is the incestuous relation between a father and his beloved daughter—with the idea that Godwin might publish the book and earn some money. Not surprisingly, Godwin found the subject "disgusting and detestable,"[75] and, two years later, Mary Shelley was still trying to retrieve her manuscript from him. In early 1822, as Godwin's eviction battles reached one climax, Mary Shelley sent her father her historical novel *Valperga*, with instructions to revise and publish it in whatever way suited his needs. Godwin wrote Mary that it was "truly generous of you to desire that I would make use of the produce of your novel";[76] he edited *Valperga* heavily and published it in 1823, receiving from the sale £400—enough to put off his creditors temporarily.[77] Mary also sent her father *Maurice*, a children's story that he did not publish and that has been lost.[78] She offered him the profits of a projected second edition of *Frankenstein;* she probably wrote, again as Mrs. Caroline Barnard, *The Fisher-Boy of Weymouth*, which Godwin published in 1819.[79] None of these daughterly efforts had any real effect on Godwin's debts, since his financial situation was so desperate, and Mary Shelley's worry only increased.

At this same time, Mary Shelley had cause for anxiety that went far beyond her sense of unfulfilled duty to her father. The years 1818 and 1819 were traumatic in Mary Shelley's own life, and most of her sorrows were associated with matters of sexuality and motherhood. Percy Shelley continued to carry on a series of flirtations with other women, including Mary's stepsister, Claire. In 1818, at the age of only twenty-one, Mary Shelley lost her baby daughter to a situation for which she never forgave her husband. Claire and Shelley had traveled to Byron's villa in Este, so that Claire could visit her daughter, Allegra, without Byron's knowledge. A few days later, Shelley insisted that Mary and their two small children make the same journey in the sweltering September heat—a ruse that Shelley concluded would mask Claire's presence from Byron. Little Clara Shelley contracted dysentery along the way; the Shelleys continued to Venice in search of a good doctor. Clara fell into convulsions as the family barged across a canal toward the city; the doctor couldn't immediately be found; and Clara died in her mother's arms in a Venice hotel lobby, a few days past her first birthday.

Mary Shelley was, predictably, "reduced . . . to a kind of despair."[80] She half blamed herself for exposing the baby to an arduous journey; she half blamed Shelley for insisting on the trip at all. In her grief, Mary began to turn cold to Shelley, who was bewildered by her withdrawal and unable to grasp the depth of her loss. In the meantime, William Godwin was totally impervious to his daughter's pain. He wrote a letter that purported to offer comfort but that must have only deepened Mary's suffering:

> I sincerely sympathize with you in the affliction which forms the subject of your letter, and which I may consider as the first severe trial of your constancy and the firmness of your temper that has occurred to you in the course of your life. You should, however, recollect that it is only persons of a very ordinary sort, and of a pusillanimous disposition, that sink long under a calamity of this nature. I assure you such a recollection will be of great use to you. We seldom indulge long in depression and mourning, except when we think secretly that there is something very refined in it, and that it does us honour.[81]

Significantly, Godwin's letter suggests that grief is a feeling reserved for the weak and that any indulgence in mourning is a perverse reversion to self-love. His daughter, he implied, should be capable of much more strength and nobility.

The next year, 1819, proved to be even more traumatic for Mary Shelley. She, Percy, Claire Clairmont, and William spent most of the winter after baby Clara's death traveling from place to place: Rome, Naples, Pompeii, back to Rome. In London, Godwin's lawsuit had come to court in February, and he wrote long letters to his daughter, describing its worrying progress and inquiring about money. She was distracted and anxious; Shelley's health was visibly failing. In Rome, little William contracted a nasty case of worms, which lasted for three days. He seemed to improve for a short time, but was prostrated by a second attack, this time of malaria. Shelley and Mary watched around the clock as their only remaining child—their little "Blue eyes," their "Willmouse"—suffered convulsions and a raging fever. On 7 June 1819, at noon, he died. He was barely three and a half years old.

Both parents were distraught. After Clara's death, Mary had felt that her existence was entirely tied up in her son; she was now "broken hearted & miserable—I never know one moments ease from the wretchedness & despair that possesses me. . . . I feel that I am no[t] fit for any thing & therefore not fit to live" (MWS *Letters*, 1:101–2). Shelley, who had not written to Godwin for a year, now wrote to his father-in-law to ask him to try to say something in his next letter to comfort Mary. Godwin's reply is lost, but Shelley describes it in this way, in a letter written on 15 August 1819:

> Poor Mary's spirits continue dreadfully depressed. And I cannot expose her to Godwin in this state. I wrote to this hard-hearted person, (the first letter I had written for a year), on account of the terrible state of her mind, and to entreat him to try to soothe her in his next letter. The *very* next letter, received yesterday, and addressed to her, called her husband (me) "a disgraceful and flagrant person" and tried to persuade her that I was under great engagements to give him *more* money (after having given him £4,700), and urged her if she ever wished a connection to continue between him and her to force me to get money for him.[82]

A few days after receiving this letter from her father, on 19 August 1819, Mary apparently wrote to protest its tone. Godwin quickly wrote her the following extraordinary reply, which deserves to be quoted in its entirety:

9 September 1819

Your letter of August 19 is very grievous to me, inasmuch as you represent me as increasing the degree of your uneasiness and depression.

You must, however, allow me the privilege of a father and a philosopher in expostulating with you upon this depression. I cannot but consider it as lowering your character in a memorable degree, and putting you quite among the commonalty and mob of your sex, when I had thought I saw in you symptoms entitling you to be ranked among those noble spirits that do honour to our nature. Oh! what a falling off is here! How bitterly is so inglorious a change to be deplored!

What is it you want that you have not? You have the husband of your choice, to whom you seem to be unalterably attached, a man of high intellectual endowments, {whatever I & some other persons may think of his morality, & the defects [rooted in this lost heart] if they be not (as you seem to think) imaginary, at least do not operate as towards you.} You have all the goods of fortune, all the means of being useful to others, and shining in your proper sphere. But you have lost a child; and all the rest of the world, all that is beautiful, and all that has a claim upon your kindness, is nothing, because a child of three years old is dead!

The human species may be divided into two great classes: those who lean on others for support, and those who are qualified to support. Of these last some have one, some five, and some ten talents; some can support a husband, a child, a small but respectable circle of friends and dependents, and some can support a world, contributing by their energies to advance their whole species one or more degrees in the scale of perfectibility. The former class sit with their arms crossed, a prey to apathy and languor, of no use to any earthly creature, and ready to fall from their stools, if some kind soul, who might compassionate, but who cannot respect them, did not come, from moment to moment, to endeavour to set them up again. You were formed by nature to belong to the best of these classes; but you seem to be shrinking away, and voluntarily enrolling yourself among the worst.

Above all things, I entreat you, do not put the miserable delusion on yourself to think there is something fine, and beautiful, and delicate, in giving yourself up and agreeing to be nothing.

Remember, too, that though at first your nearest connections may pity you in this state, yet that, when they see you fixed in selfishness and ill-humour, and regardless of the happiness of everyone else, they will finally cease to love you, and scarcely learn to endure you.[83]

When Mary Shelley received this letter from her father, she was writing her novel *Mathilda.* As she ruefully remarked to Amelia Curran a few days later, "I have no consolation in any quarter for my misfortune has not altered the tone of my father's letters" (MWS *Letters*, 1:106).

Godwin's letter to Mary is remarkable on a number of counts. Most obviously it reveals, like his letter on the death of Clara, Godwin's inability to grasp the depth of his daughter's grief over the loss of her beloved child. In belittling Mary for mourning the death of a mere "child of three years old," Godwin refuses to recognize the child's importance to his daughter and fails to acknowledge the child's claims to its mother's love and grief. Godwin's letter is also notable for the way it refers to Mary's husband. Godwin's negative comments about Percy Shelley have been excised from the printed version of the letter, probably by Lady Jane Shelley. But it is revealing of Godwin's hostility toward his daughter's husband that, at a juncture in Mary's life so charged with the losses of love and sexuality, Godwin should attack Shelley's morality and essentially berate Mary for siding with Shelley against him.

Godwin's letter is most revealing, however, for the way it divides the human species into "two great classes: those who lean on others for support and those who are qualified to support." Upon closer inspection, it seems that Godwin's remarks really refer to the female species, and praise those women who "can support a husband, a child, a small but respectable circle of friends and dependents," or even "a world." Godwin's praise for women who stifle their individual grief to support and comfort others purports to have a philosophical basis—after all, Godwin addresses his daughter as "a father and a philosopher," and he observes that the energies of these women "advance their whole species one or more degrees in the scale of perfectibility." But Godwin's praise for selfless, silent, consoling women also carries an implicit and self-serving message: the suggestion that his daughter's energies would be better spent supporting living persons who really need help—that is, fathers like Godwin himself. It is in this sense that Mary's abject depression lowers her "character in a memorable degree, and put[s her] quite among the commonalty and mob of [her] sex." A truly noble and socially useful woman, Godwin implies, would rise from the ashes of her grief to comfort and aid those around her. And if she does not, her "nearest connections" might abandon her. This is the veiled threat conveyed in the last paragraphs of Godwin's letter to Mary. If his daughter doesn't put aside her own "selfishness and ill-humor" and learn to regard the "happiness of everyone else," her "nearest connections"—who certainly include her father—"will finally cease to love [her], and scarcely learn to endure [her]."

Godwin's letter to Mary on the occasion of her favorite child's death is a remarkable revelation of Godwin's paternal assumptions, as well as his jealous craving for his daughter's support and consolation. This letter and the kind of paternal expectations it implied set the stage for the way Godwin related to his daughter over the next three years, until Shelley's death in 1822. Mary bore her last child, Percy Florence, on 12 November 1819, some six weeks after she received Godwin's letter. Godwin continued to demand support; Mary became increasingly agitated over the state of his finances and her inability to do anything about them. Shelley became angrier and angrier, calling Godwin "my bitterest enemy."[84] In 1820, "in her agony,"[85] Mary begged her friends the Gisbornes to loan Godwin £400; at this same time, she wrote and sent Godwin the manuscript of *Mathilda,* and then in 1822 the manuscript of *Valperga* to pay his debts. Events reached one crisis in August 1820, when Mary became so upset over her father's exactions that she became physically ill, and Shelley wrote Godwin a bitter letter, the last he ever addressed to him, in which he forbade Godwin to write Mary about money and indicated that, with Mary's approval, he intended to screen all of Godwin's letters before they reached her. Mary had no control over his money, Shelley said. "If she had poor thing, she would give it all to you . . . I cannot consent to disturb her quiet & my own by placing an apple of discord in her hand."[86] Events reached a second crisis in April 1822, when Godwin lost his lawsuit and faced eviction from his home. In a letter designed to exacerbate all Mary's feelings of guilt, Godwin wrote her pathetically to "forget that you have a Father in existence. Why should your prime of youthful vigor be tarnished and made wretched by what relates to me? . . . I think I ought for the future to drop writing to you."[87]

Godwin did not, of course, stop writing his daughter—his next letter, as pathetic as the last, is dated only two weeks later. Mary's own difficulties, in the meantime, only continued to increase, along with Godwin's incomprehension of them. Her unshakable stepsister Claire had finally moved out of the Shelley household in October 1820, but Shelley immediately became involved in a series of other flirtations. In April 1822, Allegra died, neglected by Byron in an Italian convent, another child victim sacrificed to Mediterranean fevers and epidemics. Two months later, Mary had a serious miscarriage and nearly died from loss of blood herself. Only Shelley's quick thinking—he made her sit in a bucket of ice until a doctor arrived—saved her life. And then in July 1822, Mary Shelley's world collapsed entirely. Percy Shelley and his friend Edward Williams set out in a new sailboat for Lerici. They were caught in a squall; both men drowned. Shelley was twenty-nine years old; Mary was twenty-four—a widow with a two-and-a-half-year-old son.

As soon as Godwin heard the news of Shelley's death, he sent his daughter two letters of consolation and reconciliation, each of which indicated the path he hoped their relation would take now that Shelley was gone. As Godwin noted on 9 August 1822, in hoping that since Mary had lost her closest friend, "your mind would naturally turn homewards, and to your earliest friend":

> Surely we might be a great support to each other, under the trials to which we are reserved. . . . We have now no battle to fight—no contention to maintain—{we have not each of us a cause to support, in which each should seek for reasons to support the two opposite sides of a question.} That is over now.[88]

Shelley's death had indeed removed, in Godwin's eyes, one obstacle to Godwin and his daughter relying on each other for mutual support and consolation. But in a letter written to his daughter a few days earlier, his first letter to his daughter after her husband's death, Godwin had been a bit more candid about the direction in which he hoped the stream of support would flow:

> All that I expressed to you about silence, & not writing to you again, is now put an end to in the most melancholy way. I looked on you as one of the daughters of prosperity, elevated in rank & fortune; & I thought it was criminal to intrude on you for ever the sorrows of an unfortunate old man & a beggar. You are now fallen to my own level; you are surrounded with adversity & with difficulty; & I no longer hold it sacrilege to trouble you with my adversities. We shall now truly sympathise with each other; & whatever misfortune or ruin falls upon me, I shall not now scruple to lay it fully before you.[89]

This letter, written in the first flood of unrestrained reaction to the news of Shelley's death, is almost as remarkable as Godwin's letter to Mary after William's death, and certainly as revealing of Godwin's expectations for his daughter. "You are surrounded with adversity and with difficulty," he says, and one expects a sentence of comfort or consolation to follow. Instead, Godwin calls up his own afflictions and announces his intention to turn his troubles over to Mary. Now that his daughter's husband is dead and she is mired in misery, Godwin says, he will "no longer hold it sacrilege to trouble you with my adversities. . . . whatever misfortune or ruin falls upon me, I shall not now scruple to lay it fully before you." Godwin's implied messages to his grieving daughter are multiple: now that her husband is dead, her father has a right to claim her support unreservedly; now that her husband is dead, her duty is to attend to her father's problems; and now that Mary is stricken with adversity, her role is to suppress her sorrow in the service of others. Most specifically, now that Percy Shelley is dead, Mary Shelley's duty is to play the maternal role to her suffering father by soothing his sorrows and supporting him in his financial and emotional need.

Notwithstanding Mary Shelley's own grief, she rapidly assumed the burden of her father's continuing expectations. As we shall see, it was a burden she eventually examined, explained, and exorcised in the pages of her last novels.

V.

With Percy Shelley's death, the relationship between Mary Shelley and her father assumed its final form, shifting into the emotional configuration it retained for the next fourteen years until Godwin's death in 1836. Mary Shelley did shortly return to England, as her father desired, where she kept in close touch with him for the rest of his life. She supplied him with money and they helped each other with publishing projects. Godwin continued to rely on Mary for emotional continuity and financial stability, though she remained poor for many years, supporting herself chiefly with her pen. Like countless other historical and fictional daughters, Mary Shelley assumed the weight of her aging father's care, supplying him with encouragement and emotional support—a form of daughterly behavior that satisfied Godwin's increasing need for maternal nurturance. Mary Shelley became in every way the model daughter, the foundation and pillar of her father's last years. And, as before, part of the currency of this emotional transaction continued to be Mary Shelley's struggle to provide William Godwin with enough money to live.

From 1822 to 1836, Mary Shelley's relationship to her father consti-tuted one of three major emotional commitments in her life. As Emily Sunstein has noted, Shelley faced three major tasks after Percy Shelley's death: securing her small son's future support and education, giving her father a "green old age" (MWS *Letters,* 2:124), and rebuilding her own life.[90] Of these three, her highest priority was providing for Percy Florence

Shelley, who was almost four years old when Shelley returned to England from Italy in 1823. Given the deaths of her three other children and the recent loss of her husband, Percy Florence Shelley quickly assumed the central position in his young mother's life. Just as Mary Shelley had felt her existence entirely tied up in William Shelley after Clara Shelley's death, so she now felt her very life linked to Percy Florence's survival. Immediately after Percy Bysshe Shelley's death, Mary Shelley wrote that her child was "necessary to the continuance of my life" (MWS *Journal*, 2:432). When Percy Florence was eleven, she told Francis Wright that she clung to her child "as my sole tie" (MWS *Letters*, 2:124). In this context, motherhood became the focus of Mary Shelley's life, a cherished responsibility to which she sacrificed many personal preferences and for which she endured much suffering. Shelley struggled to make enough money by her writing to support her son and give him a good education. She contended with Sir Timothy Shelley, Percy Florence's grandfather, over the matter of an allowance for herself and the boy. When Sir Timothy demanded that Percy Florence remain in England, Shelley gave up her plan of resettling in her beloved Italy. Later, as Percy Florence grew older, Shelley's sense of the necessity of maternal sacrifice—and of her own financial impoverishment—increased. When Percy Florence reached adolescence, Shelley enrolled him at Harrow, to make certain he received an education worthy of his father's. Two of the loneliest years of Shelley's life followed. She moved to Harrow herself, so that she could reduce school fees by having Percy Florence attend as a day boy. She felt entirely cut off from her accustomed life in London, and she suffered a devastating rejection by a suitor. As she wrote Maria Gisborne of her Harrow sojourn: "I am being killed by inches here" (2:258).

Meanwhile, over this same fourteen-year period until Godwin's death, Mary Shelley struggled to reconstruct her own life. Motherhood constituted her primary emotional tie, but she also craved a loving relationship with an adult, a relationship that might provide a sense of stable emotional commitment. As soon as Percy Bysshe Shelley died, Mary Shelley began to idolize, and even canonize, his memory—an imaginative process documented in the pages of her journal and described by many commentators as the expression of her lingering feelings of passion and guilt. When Mary Shelley returned to England, she devoted herself to Jane Williams, the wife of the man who drowned with Shelley, and a woman who therefore constituted a palpable link to her lost past. After the relationship with Jane Williams soured, Mary Shelley dedicated most of her emotional energy to relationships with other women: Isabel Robinson, Julia Robinson, Francis

Wright. As Shelley herself put it, writing of this period in 1835, "Ten years ago I was so ready to give myself away—& being afraid of men, I was apt to get *tousy-mousy* for women" (2:256). In 1832, Mary Shelley fell in love with, and apparently hoped to marry, Aubrey Beauclerk, a wealthy political reformer. When this relationship also went awry—Aubrey Beauclerk apparently became engaged to another woman in 1833 without telling Mary—she felt abandoned yet again and wrote in her diary that "my life is a burthen I would fain throw on one side" (MWS *Journal,* 2:531).

Against this backdrop of struggle on behalf of her son and struggle to fashion an enduring emotional tie to an adult her own age, Mary Shelley also fought to maintain her aging father. Godwin was sixty-six years old when Percy Bysshe Shelley drowned; Godwin died on 7 April 1836, at the age of eighty. In his declining years, William Godwin relied more and more on his eldest daughter for emotional and financial support. Following a pattern sanctioned by social custom and brought to life by the actions of numerous fictional and historical fathers, William Godwin turned his care over to his daughter and depended on her increasingly for consolation, cheer, and (in Godwin's case) infusions of cash. This expectation surfaced clearly in Godwin's letter to his daughter upon her husband's death when he promised to lay all his misfortunes before her; it was articulated just as plainly in one of Godwin's letters to Mary immediately before she set sail from Italy for England. "I am grown an old man, and want a child of my own to smile on and console me," he wrote. "I shall then feel less alone than I do at present."[91] Godwin's desire for his daughter's support and consolation continued and grew over the next years. Once Mary arrived in London, Godwin let her know he expected her to stay in England to care for him. She longed to return to Italy where she could still be "part of my Shelley," but as she told Leigh Hunt, "My father intends to make my returning to Italy an affair of life and death with him, and makes my society appear so necessary to him, that I hardly know what to think or say" (MWS *Letters,* 1:385). A few days earlier, Mary had written to Hunt in the same vein, complaining that "but for my father, I should be with you [in Italy] next spring—but his heart & soul are set on my stay, and in this world it always seems one's duty to sacrifice one's own desires, & that claim ever appears the strongest which claims such a sacrifice" (1:379). As time passed, Godwin increasingly made Mary feel that her daughterly duty to him was paramount. Even though Godwin had pulled away from his daughter during the formative years of her adolescence, he clung to her during his old age. Until the day he died, they saw each other several times a week whenever Mary was in London; he complained of her absences when she left town. Godwin depended on and rejoiced in his tie to his daughter, and even celebrated it in his last novel, *Deloraine*.

When William Godwin cast his oldest daughter into the role of domestic caretaker to her father—that is, the role of substitute mother and wife—he was enacting a pattern of paternal behavior that is not only culturally prevalent and sanctioned but also highly suggestive from a psychoanalytic perspective. Several contemporary commentators have discussed the manner in which a father metaphorically "seduces" his daughter by turning her into a figure for his wife or lover. Concentrating on Sophocles' *Oedipus at Colonus*, Lynda Boose specifically analyzes how a father's search for domestic comfort and support in his daughter expresses the father's fundamental desire to reexperience his lost tie to the pre-oedipal mother. As Boose puts it:

> Freud might have recognized the way that *Oedipus at Colonus* dramatizes the father's seduction of his daughter as embedded within the attempt to reconstruct his lost union with the mother, an adult reversion to infantile dependency and a state of helplessness to which women—and, in particular, daughters—are expected to respond. By playing the son, the father impels his daughter into the role of mother; and where a daughter stands for the mother there is no superior father to make the son give up his (surrogate) mother.[92]

Such an explanation seems to account for the prevalence of the cultural pattern of fathers turning to their oldest daughters for comfort, consolation, and emotional support. In Godwin's case, such a description seems to have particular resonance, since he displayed an intermittent tendency to view the important women in his life as mothers. As we have seen, Godwin told his second wife that, with the death of his actual mother, "You shall now be my mother" (Paul, *William Godwin*, 2:180). Godwin eventually betrayed this same expectation first with Fanny Imlay and then with Mary Shelley. And, as we shall see, it may be argued that William Godwin had resurrected and recreated in his mind, along these same lines, another important—though unlikely—mother figure: Mary Wollstonecraft herself.

For her part, Mary Shelley responded to her father's need with dedication and solicitude. Though her motherly emotions were primarily directed toward her son, Mary managed to give a good portion of daughterly devotion, bordering on the maternal, to her "dear darling Father" (MWS *Journals*, 1:549). Shelley did everything in her power to buttress Godwin emotionally and financially. She tried to stay with her father when his wife traveled abroad—remarking that "my father needs my society" (2:540)—and she visited him in London in 1834, when Mary Jane Godwin left for a rest cure. It was during this same period that Godwin's wife jealously complained that her husband did not want his wife's company, preferring his daughter's instead (Paul, *William Godwin*, 2:296–97). And Shelley's daughterly devotion took the form of years of financial support. Godwin continued to feel it was "contrary to the course of nature that a father should look for supplies to his daughter,"[93] yet he let Mary know her "supplies" of money were essential. Shelley finally managed to extract a small allowance for herself and her son from Sir Timothy Shelley: £200 annually at first, and then up to £300 when Percy Florence entered Harrow. Although the allowance was usually regular, it was not at all lordly, and Shelley struggled to supplement it with her writing. Nevertheless, Shelley always made certain her father had at least £300 annually, an amount that initially exceeded her own income.[94] Shelley's underwriting of her father's affairs forms a recurrent theme in her correspondence and journals. When Godwin was finally forced to declare bankruptcy in 1825, Mary told Hunt that "nothing will be left him but his pen & me" (MWS *Letters,* 1:476). She then tried to raise an annuity for Godwin from an insurance company and drained her own resources to pay for the Godwins' move to a different house. In 1828, Shelley obtained an advance on *Perkin Warbeck* so she could give Godwin £100 he desperately needed; in 1830, she wrote a complimentary review of Godwin's new novel, *Cloudesley*, in the hope that her positive comments would increase sales and generate more funds. Shelley published a laudatory memoir for a new edition of Godwin's *Caleb Williams* in 1831, again with the purpose of boosting sales; two years later, Shelley completed *Lodore* and worried about how much she would make by it, since "[Father's] & my Comfort depend on it" (MWS *Letters*, 2:183). In 1832, Shelley also worked with a friend to help Godwin solicit a sinecure from the governing Whigs on the grounds that Godwin had devoted his lifetime to serving their cause. This project secured Godwin a house and small pension the following year.

When Shelley was not writing for her father's benefit herself, she interceded on his behalf with her own publishers. She took one of Godwin's projects to John Murray in April 1830;[95] in 1832, she implored Murray to accept Godwin's *Lives of the Necromancers* or to suggest some other assignment Godwin might take up for pay (MWS *Letters*, 2:160). When Godwin was ill, or in such low spirits he could not write, she even provided information and ideas for his novels. Mary helped with the Italian scenes of *Cloudesley*, while Charles and Claire Clairmont furnished background for the Austrian and Russian scenes. Later, when Godwin was writing *Deloraine*, his last novel, his imagination went blank at a crucial juncture of the plot. He wrote his daughter and she provided him with the "single spark" that set his mind "in motion and activity."[96]

All these acts of protective support and consolation—acts in which Shelley assumed responsibility for her father's care and happiness—gratified Shelley's lifelong "excess of attachment" (MWS *Letters*, 1:295) to William Godwin. They grew from her enduring love for her father; maternal acts themselves, they were shaped and bolstered by Shelley's experience as mother to her child. But, though motivated by daughterly fidelity and tinged with motherly solicitude, Shelley's ministrations to her father were finally a burden to her. Even before she arrived in England in 1823, Shelley foresaw the toll that responsibility for her father would exact. Having been told by friends that "my father is anxious to see me," Shelley wrote Leigh Hunt that "I dread that tie" (1:376). Her fears were well-founded. Once in England, she discovered that "My father's situation his cares and debts prevent my enjoying his society" (MWS *Journal*, 2:472). She went so far as to tell Louisa Holcroft that she felt "tied by the leg" to Godwin's need for her: "If I talk of cloudless skies, my father becomes cloudy, & seems to have my stay so much at heart, that it seems selfish in one so useless as I am, to be worse than useless and give pain" (MWS *Letters*, 1:387).

Shelley's sense of the burdensomeness of supporting her father echoes through her letters and diaries over the following years.[97] When she longed to leave London after being wounded by Jane Williams, she wrote that her father's "claims only prevent me now from burrying myself in the country" (2:26). She told Trelawny that "the peculiar situation of my relations is heavy on me" (2:93); she wrote Maria Gisborne that she wished "for nothing but an exemption from pecuniary annoyances, both for myself & my father" (2:170–71). Shelley was painfully aware of the one-sidedness of their relation—that is, the fact that the current of emotional and financial support flowed from daughter to father, but seldom in the opposite direction. As she put it in 1838, "Shelley died & I was alone—my father from age & domestic circumstances & other things could not *me faire valoir*" (MWS *Journal*, 2:555). Shortly after William Godwin died, Shelley summed up their relation for Trelawny quite succinctly: "Since I lost Shelley—I have been alone—& worse—I had my father's fate for many a year a burthen pressing me to the earth" (MWS *Letters*, 2:281).

During this final stage of her relationship to her father, Mary Shelley came to use her writing to celebrate, at least apparently, the precise womanly virtues

William Godwin expected of her in his last years: devotion to fathers, maternal sympathy and support, and the silencing of one's own needs in the service of others. But this celebration of daughterly devotion evolved late in Shelley's career with her final fictional works; it marked a shift in style and attitude from her earlier and better-known novels. As Shelley began her career in the years 1816 to 1819, a period gilded by the discoveries of love, darkened by a father's exactions, and made tragic by the deaths of two children, she used her fiction to explore the deep ambiguities of daughterhood. In doing so, she called upon her adolescent past and her relation to her father to examine and explain the tragic condition of being female. She produced two works—*Frankenstein* and *Mathilda*—that express remarkable attachment to fathers, as well as a deep reservoir of resentment and anger against them.

2

Frankenstein

The pivotal relationship of *Frankenstein*—the interactions between a reject-ing father and his rejected creature—certainly has biographical resonance in Mary Shelley's life. When Mary Shelley began *Frankenstein* at the age of eighteen in the summer of 1816, she had been most definitively cast out of the circle of her father's favor. As we have seen, Godwin severed all direct contact with his daughter when she ran away with Percy Bysshe Shelley in 1814; he did not meet or speak with her again until the very end of 1816, when her marriage to Shelley legitimized their elopement. By this time, *Frankenstein* was well underway. During their two-and-a-half-year estrange-ment, from the time Mary was nearly sixteen until she had just passed her nineteenth birthday, Godwin spurned his daughter as she passed out of adolescence, into adult womanhood, and through hardships and joys alike. He ignored the death of her first child; he refused to communicate with her on the occasion of the birth of her second, though she named the child William in his honor. In Godwin's eyes, Mary was, like Frankenstein's rejected creature, "guilty of a crime."[1] The dedication of *Frankenstein* makes it clear that Mary Shelley had her father in mind as she finished the book. She "respectfully" inscribed it "To William Godwin, Author of *Political Justice, Caleb Williams,* &c." Yet the epigraph on the title page of *Franken-stein* focuses the biographical resonances of the novel—and directs the father's attention to his child—in a decidedly different manner. Quoting the bitter and rebellious Adam of Book 10 of *Paradise Lost* in his retort to God the Father, Shelley writes, "Did I request thee, Maker, from my clay / To mould me man? Did I solicit thee / From darkness to promote me?" (lines 743–45).

Much recent criticism of *Frankenstein* has focused on the way the novel examines female anxieties about sexuality. Ellen Moers was one of the first to describe *Frankenstein* as a "birth myth" and to outline the ways the novel traces a young woman's responses to her burgeoning sexuality and capacity for maternity.[2] Other writers, following Moers's lead, have studied the way *Frankenstein* evokes pregnancy or engages in a quest for identity with the lost mother.[3] Pursuing a different line of inquiry, a second group of critics has applied psychoanalytic models to *Frankenstein* and argued that the monster personifies Victor Frankenstein's incestuous desire for his mother.[4] Yet a third group of critics has argued that Frankenstein's monster may be read as a daughter, in particular a daughter who embodies some of Mary Shelley's specific anxieties about daughterhood and writing.[5] All these different approaches yield useful insights into the meaning of Mary Shelley's first and most puzzling novel, but none grasps the centrality of the incest theme to the daughter's story rather than the father's. Those critics who read *Frankenstein* as an incest tale see the monster as a psychoanalytic symbol, as a living psychic projection whose importance lies in what he means to Frankenstein rather than in what the monster himself feels and suffers. Those critics who read the monster as a daughter focus on the monster's anger and pain, but tend to skirt the importance of the incest theme to the monster's anguish. When *Frankenstein* is read through the lens of *Mathilda,* the tale of father-daughter incest that Shelley wrote immediately after *Frankenstein,* one can propose a fuller interpretation: *Frankenstein* tells the story of a father and daughter locked in bitter conflict; more specifically, Mary Shelley portrays Victor Frankenstein as a paternal figure who projects his own incestuous guilt upon his creature and, having made it monstrous, rejects it. As we shall see, *Frankenstein* examines what followers of Freud would call a family romance. And the novel's composition is in itself a remarkable family romance, since Mary Shelley read and revised the works of both her father and her mother to tell the tale of Frankenstein's spurned, desolate offspring.

Victor Frankenstein, the overreaching scientist who gives the novel its name, can certainly be read as a father figure. Part of his motivation in fashioning his creature, after all, is his desire to receive the homage and thanks of beings dependent on him for their generation. As Frankenstein puts it, describing the sources of his enthusiasm for his work, "A new species would bless me as its creator and source; many happy and excellent natures would owe their being to me. No father could claim the gratitude of his child so completely as I should deserve their's."[6] Once brought to life, Frankenstein's nameless creature responds to its maker as a child to its father, first swearing to be "mild and docile to my natural lord and king" (95) and eventually rebelling in anger and vengeance when Frankenstein first rejects him and then refuses to complete work on a monstrous companion. *Frankenstein* is packed with allusions to Milton's *Paradise Lost,* and these allusions serve to underscore the creature's situation as the offspring of a powerful father: the creature repeatedly describes himself as an Adam or Satan figure (95, 125), in both cases casting Victor Frankenstein as a type of God the Father.

The characterization of Victor Frankenstein as a paternal figure carries over into other relationships in the novel as well. He sees himself as the protector and guide of Elizabeth Lavenza, the cousin who comes to live with the Frankenstein family and who will one day be Victor's wife. As Victor himself puts it, he sees Elizabeth as his pampered pet: "While I admired her understanding and fancy, I loved to tend on her, as I should on a favourite animal" (30).[7] And, once his mother dies, Victor holds himself responsible for the well-being of his younger siblings, though his father, Alphonse, is still alive.[8]

In portraying the details of Victor Frankenstein's background and up-bringing, Mary Shelley uses a technique she later employs in *Mathilda:* she draws upon data from the life and work of both William Godwin and Percy Bysshe Shelley, thus casting Victor Frankenstein as a composite of her father and her husband. Numerous critics have remarked upon the many ways Victor Frankenstein may be read as a Shelley figure. Shelley published early poetry under the pseudonym "Victor," after all, and had a passionately loving attachment to his sister Elizabeth. Victor Frankenstein's intellectual development follows the same path as Shelley's, beginning in a fascination with magic and the occult and shifting into a passion for what seemed the nearly limitless borders of the "new" natural sciences.[9] Even the details of Victor Frankenstein's preoccupation with death are drawn from a source in Shelley: just as Victor Frankenstein's curiosity forces him "to spend days and nights in vaults and charnel houses" (47), so the narrator of *Alastor,* one of Shelley's versions of himself, makes his "bed / In charnels and on coffins . . . / Like an inspired and desperate alchymist" (lines 24–25, 31).[10]

But the specific contours of Victor Frankenstein's situation and imagination can also be associated with William Godwin. Like William Godwin, Victor Frankenstein's intellectual preoccupations draw him away from the bosom of his family, so that his closest family relations feel abandoned, emotionally or literally. Like William Godwin, Victor Frankenstein begins his work convinced of the power of benevolent intentions—a conviction rudely erased by the realities of human unpredictability. And Mary Shelley draws heavily on autobiographical sources in William Godwin's own work to portray some aspects of Victor Frankenstein's peculiar transgression. Before Shelley wrote *Frankenstein,* she reread Godwin's autobiographical *St. Leon.* She then used St. Leon as a model for Victor Frankenstein. Both

Victor Frankenstein and the Count Julian de St. Leon, blinded by a flaw in their early educations, seek and obtain the elixir of life. Both spend the rest of their days trying to conceal this equivocal secret from family and friends. For Victor Frankenstein, as for St. Leon, the terrible "secret" drives a wedge between himself and his chosen mate, eventually killing her. For both characters, possessing the "secret" results in the total annihilation of family ties, leading Victor Frankenstein to echo St. Leon in his condemnation of any knowledge that interferes "with the tranquillity of [a man's] domestic affections" (51). Victor Frankenstein seems intermittently to grasp the lesson that William Godwin worked out for himself in the pages of *St. Leon:* domestic emotions are among the greatest of human treasures and their loss the greatest of human tragedies.[11]

Critics have generally agreed that Shelley's portrayal of Frankenstein as a composite of her father and husband expresses her negative reaction to the ideas and behavior of both William Godwin and Percy Bysshe Shelley. But when Shelley conflates the figures of the father and the lover in her central character, she also suggests the centrality of the theme of incest to her story. The issue of incest surfaces early in *Frankenstein;* it is imbedded in the familial relationships between Shelley's characters and in the language the characters use to describe their feelings for each other. Most important, the question of incest haunts the relation between Frankenstein and his creature, locking them in mortal conflict and dooming them to destroy each other.

The issue of incest is clearly involved in Victor Frankenstein's animation of his creature. The generation of the "monster" is an act tinged with sexuality—a sexuality that has its roots in Frankenstein's desire to possess his mother. Shelley goes so far as to portray Frankenstein's scientific research as reminiscent of an act of intercourse. Frankenstein throws himself into his scientific labors with an "ardor" that astonishes his fellow students (45). When Frankenstein first discovers the secret of the generation of life, he feels an orgasmic "delight and rapture": "to arrive at once at the summit of my desires, was the most gratifying consummation of my toils" (47). To pursue his discoveries further, Frankenstein enters a womblike place: "a solitary chamber, or rather cell, at the top of the house . . . separated from all the other apartments by a gallery and staircase" (50). There, Frankenstein loses himself in "midnight labours"; warmly enclosed in the womb of his study, Frankenstein, as he puts it, "pursue[s] nature to her hiding places . . . with unrelaxed and breathless eagerness" (49). Shelley even describes the animation of Frankenstein's creature in sexually suggestive terms. With "an anxiety that almost amounted to agony," Frankenstein collects the "instruments of life" around him. As the creature lies prone at Frankenstein's feet, Frankenstein applies the "instruments of life." The creature responds with an orgasmic shudder as it comes to life: "it breathed hard and a convulsive motion agitated its limbs" (52).[12]

Shortly after the sexual shudder that animates the creature, Victor Frankenstein falls asleep. As he tosses on his bed, he has an incestuous dream that ends with another convulsively sexual movement, this time Frankenstein's:

> I was disturbed by the wildest dreams. I thought I saw Elizabeth, in the bloom of health, walking in the streets of Ingolstadt. Delighted and surprised, I embraced her; but as I imprinted the first kiss on her lips, they became livid with the hue of death; her features appeared to change, and I thought that I held the corpse of my dead mother in my arms; a shroud enveloped her form, and I saw the grave-worms crawling in the folds of the flannel. I started from my sleep with horror; a cold dew covered my forehead, my teeth chattered, and every limb became convulsed; when, by the dim and yellow light of the moon, as it forced its way through the window-shutters, I beheld the wretch—the miserable monster whom I had created. (53)

On one level, Frankenstein's incestuous dream is the perfect revelation of something he cannot grasp in his waking moments: his desire to animate lifeless matter is ultimately traceable to his desire to bring his dead mother back to life and possess her. Frankenstein had an intensely close relationship to his mother; her sudden death was a "most irreparable evil" (38) that cast his soul into a "void" of despair. Frankenstein departs for the university at Ingolstadt shortly after his mother's death, and it is there that his fascination with science specifically fastens upon the possibility of creating new life from dead matter. As we have seen, Frankenstein's first stated reason for building his creature is his desire to father a new species. But behind this desire lies a second, less articulated motivation:

> A new species would bless me as its creator and source; many happy and excellent natures would owe their being to me. No father could claim the gratitude of his child so completely as I should deserve their's. Pursuing these reflections, I thought, that if I could bestow animation upon lifeless matter, I might in process of time (although I now found it impossible) renew life where death had apparently devoted the body to corruption. (49)

Behind Frankenstein's wish to father a new species lies his desire to resurrect the dead. Because at this point in the novel Frankenstein has experienced only one death—his mother's—the reader can infer a motivation that Frankenstein cannot quite put into words for himself: If Frankenstein can learn to "renew life where death had apparently devoted the body to corruption," he will possess the power to bring his beloved mother back from the realm of the dead.[13]

Frankenstein's dream expresses his own sense of the connection between his desire to create life and his desire to resurrect his mother, as well as his physical longing to possess his mother in an act of incest. Frankenstein has his dream, after all, immediately after he has brought his "monster" to life—giving life to his creature results in a dream-vision of Frankenstein's mother rising from the dead. But the mother rises from the dead in a manner that reveals Victor Frankenstein's incestuous longing for her: she appears in the guise of Frankenstein's lover. Frankenstein dreams he sees Elizabeth Lavenza walking in the streets of Ingolstadt and kisses her. At the first imprint of his lips, Elizabeth is revealed for what she really is, that is, the body of a ghastly dead mother, whose garments are covered with grave-worms. Frankenstein's dream thus pictures for him what, in his waking life, he seeks to accomplish in his relation to Elizabeth: to possess his mother sexually, to recreate with Elizabeth the blissful, undisturbed union of mother and child. As Frankenstein dreams, the sight of the mother/lover—and the sexually suggestive worms covering her body—make Frankenstein shudder awake, thus completing the fantasy union with the mother that began when Frankenstein applied the "instruments of life" to his creature.

Because Frankenstein vaguely connects his desire to generate life to incest and death, it is no wonder that he finds his work detestable even as he is driven to complete it. Frankenstein is inexorably drawn to what he calls his "work-shop of filthy creation"; he castigates himself even as he "disturb[s], with profane fingers, the tremendous secrets of the human frame"; his spirits turn "with loathing" from his occupation as he is "still urged on by an eagerness which perpetually increased" (50). And Frankenstein's guilt over his incestuous longing leads him to commit one other instinctive and irrevocable act: he rejects the creature he has just brought to life, a creature too closely associated in Frankenstein's mind with death, incest, and illicit sexual desire.

There is, consequently, more to Frankenstein's repudiation of his creature than Frankenstein puts into words for his listener, Robert Walton, and the reader. Shelley deliberately makes Frankenstein's stated motive for rejecting his creature seem implausible and unconvincing. According to Frankenstein, he repudiates his creature solely because he finds it ugly:

> How can I describe my emotions at this catastrophe, or how delineate the wretch whom with such infinite pains and care I had endeavoured to form? His limbs were in proportion, and I had selected his features as beautiful. Beautiful—Great God! His yellow skin scarcely covered the work of muscles and arteries beneath; his hair was of a lustrous black, and flowing; his teeth of a pearly whiteness; but these luxuriances only formed a more horrid contrast with his watery eyes, that seemed almost of the same colour as the dun white sockets in which they were set, his shrivelled complexion, and straight black lips. (52)[14]

Frankenstein has, by his own description labored many months to construct the creature;[15] it not entirely credible that, after months of looking at the creature's face, Frankenstein should suddenly find the creature's appearance unbearable. Further, a number of physical details in Frankenstein's description of his "monster" do not seem loathsome to the reader. Aside from his gigantic stature, the creature's facial "deformities" consist of three things: unnaturally light, watery eyes; shriveled, jaundiced skin; and straight black lips. Frankenstein's reaction to his offspring, in short, seems out of proportion to the facts as Frankenstein himself states them.[16] There is clearly some other deep-seated and unarticulated taboo at work in Victor Frankenstein's imagination.

It is the creature's "straight black lips," in fact, that provide the clue to the real source of Frankenstein's aversion to his offspring. Frankenstein falls asleep and dreams his incestuous dream immediately after running away from his creature in disgust. When his lover Elizabeth appears in Frankenstein's dream and he kisses her, her lips undergo a telling transformation: "[T]hey became livid with the hue of death; her features appeared to change." The word "livid" describes a deep, bruised color—specifically black and blue (OED). In this light, Elizabeth's "livid" lips are linked in Frankenstein's dream to the creature's "straight black lips." Suggestive of the vulva,[17] both sets of "lips" repulse Frankenstein because of their incestuous associations. The creature has not only been animated by an act whose sources lie in incestuous longings—the creature becomes, in Frankenstein's mind, another embodiment of his lover, Elizabeth, and, by extension, Frankenstein's dead mother. This association is solidified in Frankenstein's mind when the first thing Frankenstein sees as he wakes from his convulsive dream is his creature, who hangs over his bed with an entreating gesture:

"[E]very limb became convulsed; when, by the dim and yellow light of the moon, as it forced its way through the window-shutters, I beheld the wretch—the miserable monster whom I had created" (53). Shelley immediately gives Frankenstein a pun that emphasizes the connection between his offspring and the figure of the mother/lover: "[N]o mortal could support the horror of that countenance. A *mummy* again endued with animation could not be so hideous as that wretch" (53—italics mine). The newly animated creature, therefore, is entangled in the troubling association of mother and lover for Frankenstein. That the creature is also in some sense Frankenstein's child makes the emotional equation yet more disturbing, so Frankenstein quickly decides his creature is a "monster" (53). Troubled by guilt over his own barely perceived incestuous desires, Victor Frankenstein dispenses with his guilt in a convenient fashion: he projects it onto his creature and then rejects the being he has labored so long to bring to life.

It is worth noting that Frankenstein's incestuous dream looks forward to an incestuous dream in Mary Shelley's last novel, *Falkner*. In *Falkner*, Rupert Falkner's lover, Alithea Neville, is a mother figure to him. Near the end of the novel, Falkner has an incestuously suggestive dream in which this mother/lover blends imperceptibly into Falkner's daughter, Elizabeth Raby. Something of the same overlapping of female roles is apparent in Franken-stein's dream. Elizabeth Lavenza, Frankenstein's fiancée, becomes the corpse of his dead mother; as Frankenstein awakes, the composite lover/mother figure immediately merges into the palpable vision of Frankenstein's off-spring, with Victor Frankenstein staring straight into the eyes of his child, "the miserable monster whom I had created." The overlapping of female roles in both dreams implies a similarity in the meaning of the figures in them. Can Frankenstein's creature be read as a wretched predecessor to Elizabeth Raby? Is the "monstrous" consciousness at the center of Mary Shelley's first novel the precursor of a whole series of other abandoned or rejected daughters who appear in the rest of her work?

Several arguments can be made for reading Frankenstein's "monster" as an embodiment of the female in some sense, and specifically as a daughter. For one thing, Victor Frankenstein's displacement of his own monstrous fears upon the head of his creature parallels and repeats the male cultural act that associates, by an act of projection, what Gilbert and Gubar have called "filthy materiality" with female otherness.[18] After Victor Frankenstein projects his sexual anxieties upon his creature—a creature who is, until then, nothing more than a blank slate—the creature becomes, in Frankenstein's eyes, the living, moving embodiment of sexuality, filth, and death. In precisely the same way, male culture can project its fear of sexuality and death upon the female and cast her symbolically as physically monstrous—deformed, dirty, "an embodiment of just those extremes of mysterious and intransigent Otherness which culture confronts with . . . fear [and] . . . loathing."[19] In this context, the repulsive physical appearance Frankenstein imputes to his creature may be read as a figure of its loathsome femininity. And, as we shall see, the creature quickly internalizes its father's "reading" of it.

If Frankenstein's creature can be read as an embodiment of the female, it can be also be read more specifically as representing the plight of the daughter. Shelley takes pains to underscore the similarities between the situation of the creature and the predicament of the other abandoned, rejected, or betrayed daughters with whom she populates the pages of *Frankenstein*. Although Frankenstein's nameless creature is emphatically male, his circumstances have much more in common with the daughters who appear in the novel than with the sons. Chief among the similarities is the fact that the creature is "an orphan and beggar" (28)—a condition to which, at some point in the novel, all the daughters in *Frankenstein* have been reduced by their fathers. On the opening page of Frankenstein's narration, Shelley presents the story of Caroline Beaufort, Frankenstein's mother. Caroline Beaufort was motherless; she was cast into helpless poverty when her father lost his fortune and died. Society did not allow her the means to support herself; she was saved from penury and wretchedness only because Alphonse Frankenstein found her and allowed her to depend on him for protection. Similarly, Elizabeth Lavenza, Frankenstein's cousin, was sent from her family home when her mother died and her father remarried. She was saved because Alphonse Frankenstein, her kindly uncle, was willing to take her into his house.[20] Justine Moritz, a Frankenstein family servant who is eventually accused of murdering Victor Frankenstein's younger brother, is made into "an orphan and a beggar" when first her father dies and then her mother. Shelley further emphasizes the connection between Justine and Frankenstein's creature when Justine, explaining why she succumbed to her confessor's pressure to admit to a crime she did not commit, exclaims, "I almost began to think that I was the monster that he said I was" (82). Even Safie, the Arabian girl who falls in love with Felix DeLacey at the center of the creature's narration, is orphaned of a mother and betrayed by her father.[21] The histories of these daughters all serve to suggest Shelley's recognition of the pitifully dependent circumstances to which female children can be brought by the absence of a mother and the abandonment of a father. But they also point to and parallel the plight of the novel's central character.

Like these daughters, Frankenstein's creature is motherless, has been abandoned by his father, and has thus been reduced to the condition of "an orphan and a beggar." The difference is that the other daughters in *Frankenstein* find some haven of male protection and are thus not driven to rebellion and revenge. For Frankenstein's offspring, devoid of any social ties or saving human affection, the story is very different.

Some details of the creature's early history link him to a very specific daughter: Mary Shelley herself. As the creature hides in the hovel behind the DeLacey cottage, he reads *Paradise Lost*, a volume of Plutarch's *Lives*, and the *Sorrows of Werter* (123)—all works that Mary Shelley read as she prepared to write *Frankenstein*. Motherless and rejected by her own father as she wrote *Frankenstein*, Mary Shelley gives the creature her own obsessive fascination with her "accursed origin" (126).[22] Most important, Mary Shelley uses Frankenstein's rejected offspring to express her own rage and aggression, in particular at William Godwin and in general at cultural fathers whose power and prerogatives rob daughters of autonomy by associating them with sexuality, filth, and death. As U. C. Knoepflmacher has persuasively argued, *Frankenstein* is to a large degree a revenge tale in which Frankenstein's creature punishes his neglectful father/creator by forcing him to experience the creature's own desolation.[23] The centrality of rage and revenge to the meaning of *Frankenstein* explain Shelley's decision to cast the figure of the betrayed daughter as a male: in the guise of a gigantic male, Frankenstein's offspring possesses vast power, specifically the physical power to avenge itself through murder.[24]

To tell the tale of the fate of the father and his "monstrous" offspring, Mary Shelley uses, in part, a revisionary literary technique: she rewrites *Caleb Williams*, her own father's most important and widely read novel. From this angle. the composition of *Frankenstein* may be seen as an extraordinary family literary romance. As Mary Shelley wrote *Frankenstein*, she made a point of reading and rereading works written by both her father and her mother. From 1814 through 1817, she read Godwin's *Political Justice*, *St. Leon*, *Caleb Williams* (twice), *Essay on Sepulchres*, *Life of the Phillips*, *Fleetwood*, *Life of Chaucer*, and *Mandeville*. During the same period, she also read works by Mary Wollstonecraft: *Mary: A Fiction*, *Letters from Norway*, *Wrongs of Woman*, *The French Revolution*, *Posthumous Works* (edited by Godwin), and *Vindication of the Rights of Woman*. For our purposes, the most important of these works are *St. Leon*, *Caleb Williams*, and *The Wrongs of Woman*. *St. Leon* provided Shelley with autobiographical material, together with the outlines of the character and situation of Victor Frankenstein. *Caleb Williams* provided

Shelley \ the
desperat
    Shell
them int of
her fathe
Williams, ...s for dealing unfairly with
citizens w ...neither social rank nor money—a criticism epitomized
in the fate of Hawkins, a leaseholder who is convicted of a murder he did not
commit, forced to confess, and then executed.[25] In *Frankenstein*, Shelley
also criticizes the English justice system by giving Justine Moritz the same
fate Hawkins meets: like Hawkins, Justine suffers unjust conviction, a forced
confession, and wrongful execution. Further, Shelley uses many of her
father's ideas and philosophical vocabulary in her description of the beliefs
of Victor Frankenstein. In *Caleb Williams*, Ferdinando Falkland, the man
who eventually pursues Caleb across England in an attempt to prevent him
from revealing Falkland's "secret," is a scion of the upper classes who pro-
pounds the importance of "benevolence" and reason, and judges all acts by
their social utility. Similarly, Victor Frankenstein is moved to act by the
principles of "benevolence" (42, 95) and reason, and seeks to discover scientific truths that will be useful to the social community.[26]

    But Shelley puts Godwin's *Caleb Williams* to use in a more significant
fashion in her portrayal of the plight and powers of the "monster." Chiefly,
Shelley adopts her father's analysis of the impact of environment upon
character, but rewrites the analysis to highlight individual paternal guilt
rather than the social system Godwin emphatically indicts. *Caleb Williams*
is, by Godwin's own description, "a general review of the modes of domestic
and unrecorded despotism, by which man becomes the destroyer of man"
(1). In *Caleb Williams*, the novel's hero learns the guilty secret of Falkland's
past: Falkland, Caleb's master and mentor, murdered Barnabas Tyrrel over
an insult to Falkland's honor. Falkland confesses his guilt to Caleb but then
feels compelled to keep Caleb in his power to prevent further revelations.
Godwin structures his plot to reveal the way that Falkland, as a wealthy
landowner, controls Caleb's environment and fate, making Caleb into an
outlaw. Falkland first refuses to let Caleb leave his employ; when Caleb insists,
Falkland determines to ruin Caleb by accusing him of robbery. The story of
Caleb Williams's abandonment and persecution begins at this point. Falkland
ceases to be his supportive mentor. He has Caleb thrown into jail, and when
Caleb escapes, Falkland pursues him mercilessly. Caleb grows to recognize
the extent to which deprivation generates immorality. "O poverty!" he

exclaims, "thou art indeed omnipotent! Thou grindest us into desperation . . . thou fillest us to the very brim with malice and revenge, and renderest us capable of acts of unknown horror!" (116). Cut off from human contact and hardened by impossible living conditions, Caleb falls in with a band of thieves. As Falkland's agents ferret Caleb out of whatever hiding place he can contrive, Caleb sinks lower and suffers more. Caleb repeatedly castigates the social system that allows a wealthy, upper-class "master" to exert such power over his servant (72, 83–85, 163, 182–83). Close to the end of the novel, Caleb blames society and his circumstances for making him what he has become:

> Pursued by a train of ill fortune, I could no longer consider myself as a member of society. I was a solitary being cut off from the expectation of sympathy, kindness and the good will of mankind. . . . I cursed the whole system of human existence. I said, Here I am, an outcast, destined to perish with hunger and cold. All men desert me. All men hate me. I am driven with mortal threats from the sources of comfort and existence. Accursed world! that hates without a cause, that overwhelms innocence with calamities which ought to be spared even to guilt! Accursed world! dead to every manly sympathy; with eyes of horn and hearts of steel! Why do I consent to live any longer? Why do I seek to drag on an existence, which, if protracted, must be protracted amidst the lairs of these human tygers? (247, 251–52)

From Godwin's point of view, the social system's support of Falkland's prerogatives as a wealthy landowner has deprived Caleb of the essential civilizing ingredient—human sympathy. As Caleb says,

> The greatest aggravation of my present lot was, that I was cut off from the friendship of mankind. I can safely affirm, that poverty and hunger, that endless wanderings, that a blasted character and the curses that clung to my name, were all of them slight misfortunes compared to this. . . . Sympathy, the magnetic virtue, the hidden essence of our life, was extinct. (308)

Deprived of human sympathy, Caleb has lost all human sympathy himself. As he puts it, "I was a monster with whom the very earth groaned!" (249).

In *Frankenstein*, Shelley ascribes her "monster's" descent into violence to similar environmental causes but focuses the responsibility for his plight more squarely on the monster's rejecting creator. Like Caleb Williams, Frankenstein's creature is subjected to countless physical deprivations —he goes hungry, he shivers with cold, he sleeps in the elements when he cannot find shelter. Like Caleb Williams, Shelley's "monster" suffers chiefly from the lack of human contact, from the fact that he is, to borrow Caleb's phrase, "a solitary being, cut off from the expectation of sympathy, kindness, and the good will of mankind." The creature knows that misery has made him evil. "I was benevolent and good; misery made me a fiend," he tells Frankenstein. "Make me happy, and I shall again be virtuous" (95). Specifically, the monster knows that his lack of "sympathy" and companionship has forced him to transgress social boundaries. Full of this recognition, he asks Frankenstein to fashion a companion for him declaring "my evil passions will [flee], for I shall meet with sympathy" (143).

But while Godwin traces Caleb Williams's suffering to the oppression of the social institutions that stand behind Falkland, Shelley has her "monster" insistently condemn a single individual—his rejecting father. According to the creature, Victor Frankenstein is to blame for the "deformity" that isolates him from other human beings. "Cursed creator!" the "monster" exclaims in agony. "Why did you form a monster so hideous that even you turned from me in disgust? . . . Satan had his companions, fellow-devils, to admire and encourage him; but I am solitary and detested" (126). And, according to the creature, Frankenstein did worse than make him physically ugly. The creature continually insists that rejection by his father is the origin of his suffering, and therefore of his vengefully malicious behavior. "No father had watched my infant days," (117) he laments, and later: "I remembered Adam's supplication to his Creator; but where was mine? he had abandoned me, and, in the bitterness of my heart, I cursed him" (127).

To reinforce and explain the creature's sense of Frankenstein's responsibility for his isolation, Shelley borrows and rewrites an important scene from *Caleb Williams*, specifically locating the father's rejection as the cause of his creature's violence. In one of Caleb Williams's encounters, he is guarded by a "venerable" and "benevolent" (246) old man whom Caleb seeks to interest in his case. Caleb tells the old man how unjustly he has been handled and asks the old man's help. The old man seems favorably disposed to becoming Caleb's "benefactor" (247) and aiding his escape, but first asks to know his name. When Caleb reveals his identity, the kindly old man is aghast—he refuses to have anything more to do with Caleb, and he tells Caleb "it would be an abuse of words to consider [Caleb] in the light of a human creature" (249). Rejected by the kindly and benevolent old man, and made to feel like a "monster" (249) by the rejection, Caleb eventually succeeds in escaping without him.

Mary Shelley adopts and revises this scene from her father's novel for a crucial sequence of *Frankenstein*. Shelley has her creature seek out the support and help of another kindly, "benevolent" (103) old man, Mr. DeLacey. Like Caleb Williams, the creature tells the old man the tale of his misfortunes; like the old man in Godwin's novel, DeLacey seems favorably disposed to helping the supplicant until circumstances reveal the supplicant's identity—in *Frankenstein* when DeLacey's son, Felix, enters the room and reacts in terror to the nameless creature's horrid appearance. Godwin's old man is kind and venerable but not particularly paternal; Shelley, on the other hand, takes pains to emphasize the importance the "monster" attaches to DeLacey as a father figure. In *Frankenstein,* the abandoned creature consistently views DeLacey as a father who might replace the one who abandoned him. The creature secretly watches the DeLaceys for months, yearning to be admitted to their family circle. When he first sees DeLacey offer fatherly comfort to his daughter, Agatha, the creature identifies with the daughter instantly and reacts powerfully to the father's love: "I felt sensations of a peculiar and overpowering nature: they were a mixture of pain and pleasure, such as I had never before experienced, either from hunger or cold, warmth or food: and I withdrew from the window, unable to bear these emotions" (103–4). Shortly afterward, the creature learns the word associated with the old man's affection for his daughter, and with the creature's own mingled emotions of daughterly pleasure and desperation: "The youth and his companion had each of them several names, but the old man had only one, which was *father*" (107–8, Shelley's italics). As the scene unfolds and the creature sees the mutual sympathy the DeLacey children share with their father, he becomes increasingly obsessed with the question of his own origins and increasingly covets DeLacey's affection, even admitting that, as he views the children's "bliss," "the bitter gall of envy rose within me" (125). Shelley's use of allusion underscores DeLacey's importance to the creature as a father who might replace Frankenstein. When the creature reads *Paradise Lost,* huddled in the hovel behind DeLacey's cottage and walled off from the warmth of the DeLacey family hearth, he understands that it is the absence of paternal protection that differentiates him from Adam. As the creature puts it, Adam "had come forth from the hands of God a perfect creature, happy and prosperous, guarded by the especial care of his Creator; he was allowed to converse with, and acquire knowledge from beings of a superior nature: but I was wretched. helpless, and alone" (125).

In this context, DeLacey's rejection of the creature represents rejection by the father figure in whom the creature has invested his hope for human sympathy. As Shelley portrays it, the creature's approach to DeLacey is the culmination of his search for a father; when DeLacey cries out "Great God! . . . who are you?" (131), the scene repeats Frankenstein's own horrified response to his first glimpse of his creature.

DeLacey's rejection, since it is a father's rejection, has an awful impact: unlike Caleb Williams, who feels "monstrous" but continues to run from his pursuers, Shelley's creature contemplates violence when the sympathy of his father figure is denied him. He retreats to his hovel in despair and, for the first time in his history, considers aggression and vengeance. Where the creature had initially envied the DeLacey children and longed to be one of them, he now yearns only for their destruction:

> [M]y feelings were those of rage and revenge. I could with pleasure have destroyed the cottage and its inhabitants, and have glutted myself with their shrieks and misery. . . . All, save I, were at rest or in enjoyment: I, like the archfiend, bore a hell within me; and, finding myself unsympathized with, wished to tear up the trees, spread havoc and destruction around me, and then to have sat down and enjoyed the ruin. (132)

The creature's reference to *Paradise Lost* again underscores his situation as the offspring of a rejecting father. Indeed, it is immediately after DeLacey's rejection that the creature commits his first act of vengeful destruction: once DeLacey has broken "the only link that held me to the world" (134), the creature bends his "mind towards injury and death" (134) and burns down DeLacey's cottage.

Caleb's encounter with the "venerable" old man is not a crucial scene in *Caleb Williams*. Caleb is wounded by the old man's repudiation, but their meeting, one in a long series of picaresque adventures, does not change Caleb's behavior in any material way. Shelley, on the other hand, places her revision of Godwin's scene from *Caleb Williams* at the emotional center of *Frankenstein*. DeLacey's rejection of the creature is the turning point in the creature's history; DeLacey's refusal to provide the creature human sympathy touches off the chain of violence and vengeance that eventually destroys both the "monster" and the original rejecting father, Frankenstein himself. In her emphasis on DeLacey as a father figure, and in the structural importance Shelley accords this scene in the organization of *Frankenstein*, Shelley in effect turns William Godwin's environmental argument against William Godwin himself: she shows that the creature is made monstrous by the lack of human sympathy his environment allows him, but she lays the blame for the offspring's vengeful violence directly at the door of the rejecting father.

Shelley borrows from and rewrites *Caleb Williams* in one final way: she inverts the structural elements of her father's plot to place the balance of power in the hands of the figure of the betrayed daughter. Numerous writers have observed that both novels are organized by the device of a relentless pursuit, in which two opponents are obsessively and fatally linked to each other.[27] In Godwin's *Caleb Williams*, Falkland controls the chase and punishes his servant through most of the novel. Caleb runs away from Falkland and his accomplices for the better part of two hundred pages, through a picaresque series of apprehensions and escapes. Finally, in the last few pages, Caleb succeeds in revealing the secret of Falkland's crime and thus frees himself from the grip of Falkland's power. The plot of *Frankenstein*, on the other hand, has two cycles of pursuit, with the figure of the daughter dominating both. In the first cycle, the creature tracks Frankenstein. Using the papers he found in Frankenstein's coat the creature learns Frankenstein's name and his origins in Geneva, and the creature makes his way there. On the outskirts of the town, the creature meets little William Frankenstein; when he realizes that William "belong[s]" (139) to his enemy, he kills him. The creature next hides a locket-sized portrait of Frankenstein's mother in the clothing of Justine Moritz, thus ensuring that Justine will be accused and convicted of William's murder. The creature finally finds Frankenstein at the foot of a glacier in the Alps; he tells Frankenstein the story of his suffering and demands that Frankenstein make him a companion. The creature then pursues Frankenstein across Europe and into England as Frankenstein prepares to build a female creature. When Frankenstein destroys the female before animating it, the creature bursts into violence again, murdering first his friend, Clerval, and, after tracking Frankenstein to his honeymoon destination, his bride, Elizabeth. Thus, throughout this first cycle of pursuit in *Frankenstein*, the outcast pursues and punishes his master in a direct inversion of the pursuit pattern of *Caleb Williams*.

In the last pages of *Frankenstein*, Shelley adds a second cycle of pursuit and ostensibly reverses her scheme by allowing Frankenstein to pursue his rejected creature. But even here it is clearly the creature who controls the terms of the chase and who manipulates Frankenstein into following him to increasingly desolate terrain. As Frankenstein prays at Elizabeth's graveside, the creature's fiendish laugh goads Frankenstein into following him. From then on, the creature taunts Frankenstein whenever his energy fails and jeers at him whenever he is about to give up the chase. The creature leaves marks on trees so Frankenstein can follow his trail (201, 202); he leaves food to keep up Frankenstein's strength (201, 202). The creature even warns

Frankenstein, in a mocking note, to wrap himself in furs and load his sledge with food before setting out after him over the Arctic wastes (203). Frankenstein obsessively pursues his rejected creature through the last pages of the novel, but the creature is clearly in control.

The point, of course, is that Shelley rewrites her father's plot to give power and authority to the rejected social outcast. As the creature puts it, after telling Frankenstein he is his creature's slave, "Remember that I have power; you believe yourself miserable, but I can make you so wretched that the light of day will be hateful to you. You are my creator, but I am your master" (165). In this way, the figure of the betrayed daughter gains ascendancy over her rejecting creator by dominating and punishing him. Frankenstein's creature does what the other daughters in the novel cannot do: he vents his fury and frustration in violence. In Shelley's first novel, her protagonist's rage is expressed openly, even if Shelley must portray her protagonist as nameless and male. As we shall see, Shelley's subsequent daughters become emphatically female but express their rage in less direct ways.

Perhaps the chief artistic triumph of *Frankenstein* is the fact that Shelley expresses her creature's malice and violence thoroughly, yet manages to keep him almost entirely sympathetic. She accomplishes this chiefly by allowing the creature to describe his suffering at great length and by placing the creature's own narrative at the structural center of the novel. Shelley uses one other strategy to manipulate her readers' sympathies in favor of the rejected creature. Victor Frankenstein repeatedly insists that his creature is monstrous and loathsome; Shelley manipulates point of view to invite an ironic response to Frankenstein, his behavior, and his assertions.

Shelley gives *Frankenstein* a complicated, concentric narrative frame. The outermost narrative frame consists of a series of letters written by Robert Walton, an arctic explorer, to his sister, Margaret Saville. Walton's narrative frames Frankenstein's narrative—told to Walton on a ship locked in the ice close to the North Pole—which in turn frames the creature's story. This structure of related framed narratives serves, among other things, to highlight a crucial fact: that Frankenstein's narrative is in fact a story, told by Frankenstein about himself and therefore open to scrutiny by the reader for its reliability. Upon close inspection, the reader discovers that Mary Shelley repeatedly casts Frankenstein as less than a completely reliable narrator.

We have already seen that Frankenstein's description of the animation of his creature is not to be taken entirely at face value—that is, that Frankenstein fails to articulate in it all his reasons for creating his creature and all his reasons for abandoning it. Having suggested that Frankenstein finds his creature "loathsome" for reasons he cannot entirely express, Shelley continues to suggest that Frankenstein's responses to his creature mask hidden motives and are therefore to be read with a questioning eye. First of all, Shelley undermines Frankenstein's credibility by her use of sight imagery. Frankenstein sees his creature as physically ugly; he consistently extrapolates from the creature's physical appearance to his moral nature, concluding that the creature's soul is as hideous as his face. When Frankenstein meets the creature on the ice at Montanvert, for example, Frankenstein is repelled by the creature's "unearthly ugliness [that] rendered it almost too horrible for human eyes." Frankenstein immediately interprets the creature's moral nature from its appearance: "[H]is countenance bespoke bitter anguish, combined with disdain and malignity" (94). As this encounter represents the first meeting between Frankenstein and his creature since the night the creature came to life, Frankenstein has little basis, except his preconception, for deciding that his creature feels "disdain and malignity." Frankenstein continues to associate his creature's appearance with moral corruption as the novel unfolds, repeatedly making assertions such as "[H]is countenance expressed the utmost extent of malice and treachery" (164) and "His soul is as hellish as his form, full of treachery and fiend-like malice" (206).

Shelley's rendering of Victor Frankenstein's reaction to William's murder also casts doubt on Frankenstein's total reliability. Frankenstein hears of William's death in a letter from his father; he quickly returns to Geneva to comfort his family. On the way there, Frankenstein gets a glimpse of his creature:

> A flash of lightning illuminated the object, and discovered its shape plainly to me; its gigantic stature, and the deformity of its aspect, more hideous than belongs to humanity, instantly informed me that it was the wretch, the filthy daemon to whom I had given life. What did' he here? Could he be (I shuddered at the conception) the murderer of my brother? No sooner did that idea cross my imagination, than I became convinced of its truth; my teeth chattered, and I was forced to lean against a tree for support. The figure passed me quickly, and I lost it in the gloom. Nothing in human shape could have destroyed that fair child. *He* was the murderer! I could not doubt it. The mere presence of the idea was an irresistible proof of the fact. (71–72)

Frankenstein again associates the creature's physical deformity with moral loathsomeness and guilt. Since the creature's aspect is "more hideous than belongs to humanity" and since "nothing in human shape" could murder a child, Frankenstein reasons, the creature must be the culprit. Yet Shelley's rendering of this speech makes Frankenstein undercut the reasoning behind his conclusions even as he asserts their accuracy. "No sooner did that idea cross my imagination, than I became convinced of its truth," admits Frankenstein, in a startling abandonment of logic. And, forsaking the scientist's insistence on corroboration and proof, Frankenstein asserts that the mere existence of an idea proves its correctness: "*He* was the murderer. . . . The mere presence of the idea was an irresistible proof of its fact." Coming from a scientist of Frankenstein's obvious powers, Frankenstein's presumptive logic suggests he is prone to read his creature in a flawed way, consistently imputing malice to a creature he barely knows. Frankenstein's irrational response to his creature undercuts his negative pronouncement about the creature's moral nature, creating sympathy for the misunderstood and abandoned wretch, and reminding the reader that Frankenstein's reactions to the "monster" disguise his own hidden feelings.

This pattern of presuming that his creature is fundamentally malevolent persists throughout the first half of Frankenstein's narrative. Frankenstein eventually admits that he does not know for certain if the creature is guilty of murder: "I had hitherto supposed him to be the murderer of my brother," he says, "and I eagerly sought a confirmation or denial of this opinion" (97). But the lack of confirmation does not prevent Frankenstein from continuing to hold firmly to his belief in the creature's malignity—and responding to this belief with a torrent of hatred and abuse. As Frankenstein puts it, after concluding that the creature is somehow responsible for Justine's death as well as William's,

> My abhorrence of this fiend cannot be conceived. When I thought of him, I gnashed my teeth, my eyes became inflamed, and I ardently wished to extinguish that life which I had so thoughtlessly bestowed. When I reflected on his crimes and malice, my hatred and revenge burst all bounds of moderation. I would have made a pilgrimage to the highest peak of the Andes, could I, when there, have precipitated him to their base. I wished to see him again, that I might wreak the utmost extent of anger on his head, and avenge the deaths of William and Justine. (87)

Of course, Frankenstein's conclusions about this creature are eventually proven true. When the creature tells his story, he admits his culpability in the deaths of William and Justine. But that the creature is eventually proven guilty does not undercut the irony implicit in Mary Shelley's treatment of

Victor Frankenstein. Through the first half of Frankenstein's story, until he hears the creature's account, all Frankenstein knows of his creature with certainty is that he finds the creature loathsome to his sight.

Shelley invites an ironic response to Frankenstein and his actions in the first half of his narration in at least one other way: she emphasizes the aggression Frankenstein displays toward his creature and contrasts it to the creature's tendency, in encounters with Frankenstein, initially to avoid violence. When Frankenstein first sees the creature by the side of the glacier, his opening statement indicates yet again the presumptively negative light in which Frankenstein has decided to construe his creature. "Devil!" Frankenstein exclaims, "Begone, vile insect!" (94). Frankenstein immediately threatens the creature with violence: "[R]ather stay, that I may trample you to dust!" And then, "My rage was without bounds; I sprang on him, impelled by all the feelings which can arm one being against the existence of another" (94–95). The creature, for his part, remains calm. He points out to Frankenstein that Frankenstein himself is guilty of the aggression he tries to assign his creature. "I expected this reception," he says. "All men hate the wretched; how then must I be hated, who am miserable beyond all living things! . . . You purpose to kill me. How dare you sport thus with life?" (94). When Frankenstein tries to jump on the creature, the creature does not attack but runs away. "Be calm!" the creature implores Frankenstein. "I entreat you to hear me, before you give vent to your hatred on my devoted head. . . . I will not be tempted to set myself in opposition to thee" (95). For much of the rest of this scene, Frankenstein rages while the creature begs him to listen to his tale before passing judgment. As the creature wryly puts it, "The guilty are allowed, by human laws, bloody as they may be, to speak in their own defence before they are condemned. Listen to me, Frankenstein. You accuse me of murder; and yet you would, with a satisfied conscience, destroy your own creature. Oh, praise the eternal justice of man!" (96).

Shelley again emphasizes Frankenstein's aggression and the creature's rationality in the scene immediately following the close of the "monster's" narration. After a brief moment of bewilderment, Frankenstein's anger at the creature flares out again: "I could no longer suppress the rage that burned within me" (141), Frankenstein cries. As Frankenstein execrates his creature, the creature again points out the irony implicit in Frankenstein's aggressive behavior toward him, and tries to calm Frankenstein. "You are in the wrong," he says, "and, instead of threatening, I am content to reason with you. I am malicious because I am miserable. . . . You, my creator, would tear me to pieces, and triumph; remember that, and tell me why I should pity man more than he pities me?" (141). The creature then makes what he sees as a "reasonable and moderate" (142) demand: that Frankenstein build him a companion, so that the creature and a partner may share a "harmless" (142) life, hidden in the jungles of South America, eating berries and living in peace with nature and human beings. Frankenstein momentarily softens and promises to construct a female creature to end his creature's desperate isolation.

In both of these scenes, Shelley subtly manipulates the reader's sympathies in favor of the spurned, desolate creature. Frankenstein presumes his creature to be malevolent and attacks it; the creature responds either by running beyond Frankenstein's reach or reasoning with him. In its encounters with Frankenstein, the creature repeatedly acts more "human" than its creator. In short, the weight of each scene casts Frankenstein's behavior in an ironic light as he plays the role of the aggressor to the creature's role of rational and miserable victim.

This is not to say, of course, that Shelley portrays the creature as essentially and consistently virtuous. The creature quickly internalizes Frankenstein's rejection and sees himself in Frankenstein's terms as loathsome, filthy, and repulsive. He is initially puzzled when local inhabitants run away from him in terror, but he grasps the horrible truth of his predicament when, in a painful parody of Eve's first glimpse of her face in *Paradise Lost*, the creature sees his reflection in a pool and starts back in horror:

> At first I started back, unable to believe that it was indeed I who was reflected in the mirror; and when I became fully convinced that I was in reality the monster that I am, I was filled with the bitterest sensations of despondence and mortification. (109)

Milton's Eve, of course, finds her reflection beautiful. As Gilbert and Gubar have pointed out, Mary Shelley's rewriting of this scene corrects Milton's portrayal of Eve's reaction to her appearance: How could any woman, created second and as an inferior type of man, find her image pleasing?[28] By the same token, how could the creature, rejected by a father because of its troubling associations with incest, sexuality, and death, see its own reflection as anything but monstrous? In part, the creature's horrified reaction to its image in the mirrorlike surface of the pool is a female reading of the mirror held up to women by the culture that shapes them: their femininity, due to its entanglement in sexuality and "filthy materiality" is loathsome. From this point of view, it is little wonder that the creature's emotions sometimes veer wildly—from the extremes of self-hatred to a startled rage directed at the creator who made him what he is.

But the monster's horrified response to its image in the pool is not only a general feminine response to self shaped by culture. It is, even more specifically, an expression of an individual daughter's self-loathing, generated by the father's inexplicable rejection of her. Just as cultural "fathers" may define femininity as repulsive and filthy, so can individual fathers cause daughters to associate themselves with sexuality and guilt when, at crucial passages, the fathers behave in an inexplicably rejecting manner. As we have seen, this situation arises most commonly as the daughter passes through adolescence and matures physically into a fully sexual being. As the daughter leaves the asexual latency of her childhood and as the father recognizes the daughter's burgeoning sexuality, he often withdraws affection, both to eliminate the possibility of incest and to erect a barrier against his conscious recognition of the desire the daughter inspires in him.[29] This pattern of paternal rejection is one of the mechanisms that moves the daughter into the cultural stream of adult femininity, and, simultaneously, perpetuates the daughter/woman's association with sex, guilt, and "filthy materiality." This paternal response, of course, also shapes the way the daughter views herself. The daughter sees her emerging sexuality as connected to her father's inexplicable rejection and as emblematic of rejection by the male world.[30] In this way, the individual father's rejection, with its attendant implication of the daughter's guilty sexuality, not only precipitates the daughter's introduction into adult womanhood but also teaches her the self-loathing that culture attaches to the female state.

In this context, it is worth examining what Mary Shelley tells us about the imaginative origins of *Frankenstein*. Shelley provides her lengthiest account of the genesis of the novel in an introduction written for Colburn and Bentley's 1831 Standard Authors edition. The purpose of the introduction, Shelley tells us in curiously sexual language, is to explain "How I, then a young girl, came to think of, and to dilate upon, so very hideous an idea" (1831 introduction, 222). Shelley relates the famous tale of the ghost story contest with Byron, Shelley, and Polidori; she then describes a waking dream, inspired by a conversation about galvanism and the reanimation of corpses. The waking dream is a "hideous phantasm" (1831 introduction, 228) that terrifies her and provides the germ of her tale:

> Night waned upon this talk, and even the witching hour had gone by, before we retired to rest. When I placed my head on my pillow I did not sleep, nor could I be said to think. My imagination, unbidden, possessed and guided me, gifting the successive images that arose in my mind with a vividness far beyond the usual bounds of reverie. I saw—with shut eyes,

but acute mental vision,—I saw the pale student of unhallowed arts kneeling beside the thing he had put together. I saw the hideous phantasm of a man stretched out, and then, on the working of some powerful engine, show signs of life, and stir with an uneasy, half-vital motion. (1831 introduction, 227–28)

Shelley's account of her nightmarish "waking dream," with its description of the "working of some powerful engine" to bring the creature to life, duplicates the sexual overtones of the animation scene in *Frankenstein* as Shelley wrote it in the summer of 1816. As Shelley explains, she began to write *Frankenstein* the day following her dream, and began composition with the sexually charged scene in which Frankenstein brings his creature to life. By Shelley's own account, this nightmarish image and the scene it produced lie at the very heart of what inspired her to write *Frankenstein,* as well as at the heart of the novel itself.

As several commentators have pointed out, Shelley's placement of the origins of *Frankenstein* in a dream diverts focus away from her authorial responsibility for telling such a hideous story.[31] But it is worth noting that the 1831 introduction, in addition to deflecting attention away from Shelley's active labor as an author, also locates the origins of *Frankenstein* in "waking dreams" that antedate the ghost story competition and conversations at Villa Diodati by several years. Shelley begins her explanation of how she came to "dilate upon so very hideous an idea" with an account of her childhood as "the daughter of two persons of distinguished literary celebrity" (1831 introduction, 222). Her favorite pastime, she says, was to "write stories," and she goes on to describe her sense of how her imagination worked in her adolescence:

Still I had a dearer pleasure than this, which was the formation of castles in the air—the indulging in waking dreams—the following up trains of thought, which had for their subject the formation of a succession of imaginary incidents. My dreams were at once more fantastic and agreeable than my writings. In the latter I was a close imitator—rather doing as others had done, than putting down the suggestions of my own mind. What I wrote was intended at least for one other eye—my childhood's companion and friend; but my dreams were all my own; I accounted for them to nobody; they were my refuge when annoyed—my dearest pleasure when free.

I lived principally in the country as a girl and passed a considerable time in Scotland . . . my habitual residence was on the blank and dreary northern shores of the Tay, near Dundee. . . . They [the shores of the Tay] were the eyry of freedom, and the pleasant region where unheeded I could commune with the creatures of my fancy. I wrote then—but in a most commonplace style. It was beneath the trees of the grounds belonging to our house, or on the bleak sides of the woodless mountains near, that my true compositions, the airy flights of my imagination, were born and fostered. I did not make myself the heroine of my tales . . . but I was not confined to my own identity, and I could people the hours with creations far more interesting to me at that age, than my own sensations. (1831 introduction, 222–23)

Several observations can be made about Shelley's account of her adolescent "waking dreams." To begin with, one wonders how William Godwin responded to Shelley's insistence that she "lived principally in the country as a girl and passed a considerable time in Scotland" when, as we have seen, Shelley lived principally in William Godwin's house in London and spent a year and a half in Scotland, the place Godwin sent his daughter for part of her adolescence to eliminate friction with his second wife. As we have seen, Mary Godwin was almost fifteen when Godwin sent her to Dundee; associated as it was with her developing womanhood and her conflicts with her father's second wife, the Scottish sojourn must have seemed to the adolescent Mary Godwin to be both a paternal rejection of the adult woman she was becoming and a definitive exile from her father's affection. Shelley's distorted emphasis on Scotland in the 1831 introduction to *Frankenstein* suggests that Scotland dominated everything else in Shelley's youth; it became for Shelley a place that shadowed and defined her adolescence, determining her perception of herself and her relation to her work as a writer. Equally important, Shelley's account locates the period of her Scottish residence as the source of her "true compositions"—her first "waking dreams" that, by Shelley's account, lay behind the very specific "waking dream" that coalesced, some four years later, into the text of *Frankenstein*. As Shelley puts it, in what seems a very accurate description of a girl coming to grips with her adolescent anxieties in fantasy, these "waking dreams" were her "refuge when annoyed" and her "dearest pleasure when free." In short, Shelley's 1831 introduction to *Frankenstein* subtly implies that the novel has its imaginative origins in a period related to, but antedating, Shelley's relationship to her husband and Byron. Specifically, Shelley implies that *Frankenstein* is rooted in the "waking dreams" of Scotland—waking dreams that perhaps allowed the adolescent Mary Godwin to grapple with paternal rejection, that rejection's incestuous implications, and the burgeoning female sexuality that seemed to have inspired both.

It is in this context that Frankenstein's creature, like Mathilda, can be read as a daughter made monstrous by incest. Shelley's rendering of Victor Frankenstein's incestuous relation to his creature is a figure for the sources of the daughter's sense of her own guilty sexuality and loathsomeness. The father's rejection teaches a daughter to see herself as different—sexual and hideous; in precisely the same way, Victor Frankenstein's rejection teaches his creature to see himself as repulsive and not of the human species:

> I was . . . endowed with a figure hideously deformed and loathsome; I was not even of the same nature as man. . . . When I looked around, I saw and heard of none like me. Was I then a monster, a blot upon the earth, from which all men fled, and whom all men disowned? (115–16)

Frankenstein's creature has learned a terrible lesson from his father's rejection, and he has acquired the daughter's awful knowledge of being like—yet horribly unlike—her father: "Cursed creator!" the monster exclaims in agony. "Why did you form a monster so hideous that even you turned from me in disgust? God in pity made man beautiful and alluring, after his own image; but my form is a filthy type of your's, more horrid from its very resemblance" (126).

Much of the creature's tragedy, then, lies in his sense of himself as loathsome and less than human. Yet in a very real way, the greater part of the creature's tragedy—and the daughter's—is the constant realization that he is not so different at all from either his creator or the people who run from him in terror. As we have seen, Mary Shelley was trained before her adolescence to expect to inherit the prerogatives of the son rather than the guilt of the daughter. Her description of the monster's baffled sense of his similarity to privileged human beings perfectly captures the daughter's confused sense of similarity, disappointment, and loss, as she enters adolescence and finds expected opportunities removed. Significantly, Shelley sets this moment of recognition in the context of the creature's literary education. As he reads *Werter, Paradise Lost,* and Plutarch's *Lives*—all definitive expressions of male culture and works that Shelley herself read—Frankenstein's creature reacts in this way: "As I read . . . I applied much personally to my own feelings and condition. I found myself similar, yet at the same time strangely unlike the beings concerning whom I read, and to whose conversation I was a listener" (124). As we shall see, Mathilda enters adolescence longing to be a boy and expecting to inherit a son's prerogatives; she is dismayed to find she is instead treated like a daughter. In the same way, Frankenstein's creature reads the stories of male protagonists and finds he is strangely like, yet strangely unlike, the favored males who populate the pages. It is in this context that Shelley's insistent doubling of the creature and his creator may be read. Shelley goes to great pains to employ imagistic patterns that make Frankenstein and his creature obvious repetitions of one another.[32] It is entirely appropriate, emotionally and psychologically, for a daughter to resemble, or double, a father. And part of the daughter's baffling tragedy of recognition begins when, despite the fact that she resembles and repeats the father, she is rejected and denied his prerogatives.

This line of argument allows us to understand the creature's explosive rage as well as some of the logic underpinning his first and last crimes—the murder of William Frankenstein and the murder of Elizabeth Lavenza. Rejected and made loathsome by a father, deprived of any legitimate social position or connection, the creature turns to revenge. "I will glut the maw of death, until it be satiated with the blood of your remaining friends" (94), he threatens Frankenstein; and later, "I can make you so wretched that the light of day will be hateful to you" (165). The creature does precisely what a repudiated daughter might be expected to do were she gigantic and powerful: he turns on his father/creator and punishes him by making the father experience his offspring's own desolation. As Knoepflmacher correctly points out, the creature's first murder—that of the child William Frankenstein, Frankenstein's youngest brother—may be read as an act of fratricide. Mary Shelley's younger brother, the first son of William Godwin and Mary Jane Godwin, was named William. As Knoepflmacher suggests, Shelley kills off William as the creature's first victim and thus triumphs imaginatively over one of the younger siblings with whom she competed for Godwin's affection.[33] This first murder may also be read from a slightly modified perspective, as a subtly different kind of fratricide. With the first murder, the creature punishes and eliminates the figure of the son, the privileged boy who stands to inherit the prerogatives offered to, but ultimately withheld from, the daughter. Yet, finally, the fact that Shelley names the first victim "William"—the name not only of her brother but also of her father and her six-month-old son—suggests a rage directed at all the male figures who define her in the roles played by a woman in the family sexual romance: daughter, sister, mother.[34] And in murdering Henry Clerval, Frankenstein's close friend and an obvious figure for Percy Bysshe Shelley, Mary Shelley has her creature kill off the person who defines her in the only remaining sexual role a female may play to a male: wife and lover. Clearly, Shelley's creature revenges himself on and destroys all the family's males who entangle the woman in guilt and sexuality. In doing so, the creature exacts a daughter's vengeance on a patriarchal society that projects its own guilt upon the figure of the daughter.

The creature's murder of Elizabeth, Frankenstein's fiancée, has a different but equally compelling logic. It is important to point out, first of all, that Shelley carefully emphasizes the incestuous nature of the relationship between Frankenstein and his cousin. As we have seen, the 1818 edition portrays them as first cousins who are raised as brother and sister, so that the tie of blood relationship between them is deepened by growing up as siblings. But Victor and Elizabeth are not only cousins and siblings; their behavior also suggests they resemble a father and his daughter. As we have seen, Shelley portrays Victor Frankenstein's relation to his fiancée largely in paternal terms. Frankenstein dotes on Elizabeth and strives to shelter and care for her—a tendency that Shelley stresses and enlarges upon in her 1831 revisions. In fact, Shelley frames all the marriages in the Frankenstein family as relationships that cast the husband in the role of a paternal figure and somehow enshrine a daughter's submission to and passion for her father. The marriage of Alphonse Frankenstein and Caroline Beaufort, Frankenstein's parents, does precisely these two things. Alphonse Frankenstein, as an intimate friend of Caroline Beaufort's father, is clearly old enough himself to be the girl's parent, yet he marries her.[35] Shelley portrays Alphonse's relation to Caroline with all the fatherly overtones the difference in their ages would imply. As Victor Frankenstein describes it, Alphonse "came like a protecting spirit to the poor girl, who committed herself to his care" (28).[36] And Shelley makes it clear that Alphonse is attracted to Caroline at the outset because of her passionate attachment to her real father. Alphonse enshrines in a portrait what he sees as Caroline's consummate virtue and then hangs the painting over the mantelpiece for all to see and admire. At Alphonse's command, the painting depicts Caroline as the very embodiment of a daughter's consuming devotion to and passion for her father: "It was an historical subject, painted at my father's desire, and represented Caroline Beaufort in an agony of despair, kneeling by the coffin of her dead father" (73).

Shelley highlights the incestuous currents of the relation between Victor and Elizabeth in other ways. In her 1831 revisions, Shelley removes the blood tie—Elizabeth becomes an Italian foundling instead of Frankenstein's cousin—but then intensifies the incestuous currents even more in the linguistic texture of the novel. Shelley has Frankenstein continually refer to Elizabeth as "my more than sister" (235, 236), while Elizabeth writes to Frankenstein and refers to his younger brothers as "our dear children" (243).

In the 1818 edition, Shelley also underlines the incestuous implications of their relationship by having key characters wonder aloud if the incest taboo interferes with the cousins' attachment to each other and therefore poses a barrier to their marriage. Alphonse Frankenstein speculates about this matter first, when he surmises that his son, having grown up with Elizabeth, might view Elizabeth as a sister, "without any wish that she might become your wife" (148). Elizabeth herself later worries over the same difficulty in a long letter to her fiancé. "But as brother and sister often entertain a lively affection towards each other, without desiring a more intimate union, may not such also be our case? Tell me, dearest Victor" (185).

For Victor himself, the difficulties posed by marriage to Elizabeth surface in his incestuous dream, which focuses not so much on Elizabeth as a sister, but rather on Elizabeth as a troubling amalgam of mother, lover, and "monstrous" offspring. Indeed, once Frankenstein has dimly grasped the nature of his emotion for Elizabeth and projected his "monstrous" desire onto his newly animated creature, he seems to go to great lengths to avoid marrying Elizabeth. As critics have noticed, Frankenstein spends an inordinately long time away from Geneva, always finding projects to postpone his marriage, even as he insists he misses and loves Elizabeth:[37] his first absence lasts six years (73), his next about two (150). When Frankenstein's father finally presses him to marry Elizabeth, Frankenstein reacts with aversion: "Alas! To me the idea of an immediate union with my cousin was one of horror and dismay" (149). This aversion, rooted in Frankenstein's troubling association of Elizabeth with incestuous guilt and the animation of his creature, continues until the day of the marriage itself. As Frankenstein returns to Geneva to marry Elizabeth, after he has been cleared of Clerval's murder, he recalls the night of the creature's animation, remembering in particular the sexual shudder that brought the creature to life: "I remembered shuddering at the mad enthusiasm that hurried me on to the creation of my hideous enemy" (181). Against such a background of guilty sexuality and fear, the impending marriage fills Frankenstein with horror and loathing. He strives to hide "in my own heart the anxiety that preyed there" (189), but "[a]s the period fixed for our marriage drew nearer, whether from cowardice or a prophetic feeling, I felt my heart sink within me" (188).

After the marriage, Frankenstein's troubled sense of the incestuous guilt implicit in his relation to Elizabeth becomes even more closely associated with his fear of confronting his creature, a fact that in itself suggests a parallel in Frankenstein's mind between Elizabeth and his "monstrous" offspring. The creature has ominously warned Frankenstein that, like Elizabeth, "I shall be with you on your wedding-night" (166). For his part, Frankenstein expresses his emotions about the wedding night in ambiguous language that conflates Elizabeth and the creature. As Frankenstein enters the gates of their honeymoon retreat, for example, an "unexplainable feeling" (191) arrests him momentarily—an aversion that can be traced either to fear of consummating his marriage to Elizabeth or fear of grappling with his creature. The implication, of course, is that the two acts are somehow the same. Later when night falls and the time to retire draws near, Frankenstein experiences the same ambiguous aversion: "[S]o soon as night obscured the shapes of objects, a thousand fears arose in my mind. I was anxious and watchful" (192). Frankenstein tells Elizabeth that this nuptial "night is dreadful, very dreadful" (192); as the hour grows late, he reflects, in language heavy with ambiguity and sexual connotation, "how dreadful the combat which I momentarily expected would be to my wife, and I earnestly entreated her to retire" (192). Just before this passage, Frankenstein has sworn to "not relax the impending conflict" of his wedding night "until my life, or that of my adversary, were extinguished" (192). In this context, it is difficult to tell whether the "adversary" Frankenstein expects shortly to confront in a "combat" dreadful to his wife will be his creature—or his bride.

Shelley's ambiguous conflation of Elizabeth and Frankenstein's "monstrous" offspring in these scenes serves several purposes. First of all, it emphasizes the connection between Elizabeth and the creature that exists in Frankenstein's own mind, a connection that first surfaced in the "straight black lips" of Frankenstein's incestuous dream. Just as Frankenstein's nightmare of the ghastly connection between his dead mother and Elizabeth gave way to his vision of a "monstrous" daughter, so, on Frankenstein's wedding night, his feverish imagination inversely links his monstrous offspring to his wife/lover and, through her, his mother. As we have seen, Frankenstein's creature may be read as the corpse of his dead mother come to life; entangled in the guilty sexuality of seeking to reanimate his mother through his love for Elizabeth, Frankenstein can possess Elizabeth physically only when she, too, has become a corpse. And this is precisely what Frankenstein does. Immediately after Elizabeth dies, he holds her in his arms for the first time in the novel and caresses her passionately: "[N]ow, as she lay, her head upon her arm, and a handkerchief thrown across her face and neck, I might have supposed her asleep. I rushed towards her, and embraced her with ardour" (193).[38]

But Shelley's ambiguous conflation of Elizabeth and Frankenstein's creature suggests that both characters are something more than figures for the dead mother. It reinforces the fact that Elizabeth, like the creature, is also a figure for the daughter; to the extent that Frankenstein's relation to Elizabeth is a paternal one, their marriage has incestuous overtones of a different sort. It is in this context that the creature's murder of Elizabeth should be discussed. Shelley portrays both Elizabeth and Frankenstein's "monstrous" offspring as daughters, but as daughters of a very different type. Rejected by the father figure and unable to become Elizabeth, the creature murders Elizabeth instead.

The Elizabeth of Shelley's 1818 edition of *Frankenstein* is a very different character from the one who appears in the 1831 version. As Mary Poovey and others have noted, the Elizabeth of 1818 is a more realistic and believable woman, while the Elizabeth of 1831 is an elevated and sentimentalized type.[39] For most critics, Shelley's sentimentalization of Elizabeth in the 1831 version constitutes an aesthetic flaw: they have argued that Shelley's artistic powers waned in her later years and that Shelley's sentimentality implies her endorsement of Elizabeth's conventional behavior.[40] It is worth examining some of the specific features of Elizabeth's personality that Shelley erased in 1831, for these features, imagined and described when Shelley first composed the novel, identify Elizabeth more closely with Frankenstein's "monstrous" offspring.

To begin with, the Elizabeth of the 1818 edition shares the creature's ability to reason and learn, intellectual tendencies almost entirely eliminated in the Elizabeth of 1831. In the 1831 version, Elizabeth's "brow was clear and ample" (235) and the mature Elizabeth's face has an "expression more full of sensibility and intellect" (245). But aside from one mention of Elizabeth's taste for "the aerial creations of the poets" (236), these are the only references to Elizabeth's mental capabilities—quite weak suggestions of intellectual vigor, at that.[41] The Elizabeth of 1818, on the other hand, possesses a strong mind and an appetite for knowledge—qualities that both make her more like Frankenstein himself and tie her to Frankenstein's creature. In 1818, Elizabeth has a great "capability of application," and Frankenstein insists that he "admire[s] her understanding and fancy" (30). Frankenstein even shares his consuming interest in Paracelsus and Albertus Magnus with Elizabeth, but she is not captured intellectually by the material: "I disclosed my discoveries to Elizabeth . . . under a promise of strict secrecy; but she did not interest herself in the subject, and I was left by her to pursue my studies alone" (33–34). Caroline Beaufort's death makes Elizabeth's mind "acquire new firmness and vigour" (39); she applies herself to the instruction of Frankenstein's younger brothers. When one of the brothers shows a taste for working out of doors, Elizabeth even presents his father with a forcefully reasoned argument—based on Godwin's principles of benevolence and utility—that the life of the farmer is superior to the life of a lawyer. Alphonse Frankenstein is so impressed by her conviction and logic that he tells Elizabeth she should become the advocate instead, a comment that, as Elizabeth ruefully says, "put an end to the conversation on that subject" (59–60).

If the Elizabeth of 1818 shares the creature's intellectual tendencies and acquirements, she shares with him a second significant quality: the capacity for feeling anger and expressing it eloquently. This quality is also entirely erased in the revised Elizabeth of 1831, who meets injustices with sad smiles and resignation. The prime example of the 1818 Elizabeth's capacity for anger appears in the scene in which she visits Justine in prison. Once Elizabeth realizes Justine is innocent, having been convicted by an unjust social system of a crime she did not commit, Elizabeth breaks into an angry denunciation of the system. Elizabeth's indictment is passionate, pointed, and filled with Godwinian vocabulary and spirit:

> [W]hen one creature is murdered, another is immediately deprived of life in a slow torturing manner; then the executioners, their hands yet reeking with the blood of innocence, believe that they have done a great deed. They call this *retribution*. Hateful name! When that word is pronounced, I know greater and more horrid punishments are going to be inflicted than the gloomiest tyrant has ever invented to satiate his utmost revenge. (83)

This speech is entirely omitted from the 1831 edition. In Shelley's revised version, Elizabeth accepts Justine's advice to "submit in patience to the will of Heaven!" After Justine's execution, Elizabeth is deprived of her angry voice entirely, and surrenders herself silently to a "deep and voiceless grief" (246).

The 1818 edition of *Frankenstein* identifies Elizabeth and Frankenstein's "monstrous" offspring in one final way, that is, through an intriguing structural juxtaposition omitted from the 1831 version. In the 1818 edition, Frankenstein travels to the valley of Chamounix with Elizabeth, his father, and brother; in 1831, he makes the journey alone. It is on this trip, of course, that Frankenstein first encounters his creature face to face outside the laboratory and talks with him. In the 1818 version, having settled Elizabeth and his family into an inn on the valley floor, Frankenstein decides to ascend to the summit of Montanvert alone. He meets his creature on the glacier; the creature tells Frankenstein his tale; Frankenstein is filled with disgust, yet agrees to construct a female companion for him. Frankenstein then returns to Elizabeth, who has waited anxiously all night for his reappearance. Sickened by the recent sight of "the filthy mass that moved and talked" (143), plagued by his promise to create a second creature, Frankenstein finds everything around him unspeakably "filthy" and hellish:

> [T]he gentle affection of my beloved Elizabeth was inadequate to draw me from the depth of my despair. The promise I had made to the daemon weighed upon my mind, like Dante's iron cowl on the heads of the hellish hypocrites. . . . Can you wonder, that sometimes a kind of insanity possessed me, or that I saw continually about me a multitude of filthy animals inflicting on me incessant torture, that often extorted screams and bitter groans? (145)

Two features in the 1818 version of this scene link Elizabeth to Frankenstein's creature. The first is a structural juxtaposition: Elizabeth waits anxiously for Frankenstein in the inn on the valley floor while the creature, filled with equal anxiety, tells Frankenstein his tale close to the mountain's summit. The juxtaposition of the two anxious figures parallels them; it also places Frankenstein between them, thus suggesting that Frankenstein's relation to the two characters is itself somehow parallel and similar. And there is a second telling similarity between Elizabeth and the creature, brought home in the language of the passage just quoted—a passage that is also omitted from the 1831 edition. In the 1831 version, Frankenstein descends from the mountaintop and meets no one; in the 1818 edition, he meets Elizabeth and simultaneously sees "continually about me a multitude of filthy animals inflicting on me incessant torture." In the 1818 version of the novel, that is, Elizabeth becomes entangled in the visions of filth and animality generated in Frankenstein's imagination by his encounter with his creature. She is thus identified in Frankenstein's mind with his "monstrous" offspring; as part of the "multitude of filthy animals" Frankenstein sees surrounding him, Elizabeth is mired in the same loathsome materiality and sexuality Frankenstein associates with his creature.

Shelley's 1831 revisions to *Frankenstein*, then, erase the specific features linking Elizabeth to the "monster" in the 1818 edition: Elizabeth's intelligence, her latent anger and ability to verbalize it, her association with filth and sexuality in the imagistic pattern of the novel. The 1831 Elizabeth is pure, celestial, and often voiceless, like so many of Shelley's later heroines. In the 1831 version of *Frankenstein*, Shelley seems to strive for a different effect, stressing the great gap in the patterns of female behavior exhibited by Elizabeth and the creature. In 1818, Shelley portrays Elizabeth as a type of the monstrous daughter; by 1831, Elizabeth instead embodies the elevated ideal of a woman committed to the domestic affections, a point to be taken up in due course.

But though the 1818 version of *Frankenstein* carefully parallels Elizabeth and the creature in significant ways, there is a crucial difference between them. Despite the intelligence and latent anger the Elizabeth of 1818 shares with the creature, she is finally a daughter of a very different sort. The 1818 Elizabeth is complete and privileged; all the different qualities of her temperament have achieved an equilibrium that suits her perfectly to the family role she plays. The symbol of this privilege is the education Elizabeth receives. The 1818 Elizabeth is educated in languages with her brothers (31) and taught that "mutual affection" (37) binds the family together. The symbolism of Elizabeth's education presents a jarring contrast, of course, to the education the creature has received: huddled in a "kennel," walled off from the warmth of the DeLacey family hearth, the creature has educated himself by overhearing the lessons meant for Safie, another daughter, who is eventually able to find protection in the paternal love of an adopted father. When Frankenstein assesses the relative status accorded to him and Elizabeth in the family circle, he insists that "Neither of us possessed the slightest preeminence over the other" (37). On closer inspection, of course, a difference between Elizabeth and her male siblings does indeed exist; it consists of the same set of qualities that differentiates Elizabeth from Frankenstein's creature. Shelley sums up the essential difference between Elizabeth, her male siblings, and Frankenstein's "monstrous" offspring in the first words of description she applies to Elizabeth:

> She was docile and good-tempered, yet gay and playful as a summer insect. Although she was lively and animated, her feelings were strong and deep, and her disposition uncommonly affectionate. No one could better enjoy liberty, yet no one could submit with more grace than she did to constraint and caprice. (29–30)

Frankenstein's creature is certainly not "docile and good-tempered." Although he initially pledges to be "even mild and docile" to his father, whom he acknowledges as his "natural lord and king" (95), the creature is, finally, utterly incapable of suffering rejection, and the pressures of isolation placed upon him, with any redeeming female "grace." For all her intelligence and latent capacity for anger, Elizabeth, unlike Frankenstein's "monstrous" offspring, finally submits to the "constraint and caprice" of her situation as a daughter. This submission is, of course, the price of the privilege and paternal protection she receives in return. But for the creature, the situation is entirely different. Having been denied the father's affection and any share in the father's privilege from the outset, the creature has developed little capacity, or taste, for compliance and submission. This analysis suggests another reason why Frankenstein's "monstrous" offspring is driven to murder Elizabeth. Elizabeth represents the figure of the compliant and therefore beloved daughter. Deprived of the love that would keep him "docile" and jealous of the paternal protection bought by Elizabeth's compliance, the creature murders Elizabeth, the daughter he despairs of becoming.

As this line of reasoning implies, Frankenstein's "monstrous" offspring simultaneously accomplishes a second purpose when he murders Elizabeth: he not only eliminates the compliant daughter, but he also eliminates his chief rival for Frankenstein's affection. In this sense, the murder of Elizabeth is an important crisis in the pattern of love-hate tensions that tie Frankenstein and his creature together. The creature has slowly attacked Frankenstein's family members and friends, destroying Frankenstein's other relational ties in a pattern of increasingly emotional closeness. When the creature murders Elizabeth, he robs Frankenstein of his most cherished possession—the figure of the wife/lover, toward whom Frankenstein extends the prerogatives of his paternal affection. Shortly afterward, Frankenstein's father, in despair at the death of "his more than daughter" (195), dies of an apoplectic fit.[42] Frankenstein is thus left entirely alone; he ceases fleeing from his "monstrous" offspring and begins to pursue him instead. In a sense, the creature has finally won what he has always most wanted—his creator's undivided attention.

The creature's murder of Elizabeth accomplishes a third and final purpose, one that draws together the incest themes structuring *Frankenstein*. When the creature murders Elizabeth, he denies Frankenstein the emotional consummation he most desires and dreads: physical union with a woman who represents, for Frankenstein, a troubling amalgam of lover, mother, and "monstrous" daughter. As critics have noted, Elizabeth's murder in one way relieves Frankenstein of his dreadful anxiety and fear about incest. Elizabeth's death removes her from Frankenstein's physical grasp and thus prevents him from breaking the incest taboo that hovers over their relationship.[43] But on another level, and read from the perspective of Frankenstein's "monstrous" offspring, the murder of Elizabeth accomplishes something quite different. When the creature murders Elizabeth, he denies the father his desire and breaks the father's sexual hold over the daughter. By murdering Elizabeth, the creature, himself a figure for the daughter, prevents the father from consummating his guilty passion on the body of another daughter. In the process, the creature gains yet another kind of power over the figure of the father and briefly removes the daughter from the realm of the father's association of the daughter with lovers, mothers, and guilty sexuality. Frankenstein's "monstrous" offspring thus punishes the father for entangling the daughter in loathsome sexuality. Elizabeth is redeemed from "filthy materiality"—but the price of her redemption is her death. From this perspective, *Frankenstein* makes the same point about fathers, daughters, and sexuality that *Mathilda* will: woman's only escape from the consequences of her sexuality is into death. As we will see, the murder of Elizabeth is the structural equivalent in *Frankenstein* of a prophetic dream Mathilda has; both express the daughter's hostility toward the guilty sexuality the father has imposed on her, and both hasten the father's death.

Though the crippling power of fathers is essential to understanding the plight of the "monster" in *Frankenstein*, mothers—and their absences—are also crucial to the work. As Gilbert and Gubar have remarked, part of the creature's quest is "a doomed search for a maternal, female principle in the harsh society that has created him."[44] The creature's violent rage is generated by his father's rejection, but behind the creature's anger at the father lies an agonized search for the mother who, eventually, proves to be dead, dying, or deadly. As we have seen, the daughters who inhabit *Frankenstein* are motherless—a situation that, as Judith Herman has pointed out, deprives the daughter of female protection and makes her more subject to the father's demands.[45] Caroline Beaufort, Elizabeth Lavenza, Agnes DeLacey, and Safie have lost their mothers to death; only Justine Moritz's mother remains alive, and she "through a strange perversity . . . could not endure" (60) her daughter. Frankenstein's "monstrous" offspring is, of course, entirely motherless; having been created by a male, from bits of dead bodies, the creature yearns not only for his father's affection but also for the soothing presence of a female companion.

The creature's motherlessness provides the context for his aggression against Justine Moritz, the only one of his victims besides Frankenstein he does not actually kill. After the creature murders William, he finds a portrait of Caroline Beaufort Frankenstein in William's clothing. The image of William's mother momentarily softens the creature, but his rage returns: "I remembered that I was forever deprived of the delights that such beautiful creatures could bestow; and that she whose resemblance I contemplated would, in regarding me, have changed that air of divine benignity to one expressive of disgust and affright" (139). The creature is infuriated by what he imagines would be the mother's rejection; he places the locket in Justine's clothing, thus assuring the execution of the only daughter in the novel whose mother remains alive. In this scene, the mother's image exerts a deadly and destructive power. Deprived of a mother's "benignity" and having learned the "lessons of Felix, and the sanguinary laws of man" (140) the creature works "mischief": he implicates another daughter in the murder of William.

Immediately after relating the story of Justine and the locket, the creature orders Frankenstein to build him a female companion of the same "deformed and horrible" species as his (140). As we have seen, Frankenstein agrees to do so. But the thought of the female creature's maternity leads Frankenstein to dismember her. As Frankenstein labors at the "filthy process" (162) of building a female creature, his heart sickens. He begins to consider reasons to break his promise to his monstrous offspring: that the female might be "ten thousand times more malignant" than her mate; that she might "turn with disgust" from the creature "to the superior beauty of man" (163). It is, finally, the possibility of the female creature becoming a mother that convinces Frankenstein to destroy her:

> Even if they were to leave Europe, and inhabit the deserts of the new world, yet one of the first results of those sympathies for which the daemon thirsted would be children, and a race of devils would be propagated upon the earth, who might make the very existence of the species of man a condition precarious and full of terror. (163)

"Trembling with passion" (164) at the thought of the female creature reproducing herself, Frankenstein tears the lifeless body to pieces. The lifeless female creature becomes, of course, another visual equivalent for Frankenstein's dead mother's corpse: when he destroys her, he expresses his own dread of the female and fear of the figure of the mother. For Frankenstein, as for his "monstrous" offspring, maternity exerts a deadly and threatening power.[46]

The figure of the dead or deadly mother is central to another novel Mary Shelley read before she wrote *Frankenstein:* Mary Wollstonecraft's *Wrongs of Woman.* Shelley's mother's novel lies behind *Frankenstein* much as her father's *Caleb Williams* does; Shelley clearly had both her parents' work in mind as she composed the tale of Frankenstein and his "monstrous" offspring. There are general similarities between all three novels. All three works incorporate a plot based on flight and pursuit, and all three feature a central character plagued by a sense of monstrosity.[47] *The Wrongs of Woman,* however, has an important feature that *Caleb Williams* does not: Wollstonecraft specifically characterizes her "monstrous" heroines as motherless daughters.

Jemima, the prison matron whose tale takes up two chapters of *The Wrongs of Woman,* is the daughter of a rejecting father and the servant girl he seduces—a girl who dies in agony nine days after Jemima's birth (102). Left to fend for herself, and without a mother's protection, Jemima becomes, by her own description, a "monster" (116) and a "wretch" (105, 107, 113). Deprived of all human ties and affection, brutalized by the harsh conditions in which she is forced to live, Jemima steals, tries to abort her illegitimate child, and finally descends into prostitution. It is, in fact, what society views as Jemima's guilty sexuality that marks her as a reviled outcast. Once Jemima has lost her virginity to the tyrannical master in whose house she works—he attacks her just as she turns sixteen and enters adult womanhood—Jemima can find no other legitimate work, no place to live, no companions. Like Frankenstein's "monstrous" offspring, Jemima is "treated like a creature of another species" (104, 107); like Frankenstein's creature, Jemima "had not even the chance of being considered as a fellow-creature" (106).[48] Jemima's situation draws inspiration from William Godwin's point that monsters are made, not born, and much of *Wrongs of Woman* adopts Godwin's criticisms of unjust social institutions. But Wollstonecraft focuses specifically on the way social institutions shape women and traces Jemima's misfortune directly to the fact she is a motherless daughter. As Jemima puts it:

> Now I look back, I cannot help attributing the greater part of my misery, to the misfortune of having been thrown into the world without the grand support of life—a mother's affection. I had no one to love me; or to make me respected, to enable me to acquire respect. (106)

Maria, the imprisoned mother who is the chief protagonist of *The Wrongs of Woman* is, like Jemima, a motherless daughter. As a girl, Maria lives with a loutish father who demands "unconditional submission" (125) from his daughters, and with a mother who has little affection for her. After Maria's mother dies, Maria and her sisters become prey to the tyranny of their father and his new mistress—a former serving girl—and Maria soon marries George Venables, mainly to escape the constraints of her father's home. But Venables, like all the husbands and fathers in *The Wrongs of*

Woman, proves to be a brutal tyrant, too. When Maria becomes pregnant and then leaves his house to make a new life for herself and her child, Venables enlists all the powers of the law to track her down and capture her. Like Jemima, "who had been hunted from hole to hole, as if she had been a beast of prey or infected with a moral plague" (80), Maria is driven from one wretched hiding place to another and treated as an outlaw. Though Maria's only crime is leaving her husband—a decision she makes to save her unborn daughter's life—society makes Maria, like Jemima, into a monstrous outcast. As Wollstonecraft puts it, Maria is "hunted, like an infected beast, from three different apartments" (178) and, finally, "hunted out like a felon" (173) and captured.

Maria's lack of a protective maternal figure thus leads ultimately to the same fate Jemima and the creature confront: Maria becomes a reviled outlaw and a spurned social outcast.[49] Maria's daughter's lack of a mother leads to something even worse: the daughter's death. When Venables finally captures Maria as she is about to flee to the Continent with their tiny daughter, he steals the baby and imprisons Maria in a lunatic asylum. There Maria, the daughter just turned mother, suffers horrifying pangs of maternal deprivation. Her breasts ache with the milk she can't give her daughter; she laments "the aggravated ills of life that her [child's] sex rendered almost inevitable," yet she cannot bear to think her daughter is dead (75–76). Maria bemoans the mother's powerlessness—that she is herself shut up in a madhouse, that "the tender mother cannot lawfully" (159) protect her fortune and her children from a tyrannical husband. And Maria is right to fear for her daughter's safety, for Jemima soon discovers that the baby daughter, deprived of its mother and confined and neglected by its father, has died (123).[50]

Mary Wollstonecraft's *Wrongs of Woman* is, like her daughter's *Frankenstein,* a novel full of tyrannical fathers, dead or powerless mothers, and abandoned daughters who become outcasts. The emotional center of *The Wrongs of Woman* is, therefore, occupied by an appropriate tale: the story of the imprisoned mother, written for and to her daughter. Fearing her own death, Maria composes a memoir of her life to leave for her daughter. Maria carefully frames her tale as a precautionary narrative—a story that emphasizes the vital importance of a mother's love, yet warns of the mother's powerlessness:

> The tenderness of a father who knew the world, might be great; but could it equal that of a mother—of a mother, labouring under a portion of the misery, which the constitution of society seems to have entailed on all her

kind? It is, my child, my dearest daughter, only such a mother, who will dare to break through all restraint to provide for your happiness—who will voluntarily brave censure herself, to ward off sorrow from your bosom. From my narrative, my dear girl, you may gather the instruction, the counsel, which is meant rather to exercise than influence your mind. (124)

Although Wollstonecraft shows Maria composing her narrative for her daughter early in *The Wrongs of Woman*, the reader does not see the narrative itself until Maria learns her daughter is dead and gives the narrative to Henry Darnford, her prison lover. Maria's narrative takes up chapters 7 through 14 of what was published as a seventeen-chapter novel. *The Wrongs of Woman* was left unfinished when Wollstonecraft died, but Wollstonecraft left notes suggesting plans for the elaboration of at least several more chapters. It is tempting to speculate that Wollstonecraft may have planned to place Maria's memoir—the tale of the imprisoned and powerless mother— close to the structural and emotional heart of the novel.[51]

History provides a poignant footnote to the composition of *The Wrongs of Woman*. Having composed Maria's memoir to her baby daughter, Wollstonecraft herself gave birth to a daughter, and she died shortly thereafter of complications arising from the birth. This circumstance must certainly have exerted a peculiar power over Mary Shelley's imagination when, a daughter turned new mother herself, she prepared to write *Frankenstein* by rereading her own mother's novel about motherhood. In any event, the imprisoned and powerless mother lies at the emotional center of *Frankenstein* in much the same way she lies at the heart of Wollstonecraft's *Wrongs of Woman*. Enclosed within layers of concentric narratives—Walton's, Frankenstein's, the creature's—lies the story of Safie's mother, the dead harem slave.[52] By placing the story of the imprisoned and powerless mother at the center of *Frankenstein,* Shelley accomplishes several things. She expresses the daughter's longing for—and natural dread of—the maternal figure the daughter needs to sustain her, yet fears becoming herself. And, as we shall see, the dead mother entombed at the heart of Mary Shelley's first novel looks forward to a dead mother buried at the center of Shelley's last novel— although, in *Falkner*, the daughter learns to use the mother's intermittent power over the figure of the father rather than fearing her.

The wretched, motherless daughter who becomes a monstrous outcast is the central figure in *The Wrongs of Woman* and *Frankenstein;* she is also the central figure in Shelley's *Mathilda*, a novel that openly examines an incestuous relationship between a father and daughter. *Mathilda* was written not two years after *Frankenstein* appeared in print. It is worth noting here that the numerous similarities between the two works confirm the importance of the theme of father-daughter incest in *Frankenstein*. Both *Mathilda* and *Frankenstein*, after all, explore intensely sexual material, and both works examine a sympathetic central character haunted by a sense of "monstrosity." Both Mathilda and the creature describe themselves as "unnatural"; both emphatically characterize themselves using the words "wretch" and "monster." Both protagonists describe themselves in language replete with images of darkness, disease, and filth, and both see themselves as "unspeakable" in some sense. Mathilda and the creature think they are cursed and set apart by nature; both sense an insurmountable barrier separating them from other human creatures; and both are "marked" in some physical sense— Mathilda with the imagined sign of Cain on her forehead,[53] the creature with an indeterminate feature of countenance that terrifies humans into wild flight and rejection. Shelley describes the situation of Mathilda and Frankenstein's spurned creature in suggestively similar terms. Not only are both motherless, but both are deserted by a father figure who comes back to haunt them or whom they haunt.

Shelley even places Mathilda and Frankenstein's creature in the same emotional landscape. As we shall see, Mathilda experiences one of the reactions of an actual incest victim: once her father leaves her, her feelings go completely cold. Shelley describes Mathilda in terms of icy, mountainous terrain, saying Mathilda is "a solitary spot among mountains shut in on all sides by steep black precipices; where no ray of heat could penetrate; and from which there was no outlet to sunnier fields" (54). In *Frankenstein*, externalizing this same emotional landscape, Shelley places Frankenstein's "monstrous" offspring in physical surroundings of precisely the same description. The creature lives alone in the place where he first talks to Frankenstein: an isolated spot walled in by Alpine peaks, among "the desert mountains and dreary glaciers . . . the caves of ice" (95). In Shelley's first two novels, it would seem, the daughter's relationship to her father dooms her to inhabit, or contain, bleak and desolate emotional landscapes.

In each of Shelley's first two novels, the daughter's relationship to her father also acts as a catalyst for the daughter's self-immolation. The closing pages of *Mathilda* and *Frankenstein*, in fact, contain a surprising number of similarities, suggesting yet again that both novels depict the fate of the daughter made monstrous by incest. Like actual incest victims, Mathilda feels responsible for her father's "fall" and subsequent death—she recalls with horror the day "three years ago that my folly destroyed the only being I was doomed to love" (79). Similarly, Frankenstein's creature assumes full responsibility for his creator's demise, uttering "wild and incoherent self-reproaches" (217) and exclaiming "that is also my victim! . . . in his murder my crimes are consummated" (216–17). Both daughters are distraught after the father's death, even though the father in each novel has entangled the daughter in guilty sexuality. After Mathilda's father commits suicide, Mathilda prostrates herself on the ground close to his grave and, in an act charged with sexual innuendo, strikes "the ground in anger that it should cover him from me" (50). For all his rage and desire to punish Frankenstein, Frankenstein's creature behaves in a similar manner. He is stricken with "grief and horror" (216) when his creator dies, and he situates himself near his father's lifeless body in a sexually suggestive pose. In a scene that echoes the creature's first glimpse of his maker, when the creature pulled back the curtains of Frankenstein's bed and reached out to detain him (53), Frankenstein's "monstrous" offspring hangs loverlike over Frankenstein's dead body (216).[54]

Both daughters express a lyrical, sensuous affection for the beauties of nature—a nature free from "unnatural" desires, in which they no longer have a place. Mathilda invokes "Your solitude, sweet land, your trees and waters" and notes that after her death the unsullied beauty of nature "will still exist, moved by your winds, or still beneath the eye of noon" (77). Frankenstein's creature displays a similar sense of loss when he realizes that "I shall no longer see the sun or stars, or feel the winds play on my cheeks" (220). Most important, both daughters—alienated from nature, bereft over the loss of the father, afflicted by guilt over the father's death—take their own lives. Mathilda becomes lost in a fantasy reunion with her father and chooses to spend the night in the elements, thus inducing the illness that eventually kills her. Mathilda craves death, "the moment I had so much desired," knowing it will be an experience "sweeter even than that which the opium promised" (76). The suicide of Frankenstein's "monstrous" offspring is more violent and self-torturing. The creature plans to burn himself alive, a self-immolation that will both punish him for his crimes against the father and put a final end to his guilty suffering. As the creature puts it, "soon . . . I shall die, and what I now feel be no longer felt. Soon these burning miseries will be extinct. I shall ascend my funeral pile triumphantly, and exult in the agony of the torturing flames" (221).

Despite the sense of triumph and exultation that his impending suicide gives him, Frankenstein's creature ends the novel in precisely the same way as Mathilda: confronting self-extinction and imminent death. From this perspective *Frankenstein* seems to convey the same message about fathers, daughters, and sexuality that *Mathilda* does: it is impossible for a woman to escape the consequences of her sexuality as long as she remains alive. In Shelley's first two novels, the figure of the daughter meets an unnaturally early end. She is associated in the father's mind with lover, wife, and mother, but the figure of the daughter is prevented by death from assuming any of these roles in a concrete way with a figure other than the father. In *Mathilda* and *Frankenstein*, that is, the daughter finally remains subject to the power and limiting scope of the father's desire. As we shall see, Shelley's last novels allow the daughter to subvert and move beyond these paternal limits.

3

Mathilda

Until recently, *Mathilda* was the most neglected of Mary Shelley's novels. Written and revised in August and September 1819, just after William Shelley's death and during a period in which William Godwin dunned his daughter for financial and emotional support, *Mathilda* did not appear in print during Mary Shelley's lifetime.[1] Yet Mary Shelley herself was acutely aware of the extent to which writing *Mathilda* was a restorative act, an imaginative endeavor that structured and expressed a complex set of feelings about fathers, daughters, and female sexuality, and thus freed her briefly from their power. As Mary Shelley put it in 1822, just after Shelley's death and remembering the death of her beloved three-year-old son, "[W]hen I wrote Matilda, miserable as I was, the *inspiration* was sufficient to quell my wretchedness temporarily" (MWS *Journals*, 2:442).

For a long while, *Mathilda* was neglected chiefly because of its inaccessibility—it remained unpublished in the Shelley family papers until Elizabeth Nitchie brought out a scholarly edition in 1959. But even with the recent renewal of interest in Mary Shelley's work, *Mathilda* has not been accorded the attention it deserves. When scholars have written about *Mathilda* they have tended to downplay or misread the importance of its central theme: incest. Nitchie, for example, dismisses the incest theme as incidental and interprets *Mathilda* as Mary Shelley's attempt to apologize to her husband for her emotional withdrawal after the deaths of their children.[2] More recently, William Veeder has concluded that "incest in *Mathilda* is a simplistic, finally sentimental response to [Mary Shelley's] involved ties to husband and father."[3] Even so acute a critic as U. C. Knoepflmacher has found Mary Shelley's use of the incest theme in *Mathilda* "melodramatic" and wonders why the heroine should "feel such inordinate guilt over the death of the incestuous lecher [her father] who can love her only after she has become a fully developed woman."[4] But far from being "melodramatic" or "simplistic," Mary Shelley's use of the incest theme lies at the heart of her fictional purposes. Like *Frankenstein*, *Mathilda* paints a portrait of a father and child locked in bitter conflict, and, like *Frankenstein, Mathilda* lays the blame for the child's misery at the father's feet. Further, given the time in Mary Shelley's life at which it was written, *Mathilda* poses an intriguing question. Confronted with the losses of motherhood, the duties of daughterhood, and the strains of being a wife in August 1819, why should Mary Shelley discover she could "quell [her] wretchedness" by writing, of all things, a highly autobiographical novel that examines the growth and tragic end of an adored father's incestuous attachment to his beloved daughter? Part of the answer lies in the extent to which *Mathilda*, like *Frankenstein*, uses the theme of incest to tell the story of the daughter's induction into womanhood and "filthy materiality."

On one level, of course, Mary Shelley wrote about incest because she, like other Romantic writers, was simply intrigued by it. Percy Bysshe Shelley had just finished his own drama about incest, *The Cenci. Mathilda* may be read as a woman's revision of a male version of Beatrice Cenci's story.[5] Percy Shelley's tale of father-daughter incest is really a tale about rebellion against tyrannical authority figures. In it Francesco Cenci is a brutal and violent man who despises his daughter Beatrice and seeks to humiliate and destroy her by forcing her into an actual act of incest. Beatrice abhors and fears her father; she has him murdered and feels no remorse. Although Beatrice acknowledges she is responsible for her father's death, she insists until the play's end that she is guiltless, since Francesco Cenci so clearly deserved to die. Beatrice's only fear as she awaits her own execution is that she might be reunited with her father after her death in some hellish afterworld. Mary Shelley's *Mathilda* reverses all of these equations and portrays the story of father-daughter incest in a much more ambiguous light. Mathilda's unnamed father, though stern and emotionally withdrawn, is an essentially good man who loves his only daughter dearly. No physical act of incest occurs—the father instead confesses to Mathilda, in a moment of guilty insight, the sexual quality of his love for her. Mathilda, for her part, adores her father until the novel's end. She is horrified to recognize his incestuous desire, but her feelings shift to guilt and then to renewed longing for him. Mathilda is consumed with remorse after her father commits suicide; her greatest hope is that, after her own death, she can finally rejoin him in some spiritual world, where she can be united with her father in eternal sexless communion.

Mathilda, in short, presents the incest situation and the daughter's response to it from the daughter's point of view—that is, much more ambiguously, and by stressing the daughter's highly ambivalent feelings for the father who loves her passionately. *Mathilda* is a remarkable novel, in fact, because of the very accuracy with which it represents what we have come to recognize as the contradictory feelings of actual victims of father-daughter incest. As Judith Herman points out in *Father-Daughter Incest*, real victims of incest lack the protection and support of a maternal figure, feel over-whelmingly guilty, and are convinced they are responsible for their father's "fall." At the same time, they sense themselves as having a privileged place in their father's affections and seek to recapture this sense of "specialness" in relations with other men. They tend to overvalue and idealize males and to suffer an impairment in their sexual response. Most important, actual incest victims feel "marked," isolated, and cut off—as if they are social outcasts, exiles outside the bounds of normal human relations. And they are weighed down by the necessity of silence, by their conviction that they must keep their history utterly secret to avoid terrible consequences.[6]

Mary Shelley's Mathilda is tormented by precisely this set of feelings. Like actual incest victims, she is motherless, wracked by guilt, and certain she is to blame for her father's "fall." When her father seems to withdraw his affection, she forces her father to tell her the truth about his feelings for her; the imagery of the tale then portrays Mathilda as an Eve whose physical allure casts both father and daughter into "hell, and fire, and tortures" (*Mathilda*, 202).[7] Like actual incest victims, Mathilda sees herself as her father's favorite and seeks to recapture the sense of specialness she felt with her father—in Mathilda's case by pining to die and be reunited with him spiritually, in a world beyond the complications of sex. Like actual incest victims, Mathilda cannot respond to other men. She tells her tale to Wood-ville, a kind young poet who loves her, to explain "the causes of my solitary life; my tears; and above all of my impenetrable and unkind silence" (176). Like actual incest victims, Mathilda is tormented by the need for secrecy and silence, so much so that she stages an apparent suicide and flees to the forest, "lest my faltering voice should betray unimagined horrors" (216). Above all, as we have seen, Mathilda is tortured by her isolation, her sense of being "marked," "wretched," and a "monster." In a long passage that could come directly from the mouth of Frankenstein's abandoned creature, Mathilda says:

> I believed myself to be polluted by the unnatural love I had inspired, and that I was a creature cursed and set apart by nature. I thought that like another Cain, I had a mark set on my forehead to shew mankind that there was a barrier between me and them . . . a gloomy mark to tell the world that

there was that within my soul that no silence could render sufficiently obscure. Why when fate drove me to become this outcast of human feeling; this monster with whom none might mingle in converse and love; why had she not from that fatal and most accursed moment, shrouded me in thick mists and placed real darkness between me and my fellows so that I might never more be seen; and as I passed, like a murky cloud loaded with blight, they might only perceive me by the cold chill I should cast upon them; telling them, how truly, that something unholy was near? Then I should have lived upon this dreary heath unvisited, and blasting none by my unhallowed gaze . . . if the near prospect of death did not dull and soften my bitter feelings. . . . I . . . should have fancied myself a living pestilence: so horrible to my own solitary thoughts did this form, this voice, and all this wretched self appear; for had it not been the source of guilt that wants a name? (238–39)

This passage repeats the very language the creature uses to describe himself—the language of wretchedness, monstrosity, namelessness, darkness, and unnaturalness. Interestingly, Mathilda's description of herself as a "living pestilence" also looks forward—to Mary Shelley's portrayal in *The Last Man* of a female plague that destroys all human civilization. Clearly, Mary Shelley thought of the daughter's situation as in some sense "wretched" and "unnatural," and in the pages of *Mathilda* she openly says what she suggests more covertly in *Frankenstein:* that the daughter's sense of "monstrosity" grows from the father's rejection and from the incestuous nature of the father-daughter relationship.

It is not entirely surprising that Mary Shelley was able to portray the feelings of actual incest victims with such precision in the pages of *Mathilda*. Shelley's relationship to her own father was not incestuous in any literal sense but, as Judith Herman notes, patterns of father-daughter incest lie at the heart of the socialization of the daughter into patriarchal society:

[W]e consider overt incest to be only the most extreme form of a traditional family pattern. For every girl who has been involved in an incestuous relationship, there are considerably more who have grown up in a covertly incestuous family. In reconstructing a picture of this kind of family, we expected to find many similarities with the families of incest victims, and thus to establish the concept that overt incest represents only the furthest point on a continuum—an exaggeration of patriarchal family norms, but not a departure from them . . . incest represents a common pattern of traditional female socialization carried to a pathological extreme.[8]

Drawing on her own "excessive and romantic attachment" to her father and on William Godwin's affection for and rejection of his daughter in adolescence, Mary Shelley was able to portray accurately the emotions of a daughter entangled in incest. In doing so, Shelley uses in *Mathilda* many of the same devices she used in *Frankenstein:* she creates a central male character who embodies aspects of both her father and her husband; she focuses on the father's rejection as the formative moment in the daughter's development; and she ties the daughter's sense of her loathsomeness to paternal desire and incest.

In this context, *Mathilda* may be read as a parable of the process by which the daughter comes of age—that is, as both the story of the process by which daughters are socialized into womanhood, and the story of the individual daughter's confrontation with the implications of her burgeoning sexuality. As we have seen, the father's rejection is the pivotal moment in the daughter's progress through adolescence. As the daughter passes out of the asexual latency of childhood and develops into physical maturity, fathers tend to withdraw affection—an action that both eliminates the possibility of incest and raises a barrier against the father's conscious recognition of the desire the daughter stimulates in him.[9] For the daughter, this rejection is deeply disturbing: it ends an idyll of passionate childhood attachment; it sets the daughter's developing sexuality in a landscape of guilt and rejection; and it confronts the daughter for the first time with the full implications of entering adult womanhood with all its associations of sin and "filthy materiality."

From this point of view, *Mathilda* is the most highly autobiographical of Mary Shelley's novels. William Godwin is clearly the model for Mathilda's unnamed father. As Elizabeth Nitchie points out, Mathilda's father is, like William Godwin, extravagant, generous, vain, dogmatic, and rigid in holding to the only feelings he could consider orthodox.[10] Like William Godwin, Mathilda's father becomes "a distinguished member of society, a Patriot; and an enlightened lover of truth and virtue" (179). He marries a highly intelligent woman who dies giving birth to their only child, a daughter. In the sixteen years following his wife's death, Mathilda's father, like William Godwin, becomes "extinct." As Mathilda puts it,

> [T]his towering spirit who had excited interest and high expectation in all who knew and could value him became at once, as it were, extinct. . . . The memory of what he had been faded away as years passed; and he who before had been as a part of themselves and of their hopes was now no longer counted among the living. (181)

In *Mathilda*, the father's disappearance results from his self-exile to remote countries; in Godwin's life, the disappearance reflects the eclipse of Godwin's intellectual reputation, his vanishing from political debate into the world of writing children's books—an absence so complete that, when Percy Shelley first wrote Godwin in 1812, he confessed he had "enrolled your name on the list of the honorable dead."[11]

Just as the nameless father is a version of William Godwin, so Mathilda plainly incorporates the history and feelings of Mary Shelley herself. Mathilda's mother dies as a result of Mathilda's birth, just as Mary Wollstonecraft died shortly after giving birth to Mary Wollstonecraft Godwin. Like Mary Shelley, Mathilda becomes passionately attached to her only remaining parent; like Mary Shelley, Mathilda is abandoned to Scotland by her father, an apparent rejection that both causes deep emotional crisis and creates the conditions for Mathilda's intellectual and imaginative growth. Like Mary Shelley, Mathilda embodies the aspirations of a son—she dreams of wandering the world in search of her father, "disguised like a boy" (185). Like Mary Shelley, Mathilda struggles with the legacy of her relationship to her father and finds it undermines her relations with other men.[12]

Of the many autobiographical details Mary Shelley draws upon for *Mathilda,* the most significant relate to the story of the daughter's socialization out of childhood and into womanhood, and the role of incestuous feelings in it. In this context, Mathilda's Scottish sojourn is important as the beginning of the drama of the daughter's development and the role of the father in her passage into womanhood and adult sexuality. Mathilda's stay in Scotland is loosely patterned on Mary Shelley's own years in Dundee; as she later did in the 1831 introduction to *Frankenstein*, Shelley portrays her Scottish years as both a confusing consequence of paternal rejection and an occasion for the daughter's liberty and growth. As we have seen, the 1831 introduction to *Frankenstein* suggests that the "waking dreams" of Shelley's years in Scotland sowed the seeds of *Frankenstein*—waking dreams that may be interpreted as the imaginative creations of a young girl attempting to understand and come to grips with her father's rejection. *Mathilda* also portrays the heroine's Scottish exile as a direct result of paternal rejection— Mathilda's father leaves her in the care of a Scottish aunt when he cannot bear to look at the baby whose birth killed his beloved wife.

The plot of *Mathilda* makes much more of the positive impact of the heroine's Scottish childhood on her development. Scotland is, for both Mathilda and Mary Shelley, a period of remarkable freedom and growth. In her portrayal of Mathilda's years in Scotland, Mary Shelley tells the story of the young girl's freedom from gender restrictions during girlhood—the tale of the daughter's passage through the asexual latency of childhood before she is expected to conform to the rigid expectations of sex roles. Mathilda lives in Scotland from her infancy until age sixteen. In Scotland, and in her father's absence, Mathilda inhabits a world of freedom and possibility. She has all the liberty of a boy. She runs "wild about our park and the neighbouring fields" (183); as she grows older, her liberty increases and she becomes "a complete mountaineer" (184). Mathilda reads voraciously, devouring the works of Shakespeare, Milton, Pope, Cowper, and Livy (184). Mathilda is a "dreamer" (185) and dwells in imaginary worlds, where she envisions herself as both male and female characters. Sometimes she acts the parts of "Rosalind and Miranda and the lady of Comus" (185)—women who either have loving father figures, or succeed in living chaste lives. But Mathilda has an even more beloved fantasy for her future:

> My favourite vision was that when I grew up I would leave my aunt, whose coldness lulled my conscience, and disguised like a boy I would seek my father through the world. My imagination hung upon the scene of recognition; his miniature, which I should continually wear exposed on my breast, would be the means and I imaged the moment to my mind a thousand and a thousand times, perpetually varying the circumstances. Sometimes it would be in a desart; in a populous city; at a ball; we should perhaps meet in a vessel; and his first words constantly were, "My daughter, I love thee"! What extactic moments have I passed in these dreams! How many tears I have shed; how often have I laughed aloud. (185)

When, as a child and adolescent, Mathilda envisions her future, her most cherished fantasy gives her the freedom of a son, a Telemachus figure who wanders the world in search of his lost father. Roaming the world "disguised as a boy" is significant: As Carolyn Heilbrun has pointed out, girls dressed in boys' clothing have more mobility and freedom, and cross-dressing often expresses emancipation from the limits placed on the girl's behavior by gender categories.[13] Mathilda's Scottish sojourn, which lasts until her sixteenth birthday, thus tells the story of the daughter's passage through childhood, a period when she is free to act and imagine herself in both male and female roles. During this time, Mathilda envisions her future with great liberty. She dreams of the moment her father will embrace her as his daughter, yet she simultaneously imagines herself as possessing the freedom and prerogatives of the son.

When Mathilda's father returns, his presence grants her something quite different from the prerogatives of the son. She receives, instead, the rejection and guilt accorded to the daughter. Mathilda's father returns on her sixteenth birthday—symbolically, the age at which the daughter's childhood ends, and she makes the transition into womanhood. At first the reunion is joyful, and her father delights in treating Mathilda in ways that avoid the confines of traditional gender roles. He trains Mathilda to be his intellectual heir. "I was led by my father to attend to deeper studies than had before occupied me," Mathilda says. "My improvement was his delight; he was with me during all my studies and assisted or joined with me in every lesson" (190). Mathilda's father initially sees their relationship in sexually neutral terms and even characterizes his love for his daughter in literary language that recalls the affection of fathers for heroic sons. Characterizing himself as Anchises, Mathilda's father casts his daughter as an Aeneas figure, saying he loved her "as Anchises might have regarded the child of Venus if the sex had been changed" (209). But the father's return has already set the stage for the next act of the daughter's tragedy. A young nobleman begins to court Mathilda; the younger man's attentions make her father "restless and uneasy" (191). Mathilda's father abruptly rejects his daughter, treating her suddenly "with harshness or a more heart-breaking coldness" (191).

As Mathilda eventually discovers, her father rejects her because of his fear of incest; he repudiates Mathilda when the appearance of a suitor makes him recognize his sexual attraction to his daughter. After Mathilda forces her father to explain the causes of his rejection, he flees from her and writes her a long letter in which he describes his feelings. In the letter he insists that he initially felt, or was conscious of feeling, "only the peace of sinless passion" (209). "Was my love blameable?" he asks. And he goes on:

> If it was I was ignorant of it . . . and if I enjoyed from your looks, and words, and most innocent caresses a rapture usually excluded from the feelings of a parent towards his child, yet no uneasiness, no wish, no casual idea awoke me to a sense of guilt. . . . But when I saw you become the object of another's love; when I imagined that you might be loved otherwise than as a sacred type and image of loveliness and excellence; or that you might love another with a more ardent affection than that which you bore to me, then the fiend awoke within me; I dismissed your lover; and from that moment I have known no peace. (209)

Mathilda's father goes on to make it clear that he rejects her out of his own "self-anger and . . . despair" (209). Unable to control his feelings for his daughter, and afraid of the result, the father ends all emotional intimacy with her. He shuns Mathilda (191) or reacts to her presence with "angry frowns" (192) and "sullen fierceness" (191). As Mathilda puts it, "We took no more sweet counsel together; and when I tried to win him again to me, his anger, and the terrible emotions that he exhibited drove me to silence and tears" (191).

When Mathilda's father rejects her as she approaches physical maturity, he replicates what we have come to recognize as a typical pattern of paternal rejection in the daughter's passage from adolescence to womanhood. As the daughter passes out of childhood and into adult sexuality, the father withdraws his affection, both to eliminate the possibility of incest and to prevent conscious recognition of his incestuous feelings. As we have seen in the case of *Frankenstein*, paternal rejection, growing out of the father's incestuous feelings, is one of the mechanisms by which the culture moves daughters into the sense of guilt and sinful physicality associated with adult womanhood. The father's rejection, associated as it is with incest, causes the daughter to regard her emerging sexuality as loathsome and horrible, and herself as in some sense "monstrous." Mary Shelley viewed William Godwin's apparent rejection of her in adolescence in this light. In fact it is significant to the daughter's story that the father's recognition of his incestuous emotions, with its consequent rejection, occurs after the appearance of Mathilda's suitor. As Judith Herman points out, the father's abrupt rejection of his daughter is often precipitated, as is Mathilda's, by the arrival of a competing male.[14] Her father's rejection is the pivotal moment in Mathilda's, and Mary Shelley's, history. As Mathilda herself puts it, the rejection casts her "in one sentence . . . from the idea of unspeakable happiness to that of unspeakable grief" (193). And when Mathilda learns that her father's rejection is related to incest, her first reaction is to feel despair and "speechless agony" (202) at the "horror and misery" (202) daughterhood holds for her.

As soon as Mathilda's father rejects her, Shelley has Mathilda express her grief in terms of a classic tale of female sexual initiation, the story of the abduction and rape of Proserpine. When Mathilda's young suitor appears and her father begins to shun her, Mathilda describes the situation in this way:

> The day before we had passed alone together in the country; I remember we had talked of future travels that we should undertake together. . . . the next hour, I saw his brows contracted, his eyes fixed in sullen fierceness on the ground. . . . Often, when my wandering fancy brought by its various images now consolation and now aggravation of grief to my heart, I have compared myself to Proserpine who was gaily and heedlessly gathering flowers on the sweet plain of Enna, when the King of Hell snatched her

away to the abodes of death and misery. Alas! I who so lately knew of nought but the joy of life; who had slept only to dream sweet dreams and awoke to incomparable happiness, I now passed my days and nights in tears. I who sought and had found joy in the love-breathing countenance of my father now when I dared fix on him a supplicating look it was ever answered by an angry frown. (191–92)

Mathilda's fantasy casts her as a Proserpine figure, an unsuspecting daughter quietly gathering flowers; her father becomes Pluto, the fierce and angry ruler of Tartarus, who abducts the innocent girl, condemning her to live in a hell of "death and misery." As Susan Gubar has shown, the story of Proserpine can be read as a tale of female sexual initiation.[15] It was a story Shelley told more extensively in another genre at about the same time she wrote *Mathilda*.

In May 1820, some six months after completing *Mathilda*, Shelley noted in her journal that she had finished "Pxxxxxxxe" (MWS *Journals*, 1:316). She eventually revised and published the work in *The Winter's Wreath* of 1832 as *Proserpine, a Mythological Drama in Two Acts*.[16] In Shelley's mythological drama, Proserpine lives happily with her mother in the first act, is abducted by Pluto offstage, and returns as an unhappy prisoner of hell in act 2. Commentators have often suggested that Shelley stuck close to her source in Ovid for *Proserpine*, but, as Alan Richardson notes, Shelley in fact revised Ovid extensively for her drama. Shelley takes Pluto out of the action of the play entirely, so that the rape occurs "in the silence between the acts";[17] Shelley portrays the female characters as angry and aggressive rather than as passively submissive to Pluto's assault. Most important, Shelley transforms Proserpine herself. Rather than portraying her as a disobedient and unreflecting child who strays in search of flowers for herself, as Ovid does, Shelley transforms Proserpine into a thoughtful and self-possessed adolescent who sends her nymphs to gather flowers for Ceres and then, realizing she is alone, begins to fear for her safety.[18] By doing so, Shelley converts Ovid's tale into a fable about the daughter's maturation and sexual initiation, a story that reflects and comments upon Mathilda as a Proserpine figure. Like Proserpine, Mathilda lives in a happy asexual world as a child; like Proserpine, Mathilda's burgeoning sexuality condemns her to a hellish world filled with "furies and all loathed shapes" (*Proserpine*, 71). And for both Proserpine and Mathilda, the figure who steals the daughter away to Hades is a fierce male figure identified with paternal power and authority.[19]

In Mathilda's case her father's behavior inducts Mathilda into womanhood by setting her emerging sexuality in a landscape of guilt and paternal rejection. Like Frankenstein's creature, Mathilda finds herself entangled in a net of incestuous feeling; like Frankenstein's creature, Mathilda grows to see herself as monstrous and inhuman. The only difference is that Mathilda specifically links her sense of wretchedness and isolation to father-daughter incest. As she puts it in a typical passage, trying to explain why she cannot respond to the affection of Woodville, the young poet:

> It was a melancholy pleasure to me to listen to [Woodville's] inspired words; to catch for a moment the light of his eyes; to feel a transient sympathy and then to awaken from the delusion, again to know that all this was nothing,—a dream—a shadow for which there was no reality for me; my father had for ever deserted me, leaving me only memories which set an eternal barrier between me and my fellow creatures. I was indeed fellow to none . . . infamy and guilt was mingled with my portion; unlawful and detestable passion had poured its poison into my ears and changed all my blood, so that it was no longer the kindly stream that supports life but a cold fountain of bitterness corrupted in its very source. It must be the excess of madness that could make me imagine that I could ever be aught but one alone; struck off from humanity; bearing no affinity to man or woman; a wretch on whom Nature had set her ban. (229)

Mathilda's sense of betrayal, guilt, and bitterness grows from her recognition of the role of incest in making her see herself as a monstrous daughter—like Frankenstein's creature, "a wretch on whom Nature had set her ban." As Mathilda herself puts it, speaking of the tragedy inherent in the daughter's recognition of the implications of her sexuality, "I had no idea that misery could arise from love, and this lesson that all at last must learn was taught me in a manner few are obliged to receive it" (189).

It is in this way, then, that *Mathilda* may be read as a parable of the daughter's initiation into womanhood. *Mathilda* portrays the daughter's ungendered, promise-filled girlhood and then links the daughter's growing sense of isolation and monstrosity as she enters womanhood to incest and paternal rejection. But though *Mathilda* lays the blame for the daughter's misery at the father's doorstep—a point to be discussed in more detail later—Mary Shelley enriches her tale by portraying the daughter's reactions to her father with all their contradictory fullness. Mathilda curses and blames her father, but she also loves him passionately. Shelley even suggests that the daughter's love for her father is as sexually charged as the father's love for her, a fact of which the daughter may not be initially aware. The sexual quality of the daughter's tie to her father emerges in the language Shelley

gives Mathilda to describe her feelings for her father, as well as in the
implications of Mathilda's behavior toward him. Even before the father's
declaration of his incestuous love, Mathilda's language is, more often than
not, the language of a lover rather than a daughter. Her father is her "beloved," her "dearest friend" (200), a partner whose "love-breathing countenance" (192) and "mutual love" (199) Mathilda strives to preserve. When
her father describes his volcanic passion for her dead mother, Mathilda's
body trembles with delight (189). She hates it when any third person shares
her solitary excursions with her father, yet "if I turned with a disturbed look
towards my father, his eyes fixed on me and beaming with tenderness
instantly restored joy to my heart" (190). Mathilda compares her relation to
her father to that between Psyche and Cupid, a comparison that in itself
reveals the sexual tension in Mathilda's feelings. In Apuleius's version of the
myth, which Mary Shelley translated in 1817,[20] Psyche spends blissful nights
sleeping with a mysterious, unnamed lover—Cupid—who disappears when
she discovers his identity. And the language in which Mathilda couches her
comparison of herself to Psyche has markedly sensuous overtones, stressing
as it does the "luxurious delight" Mathilda derives from her father. As
Mathilda puts it, her months of happiness with her father constitute a kind
of "enchantment": "Like Psyche, I lived for awhile in an enchanted palace,
amidst odours, and music, and every luxurious delight" (190).

    Mathilda repeatedly threads her conversations with her father with
references to literary works about father-daughter incest—a pattern of allusion that serves as appropriate foreshadowing for Mathilda's own situation,
but that also reveals Mathilda's preoccupation with incestuous emotions.
On one occasion, Mathilda mentions that she thinks "*Myrrha* the best of
Alfieri's tragedies" (192), and her father jumps with surprise and concern at
the reference to a play about incestuous love between a father and daughter.[21] On another occasion, Mathilda quotes lines from Fletcher's *Captain*—lines spoken by Lelia, a daughter who attempts to seduce her father
(192). Mathilda finally decides to force her father to tell her why he has
rejected her, and the language describing her motivation is again heavy with
sexual innuendo. Mathilda tells her father that, if he reveals his secret to her,
father and daughter will cross a chasm, flying on the wings of "mutual love."
There, they will "find flowers, and verdure, and delight on the other side . . .
we shall love each other as before, and for ever" (200). Earlier, Mathilda has
phrased her intentions to herself using even more sexually suggestive language. "I will win him to me," she says; "he shall not deny his grief to me and
when I know his secret then will I pour a balm into his soul and again I shall

enjoy the ravishing delight of beholding his smile, and of again seeing his eyes beam if not with pleasure at least with gentle love and thankfulness" (167). Mathilda's desire to "win" her father to her, as well as her desire to experience "ravishing delight" from him, and her determination to prevent him from "denying" himself to her, certainly suggest the sexuality of her feelings—even if her "ravishing delight" comes from the father's smile and what she will stop him from denying her is his grief rather than physical intimacy. Clearly, Mathilda's feelings for her father are charged with sexual tension; just as clearly, Mathilda's eventual recognition of this sexual tension contributes even more to her sense of her daughterly guilt and loathesomeness.[22]

For Mathilda does, at some level, discover the sexual quality of her feelings for her father. Although no physical intimacy takes place between them, she finally calls him what she perceives him to be: "a lover, there was madness in the thought, yet he was my lover" (211). And Mathilda recognizes one other aspect of her guilt: her guilt in forcing her father to admit to her his passionate love. As the text makes clear, Mathilda's father struggles to contain and eradicate the incestuous currents in his love for his daughter, but Mathilda dooms his struggle to failure when, unaware of the implications of her insistence, she forces him to explain why he has rejected her. Mathilda's father warns her not to question him on the reasons for his emotional withdrawal, because his "uneasiness," he says, "will pass away, and I hope that soon we shall be as we were a few months ago" (199). Mathilda, too, eventually realizes that her father has fought to stamp out his incestuous passion. She says that her father's "paroxisms of passion were terrific but his soul bore him through them triumphant" (197). Nevertheless, driven by love and anguish, Mathilda presses her father for an answer. Mathilda acknowledges her guilt in both bringing the incestuous situation to light and dooming father and daughter to suffering and death:

> [T]he day would finally have been won had not I, foolish and presumptuous wretch! hurried him on until there was no recall, no hope. My rashness gave the victory in this dreadful fight to the enemy who triumphed over him as he lay fallen and vanquished. I! I alone was the cause of his defeat and justly did I pay the fearful penalty. I said to myself, let him receive sympathy and these struggles will cease. . . . Half I accomplished; I gained his secret and we were both lost forever. (197)

Several observations may be made about the way Shelley frames Mathilda's guilt and participation in the incestuous situation that entangles father and daughter. Mathilda's motivation in pressing her father to reveal his "secret" is decidedly ambiguous. Mathilda has no way of knowing her father will confess a sexual attachment to her, yet his confession of love is clearly something for which Mathilda, at some buried level, deeply yearns. The father's confession of love, after all, only mirrors and articulates the desire implied in the sexual innuendo of Mathilda's own language. Even more important, however, is the way Shelley frames Mathilda's situation in terms of the classic story of Oedipus. Shelley examines the question of incestuous guilt from this perspective, too: she places Mathilda in Oedipus's situation and then retells the tale from the point of view of the daughter rather the son. In doing so, Shelley rewrites a male cultural myth to show the impact of incest on the daughter, suggesting that the daughter's fate is even more terrible than the son's.

If there is a classical tragedy upon which Shelley models *Mathilda*, it is the story of Oedipus. The parallels between Mathilda and Sophocles' Oedipus are plentiful and striking. Both are unwitting participants in an incestuous situation; both unwittingly cause the death of one parent and then lose the other parent—who has become a lover—to suicide. Both leave the scene of revelation overwhelmed by a sense of guilt; both find peace as they are about to die.[23] Shelley sets up the Oedipus parallel on the opening page of her novel when she portrays Mathilda, on the verge of death, about to tell her tale. Like Oedipus, Mathilda is transfixed by the "sacred horror" (175) of her story. Mathilda describes herself as an Oedipus figure and declares: "It is as the wood of the Eumenides none but the dying may enter; and Oedipus is about to die" (176). Once Shelley has established the importance of the Oedipus parallel to Mathilda's situation, she draws upon Sophocles' play for the details of her novel in a number of ways. To begin with, the discovery scenes of *Mathilda* repeatedly use the sort of dramatic irony that is characteristic of *Oedipus the King*. Specifically, Shelley draws upon Oedipus's famous curse: the scene in which Oedipus, seeking to learn the identity of Laius's murderer, unwittingly calls a curse down upon his own head. Shelley sets up a similar situation in *Mathilda*. Eager to know the secret behind her father's rejection, Mathilda vows to wring an explanation from him. As she speculates about her father's feelings, and the "unworthiness" of the person who must inspire them, she unwittingly implicates herself in the crime, as does Oedipus:

> It may easily be imagined that I wearied myself with conjecture to guess the cause of his sorrow. The solution that seemed to me the most probable was that during his residence in London he had fallen in love with some

unworthy person, and that his passion mastered him although he would not gratify it: he loved me too well to sacrifise me to this inclination, and that he had now visited this house that by reviving the memory of my mother whom he so passionately adored he might weaken the present impression. (196)

Mathilda's speculation describes the pieces of her situation exactly. Her father has fallen in love with some "unworthy person" in London; he refuses to gratify his passion for this person because to do so would sacrifice Mathilda to his "inclination"; he has fled to the home he shared with his beloved wife to erase the influence of the person from his mind. All Mathilda lacks is the key that fits the pieces of the puzzle together: the identity of her father's unnamed lover. Like Oedipus, Mathilda does not suspect that the "unworthy person" at the center of the crime is the speaker herself. Little does Mathilda realize that in pressing to know her father's secret lover and thus understand why he has rejected his daughter, Mathilda will press to learn, like Oedipus, about her own incestuous guilt.

Shelley draws upon Sophocles's Oedipus in a second way. Both Oedipus and Mathilda actively, if unwittingly, create the conditions for their tragedy by their desire to know too much. Shelley is careful to point out that Mathilda, like Oedipus, is "presumptious and very rash" (199) in her drive to know the truth of her situation. Once her father has withdrawn all his affection and Mathilda decides to get to the bottom of the matter, Shelley gives Mathilda all of Oedipus's reckless determination in searching out the truth. Echoing Oedipus's declaration that he must know the truth of Laius's murder and his own origins even if it means his doom, Mathilda cajoles and entreats her father, saying, "I must not be repulsed; there is one thing that although it may torture me to know, yet that you must tell me" (200). Later, Mathilda presses still more insistently: "I will not be put off thus. . . ." she says; "I demand that dreadful word; though it be as a flash of lightning to destroy me, speak it" (201). Significantly, Mathilda's father urges her to be silent and play her proper womanly role. "Do not again speak to me in this strain," he says, "but wait in submissive patience the event of what is passing around you" (199). Unwilling to be restrained in dealing with her father, Mathilda continues to push for the truth until her father blurts out the secret of his incestuous love for her. It is at this point that Mathilda, like Oedipus, is precipitated into her tragedy of recognition. Both Oedipus and Mathilda are entangled in incestuous love; both have destroyed themselves by insisting on bringing the knowledge of incest to light.

There is a third way in which Shelley models *Mathilda* upon *Oedipus the*

King, a way that simultaneously draws upon the story and departs from it. Both Mathilda and Oedipus are foredoomed to participate in an incestuous situation—though he struggles to escape his fate, Oedipus cannot avoid sleeping with his mother any more than Mathilda can escape stirring up incestuous feelings in her father. But though the incestuous situation is inevitable in both cases, what actually transpires in the incestuous situation is quite different. Oedipus marries his mother and mates with her; Mathilda does not sleep with her father but simply comes to recognize the sexual character of their relationship. Yet Mathilda's recognition of the sexuality of her father's love is as tragic for her as Oedipus's committing actual incest with his mother is for him. For the daughter, it would seem, the knowledge of the inclination to transgress a taboo is as treacherous as the literal transgression of that same taboo is for the son. As Mathilda herself puts it, speaking of both her emotions and her father's, "I did not yet know of the crime there may be in involuntary feeling" (197).

For the daughter to locate "crime" in her knowledge of "involuntary feeling" rather than action implies several things about the daughter's situation. To begin with, for the daughter, the simple act of existence is tinged with guilt, while for the son, some act must be performed for guilt to arise. Mathilda finds guilt in the intrusions of her "involuntary feeling," while Oedipus is guilty because he actually breaks the incest taboo. This essential difference suggests Mary Shelley's grasp of the disadvantage at which culture has placed women: their very existence is fraught with guilt; they have so internalized the culture's association of them with sinful physicality that their involuntary emotions become criminally suspect. Further, Mathilda's "crime," unlike Oedipus's, resides exclusively in her need for knowledge. Oedipus breaks a taboo and then comes to recognize his guilty action; Mathilda simply recognizes a desire to break a taboo. Shelley defines Mathilda's "rashness" not so much as an affront to the gods—Oedipus's crime—but instead as a dangerous desire to understand an inevitable situation. In some sense Mathilda courts her fearful destiny precisely because she cannot be submissive and patient, as her father recommends, but insists instead on understanding the exact nature of her position as a woman. Mathilda's real crime is the need to know too much, the irresistible urge to push the unconscious into daylight. And once Mathilda recognizes that her "involuntary feeling"—and that of her father—centers on the secret of father-daughter incest, she assumes a burden of guilt that kills her. Mathilda is undeniably accurate when, close to the end of the novel, she utters this reflection on the condition of being a daughter: "I am, I thought, a tragedy" (233).[24]

Before Mathilda dies, her recognition of the sexual quality of her feelings for her father, combined with the guilt engendered by his declaration of passionate love, drives Mathilda to reject her sexuality entirely. When her father confesses his secret, Mathilda immediately resolves to enter a convent: "I would retire to the Continent and become a nun; not for religion's sake, for I was not a Catholic, but that I might be for ever shut out from the world" (204). After her father commits suicide, Mathilda instead withdraws into a solitary life in the wilds of nature. Tortured by her sense of monstrosity, she becomes, like Frankenstein's creature, a hermit. Away from the prying eyes of society, Mathilda obliterates any sign of her sexuality by adopting a "fanciful nunlike dress" (219). When the gentle poet Woodville appears, Mathilda realizes she cannot love him. Like actual incest victims, Mathilda cannot respond to other men. She values Woodville as a friend but insists that his sympathy for her must be "pure," totally devoid of the "gross materials that perpetually mingle even with [the world's] best feelings" (222). Once she has gained the poet's friendship, Mathilda discovers that even this disinterested affection, "the best gift of heaven" (223), does not touch her: "[A]lthough the spirit of friendship soothed me for a while it could not restore me. It came as some gentle visitation; it went and I hardly felt the loss" (223). Indeed, Mathilda finds that once her father/lover has left her, she feels nothing at all. Her father's incestuous passion has imprisoned Mathilda in the same bleak emotional landscape that Frankenstein's creature inhabits:

> I might feel gratitude to another but I never more could love or hope as I had done; it was all suffering; even my pleasures were endured, not enjoyed. I was as a solitary spot among mountains shut in on all sides by steep black precipices; where no ray of heat could penetrate; and from which there was no outlet to sunnier fields. . . . The spirit of existence was dead within me. (223)

Mathilda's discovery "has changed [her heart] to stone" (215). She internalizes the precise emotional terrain into which Shelley exiles Frankenstein's creature. Just as the creature lives in an isolated spot walled in by Alpine peaks, among "the desert mountains and dreary glaciers" (95), so Mathilda contains within her "a solitary spot among mountains shut in on all sides by steep black precipices; where no ray of heat could penetrate." Devoid of all feeling and divorced from her sexuality by her sense of guilt, Mathilda soon craves death, where she can rejoin her father in an eternal union purged of sensuality.

In writing about the incestuous patterns of behavior that structure a young girl's upbringing—and especially in revealing the young girl's unwitting complicity in them—Mary Shelley sets herself an intimidating task. She reveals deeply personal and hidden attachments; she brings to consciousness the unconscious and forbidden. In short, she delivers a deeply subversive message about the fundamental nature of a young girl's socialization. And, like many women writers who compose subversive fictions, Shelley feels compelled to couch her narrative in the sort of evasions that Gilbert and Gubar have taught us to expect. The most important of these evasions in *Mathilda* is Shelley's use of what Gilbert and Gubar call "trance-writing"—the author's insistence that her tale originates in a some force outside her and is imposed upon her almost against her will.[25] When Mathilda begins her story, she asserts that she is not totally responsible for telling her tale. "I am in a strange state of mind," she says. "Perhaps a history such as mine had better die with me, but a feeling that I cannot define leads me on and I am too weak both in body and mind to resist the slightest impulse" (175). According to Mathilda, her tale emerges by a sort of automatic writing, an involuntary agency akin to the "waking dreams" Shelley describes in her 1831 introduction to *Frankenstein*. Telling her story is something she is compelled to do by forces beyond her control. This "trance-writing" serves a useful purpose for the narrator/author of *Mathilda*: If Mathilda/Mary Shelley is forced to tell the daughter's incest story by some power beyond her, none of the blame for revealing the hideous secret can fairly be ascribed to her.

Yet even guided as Mathilda is by a power outside her, she is still ambivalent about telling her tale. She further seeks to ward off blame by openly admitting that her story is "unfit for utterance." Or is it? While confessing that her telling of the tale is an act of "pollution," the story itself, because of its horror, is still somehow sacred. As Mathilda puts it, "While life was strong within me I thought indeed that there was a sacred horror in my tale that rendered it unfit for utterance, and now about to die I pollute its mystic terrors" (175–76). The images of "sacred horror" and "mystic terror" suggest why Mathilda's tale is central to the young girl's experience: it is the story of a secret rite of passage that has all the force of religious ritual, a mystery of induction to which all girls must submit. The language also suggests why the narrator is ambivalent about telling her story. If the story is "sacred," it is also horrible; the narrator wants to tell it but does not want to "pollute" either the tale or the world she gives it to. Hidden in the tangle of Shelley's ambivalent language is a desire to reveal the truth, accompanied by a deep fear—and desire to evade—the fearful consequences of her revelation.

The narrator/author of Mathilda seeks to avoid responsibility not only because of her story's content. The use of "trance-writing" also allows her to evade blame for revealing a very different aspect of the daughter's history: the story of the way the daughter struggles to control and punish the father for his transgression. Although Mathilda becomes aware of her complicity in the incestuous situation, she seeks to focus guilt on her father. In a revealing passage, she compares herself to Eve, thus suggesting she sees herself as a temptress, yet simultaneously insists that she has done no wrong. "I must ever lament, those few short months of Paradisaical bliss," she says. "I disobeyed no command. I ate no apple, and yet I was ruthlessly driven from it. Alas! my companion did, and I was precipitated in his fall" (189). And Mathilda does more than blame her father. She also seeks to punish him. Using the same imagery of original sin, but this time casting her father as the serpent rather than Adam, Mathilda vents her rage as Eve does: "[S]tarting back with horror I spurned him with my foot; I felt as if stung by a serpent, as if scourged by a whip of scorpions which drove me—Ah! Whither—Whither?" (202). Later, assuming the role of the punishing God in the paradise story, Mathilda utters what she calls "a daughter's curse." Her curse sentences her father to Adam's punishment after the first transgression in the garden of Eden—wandering the face of the earth at the mercy of the elements:[26]

> Let him spend another sixteen years of desolate wandering: let him once more utter his wild complaints to the vast woods and the tremendous cataracts of another clime: let him again undergo fearful danger and soul-quelling hardships: let the hot sun of the south again burn his passion worn cheeks and the cold night rains fall on him and chill his blood.
>
> To this life, miserable father, I devote thee!—Go!—Be thy days passed with savages, and thy nights under the cope of heaven! Be thy limbs worn and thy heart chilled, and all youth be dead within thee! . . . and then return to me, return to thy Mathilda, thy child, who may then be clasped in thy loved arms, while thy heart beats with sinless emotion. Go, Devoted One, and return thus!—This is my curse, a daughter's curse: go, and return pure to thy child, who will never love aught but thee. (204)

The "daughter's curse" is revealing on a number of counts. It embodies the daughter's determination to gain power over the father by rejecting him—not only does she condemn the father to wander, but she condemns him to wander, unlike Adam, alone, deprived of the company of his companion in sin. Clearly, however, the "daughter's curse" has another, very different, edge: if it condemns the father, it also punishes the daughter, since the father's exile sentences the daughter to isolation and dissatisfaction in the absence of the only person she can ever love.

This same combination of hostility and attachment surfaces in the murderous dream Mary Shelley gives Mathilda. In a neat variation on the oedipal triangle, Mary Shelley allows Mathilda to avenge herself upon her father and all he represents by killing him. The night after Mathilda's father declares his incestuous love and implores her to "let me lay my head near your heart" (202), she fantasizes about his death, a fantasy that takes the form of a prophetic dream. In the dream, Mathilda's father is deathly pale and dressed in flowing garments. She follows him over fields and through woods as he races toward the sea. As they reach a high cliff over the ocean, he pauses; just as Mathilda reaches him and touches his garments he plunges over the side to his death. The dream is intriguing for its deliberate ambiguities. Mathilda may simply be following her father as he runs to the sea; yet Shelley says that Mathilda "pursued" him (205) and thus suggests that Mathilda might be chasing her father toward the ocean, aggressively driving him to his death. Similarly, as father and daughter reach the brink of the precipice, she reaches out for him and touches his garments—to pull him back from the edge or to push him over? In either case, Mathilda's fantasy about her father's death becomes literal truth when she awakes next morning. As she leaves her room, she learns that her father has fled the house, vowing never to see her again. She chases him across fields and roads, driving always *"towards the sea"* (212, Shelley's italics).[27] By the time she catches him, he has committed suicide by running off a cliff into the ocean. Mathilda feels desolate and responsible, possessed of enough "superstition" (212) to imagine that her dream murdered him. And in some sense it has: Mathilda got what she wished for; her father's death is her dream come true.

Although the story of the daughter's hostility and attachment to her father occupies center stage in *Mathilda,* a second story lies parallel to and entangled in the incest tale: a story about mothers. In *Mathilda* as in *Frankenstein,* the mother's absence is as important to the daughter figure as the father's troubling presence. It is the mother's absence that creates the conditions for the daughter's peculiar socialization; it is the mother's absence that reveals why the father's emotional need focuses on his daughter.

As we have seen, victims of incest are, like Mathilda, products of a family in which the mother is in some sense absent.[28] In the case of Mathilda, her mother Diana dies in childbirth, in the act of giving life to the daughter who eventually takes her place. We have examined the father's initial rejection of the infant daughter who causes his beloved wife's death. When

Mathilda's father returns to claim her after sixteen years, however, this rejection melts into an intermittent strategy of replacement: the father often seems intent upon making Mathilda the living embodiment of his dead wife. The father tells Mathilda she is "the creature who will form the happiness of my future life" (186); later, he insists that she is, like Diana was, "my consolation, and my hope" (187). He talks of Mathilda's mother "as if she had lived but a few weeks before" (188); most significant, he takes Mathilda back to the Yorkshire home he shared with Diana and there asks Mathilda to reenact his wife's presence for him. Mathilda describes what happens:

> When we arrived, after a little rest, he led me over the house and pointed out to me the rooms which my mother had inhabited. Although more than sixteen years had passed since her death nothing had been changed; her work box, her writing desk were still there and in her room a book lay open on the table as she had left it. My father pointed out these circumstances with a serious and unaltered mien, only now and then fixing his deep and liquid eyes upon me; there was something strange and awful in his look that overcame me, and in spite of myself I wept, nor did he attempt to console me, but I saw his lips quiver and the muscles of his countenance seemed convulsed.
>
> We walked together in the gardens and in the evening when I would have retired he asked me to stay and read to him; and first said, "When I was last here your mother read Dante to me; you shall go on where she left off." And then in a moment he said, "No, that must not be; you must not read Dante. Do you choose a book." (194–95)

Mathilda's father eventually explains his motivation in taking Mathilda to Yorkshire: he hoped that immersion in Diana's Yorkshire milieu would drive away his incestuous passion for his daughter. Just the opposite happens, of course. Once the father installs Mathilda in her mother's house, he cannot help but see Mathilda as his wife come back to life. He asks Mathilda to read Dante to him, as his wife did. But then the implications of asking his daughter to "go on where [Diana] left off" become troubling to the father, and he withdraws his request.

This scene reveals Mary Shelley's grasp of another fundamental aspect of the daughter's socialization: that, in the absence of a mother, fathers socialize their daughters by expecting them to behave as "little wives." Judith Herman points out the pervasiveness of this pattern in incestuous families and discusses its sexual implications.[29] But this pattern of behavior is not confined to incestuous or dysfunctional families. Far from it. It is, instead, the pervasive pattern of the daughter's socialization in patriarchal culture, and appears in its most common and acceptable form whenever, in the mother's absence, the oldest daughter is expected to minister to the needs of the father and younger children.

Shelley also grasps and portrays one final, essential fact of the daughter's history: when the father casts his daughter as his missing wife, he expresses a prior and less articulate need—the desire to reanimate and possess his lost mother. In this context, *Mathilda* clarifies some of the incestuous connections implied in a more covert way in *Frankenstein*. Just as Frankenstein desires to reanimate his dead mother and ends up creating a monstrous creature whom he dimly identifies as a lover and daughter, so Mathilda's father seeks to resurrect his dead mother first in Diana and then in Mathilda. Shelley makes this dynamic clear in her history of the father's relationship to his wife. Shelley describes Diana as noble, intelligent, and strong—but primarily as a mother-substitute for a grieving son. "Diana, even in her childhood had been a favourite with [Mathilda's father's] mother" (178), Shelley tells us. When his mother dies, Mathilda's father immediately abandons college and "retire[s] to the neighbourhood of his Diana and receive[s] all his consolation from her sweet voice and dearer caresses" (179). In his grief, Mathilda's father finds all his comfort in the maternalism of Diana's embrace. Within a few months they marry.

Just as the father's marriage to Diana continues his relation to a mother figure, so does his return to Mathilda express his persistent desire to possess the lost mother. Shelley makes this inarticulate aspect of the father's motivation clear in several ways. To begin with, Shelley stresses the father's sense that no time has elapsed in the sixteen years of his absence—that is, Mathilda very directly continues Diana, just as Diana very directly continued his mother. As Shelley describes it,

> There was a curious feeling of unreality attached by him to his foreign life in comparison with the years of his youth. All the time he had passed out of England was as a dream, and all the interest of his soul, all his affections belonged to events which had happened and persons who had existed sixteen years before. It was strange when you heard him talk to see how he passed over this lapse of time as a night of visions; while the remembrances of his youth standing separate as they did from his after life had lost none of their vigour. He talked of my Mother as if she had lived but a few weeks before. . . . He was, as it were, now awakened from his long, visionary sleep, and he felt somewhat like one of the seven sleepers. . . . Diana was gone; his friends were changed or dead, and now on his awakening I was all that he had to love on earth. (188)

If Diana reanimated the lost mother for Mathilda's father, and the father awakes from a sixteen-year-long "dream" to find that Mathilda has taken Diana's place, then Mathilda also in some sense resurrects or embodies the dead mother for him. This fact becomes even more apparent in the suggestive language Shelley puts in the mouth of both father and daughter. At the climactic moment of the story—just after the father has confessed his passionate attachment to his daughter, while his "blood riots through [his] veins" and he is "burnt up with fever"—he asks Mathilda to grant him a last wish: "Oh, Beloved One, I am borne away. . . . Let me lay my head near your heart" (202). Curiously, the father does not ask for a kiss, an embrace, or some other gesture of affection and attachment. He instead requests the privilege of lying, infantlike, close to Mathilda's breast, and thus implicitly casts Mathilda in a maternal pose. A few pages later, Shelley gives the father an ambiguous pronoun that underscores yet again the maternal terms in which he views his daughter. Writing of the effect of the Yorkshire visit on his feelings for Mathilda, he says:

> And now, Mathilda I must make you my last confession. I have been miserably mistaken in imagining that I could conquer my love for you; I never can. The sight of this house, these fields and woods which my first love inhabited seems to have encreased it: in my madness I dared say to myself—Diana died to give her birth; her mother's spirit was transferred into her frame, and she ought to be as Diana to me. (209–10)

This passage certainly reveals the extent to which the father sees his daughter as a replacement for his dead wife—Mathilda, he insists, "ought to be as Diana to me." Yet it also expresses the father's submerged desire to recapture his relation to his lost mother. "Diana died to give her birth," the father says; "*her* mother's spirit was transferred into her frame" (italics mine). If the italicized pronoun is read as referring to Mathilda, then the phrase clearly declares that Mathilda embodies Diana's spirit, that is, Mathilda's mother's spirit. But if the ambiguous pronoun is read as referring to Diana, the phrase also declares that Mathilda reincarnates Diana's maternal spirit, that is, all Diana's ability to respond to the father in a motherly, protective, and consoling way.

Several observations may be made about the way Shelley portrays Mathilda as a mother-figure to her father. First of all, Mathilda is to some extent aware of the maternal aspects of her position, or at least responds to her father with emotions that have a motherly component. Mathilda, after all, uses at least one literary allusion in which she casts herself as mother to her father's role of son. She compares herself to Constance, the grieving mother of Prince Arthur in Shakespeare's play *King John* (217–18).[30] Second, this pattern of a father seeking maternal comfort from a daughter is very common, even if it is not often recognized and described for what it is. We have discussed Boose's assertion that the father's seduction of his daughter is embedded within his attempt to reconstruct his lost union with the mother. Judith Herman discusses this same dynamic specifically in the case of the incestuous family.

> Some researchers who have studied incestuous fathers directly emphasize the father's unfulfilled dependent wishes and fear of abandonment. In the father's fantasy life, the daughter becomes the source of all the father's infantile longings for nurturance and care. He thinks of her first as the idealized childhood bride or sweetheart, and finally as the all-good, all-giving mother. The reality, that she is the child and he the adult, becomes quite immaterial to him. In the compulsive sexual act he seeks repeated reassurance that she will never refuse or frustrate him.[31]

As Herman implies, the intense sexuality of the father's tie to his daughter derives from deeply buried sources. Specifically, the father's "seduction" of his daughter is rooted in the powerful sexuality of his pre-oedipal tie to the mother and his desire to reconstruct that tie, in the absence of a wife, through the affections of a daughter. In this sense, father-daughter incest and the maternal behavior of the daughter intersect in both *Mathilda* and in the second play of Sophocles' trilogy, *Oedipus at Colonus*:[32] the father's relationship to Mathilda is sexually charged because it repeats his relationship to his wife and, lying prior to that, his relationship to the pre-oedipal mother. Conversely, whenever Mathilda behaves in a maternal way toward her father, her acts of motherly support and consolation inspire the father to experience emotions tinged with sexual energy. As we shall see, Shelley portrays this same intersection of the themes of father-daughter incest and the daughter's maternalism in her last novel, *Falkner*. In *Falkner*, the daughter's maternal behavior becomes a weapon to diminish and control the father; but in *Mathilda*, the daughter's maternalism, with all its bewildering incestuous implications, only catapults the daughter into suicidal desires and eventual death.

For this is the note on which *Mathilda* ends. Afflicted by her sense of guilt, yet yearning to be reunited with the father she both spurns and adores, Mathilda hungers for death. As the novel draws to a close, Mathilda becomes increasingly tormented by her guilt and sense of monstrosity. She agonizes over "that within my soul that no silence could render sufficiently obscure" (239); she is paralyzed by the conviction that "my soul [was] corrupted to its core by a deadly cancer," and by "the withering fear that I was in truth a marked creature, a pariah only fit for death" (239). First Mathilda seeks complete isolation, because only "on a lone heath at noon or at midnight, still I should be near him [her father]" (217). But nearness is not enough; she wants to be united to her father more closely, a mingling possible only if she, too, dies. First she lingers over her father's grave, pounding the ground to get inside with him (218). Then, in her frustration, she tears the hair from her head and releases it to the wind, hoping that at least that part of her can find her father quickly. Mathilda contemplates suicide but initially rejects the idea (221);[33] she then proposes a suicide pact to Woodville, arguing that in this way both she and the poet can be reunited with beloved figures who have already entered the realm of the dead (235). Finally, Mathilda fantasizes a sexless reunion with her father in Dante's terrestrial paradise. Her father will run to her from his bower; their eyes will beam at each other "with the soft lustre of innocent love" (241). And this fantasy kills her as surely as her earlier dream killed her father. Mathilda has been wandering the woods as she daydreams; she cannot find her way home and becomes soaked in a rainstorm; the resulting illness leads to her death. As she awaits her reunion with her father, her thoughts, for all their insistence on the "mental" character of her reunion with her father, still portray her as her father's bride:

> I feel death to be near at hand and I am calm. I no longer despair, but look on all around me with placid affection. . . . I shall not see the red leaves of autumn; before that time I shall be with my father. . . . In truth I am in love with death; no maiden ever took more pleasure in the contemplation of her bridal attire than I in fancying my limbs already enwrapt in their shroud: is it not my marriage dress? Alone it will unite me to my father when in an eternal mental union we shall never part. (244)

Mathilda's death is in one way the perfect fantasy solution to the daughter's predicament: she can become her father's wife/lover without the guilty sensuality of it; she can possess her father entirely, yet escape the filthy sexuality of the female condition.

At the same time, of course, Mathilda's death is not a solution to her predicament at all. It is rather an indication that it is impossible for a woman to escape the consequences of her sexuality, at least as long as she remains alive. Mathilda can be purged of the incestuous guilt associated with being a female, but only if she dies. From this point of view, Mathilda's suicide parallels the fate of Frankenstein's tormented creature. Like the creature, Mathilda eradicates her "filthy materiality" by killing herself; like the creature, Mathilda punishes herself for the crime of femaleness by self-annihilation. And to this extent, the fate of Mathilda, the female Oedipus, is again different from the fate of the male Oedipus. While Oedipus leads a long life, Mathilda, the daughter who seeks to know the truth of her genesis, is driven to suicide by the horror of her situation in her twentieth year.[34]

When Shelley sat down to *Mathilda* in the late summer of 1819, she was besieged in every aspect of her womanly role. She was almost twenty-two years old and had already suffered the deaths of three children, two of them within the previous twelve months. As a wife, she stood in fear of losing her husband. As a daughter, she was weighed down by William Godwin's inability to grasp her grief and his incessant demands for financial and emotional support. Shelley was seven months pregnant with her last child. As she wrote *Mathilda*, Shelley examined the ambivalence, horror, and loss characteristic of the female condition, and she located their sources in an individual paternal rejection that became emblematic of the culture's general rejection of the female. She expressed the daughter's affection, guilt, and hostility toward individual and cultural fathers who give too little and expect too much, and expressed her sense that daughterhood, which is a version of and doorway to motherhood, is a deadly proposition.

In *Mathilda* and *Frankenstein*, the daughter finally remains subject to the power and limiting scope of the father's desire. The daughter is associated in the father's mind with lover, wife, and mother, but the figure of the daughter is prevented by death from assuming any of these roles in a concrete way with a figure other than the father. As we shall see, Shelley's last novels allow the daughter to subvert and move beyond these paternal limits, through the apparently conventional act of behaving like a mother.

A few months after Mary Shelley completed *Mathilda*, she sent it to William Godwin. It was a perfect act of daughterly ambivalence. When she sent her father her manuscript, she complied perfectly with his desire that she assume the wifely/daughterly role and support him. Godwin was facing eviction from his home; he continued to mail her letters asking for money; she sent him *Mathilda* so he could publish it and use the profits to pay his debts.[35] At the same time, of course, sending her father *Mathilda* was an act of unvarnished rebellion. How could she think he could condone a work so transparently autobiographical, so passionately loving and hostile toward him, so boldly open about the incestuous currents of father-daughter relationships? Indeed, Godwin was shocked, and called *Mathilda* "disgusting and detestable."[36] He made no move to publish it; several years later, Mary Shelley was still trying to get the manuscript back from him. In the pages of *Mathilda*, Mary Shelley casts her heroine as an Oedipus. But Shelley's own behavior with her novel about father-daughter incest identifies the author as an Antigone as well—a daughter who cares for her elderly father in his old age but who also rebels against patriarchal norms that oppress her.

4

Lodore

For the next decade of Mary Shelley's life—from 1819 when she finished *Mathilda*, to 1831 when she began *Lodore*—the story of the daughter's conflict with the father receded from the foreground of her fiction. The father/daughter story reclaims center stage in *Lodore* and also organizes her last novel, *Falkner*. But daughters, fathers, and their vexed relations do not disappear entirely from Shelley's fiction during this middle period. They populate the peripheries of Shelley's work in ways that look back to *Frankenstein* and *Mathilda*, and forward to *Lodore* and *Falkner*. Indeed, in *Valperga* and *The Last Man*, Shelley portrays versions of daughterhood that are remarkable either for their overt sexuality or for their violently destructive power.

I.

Shelley published numerous short stories between 1819 and 1831; for our purposes the most significant is "The Mourner" (1829).[1] The relationship between father and daughter in "The Mourner" is as passionate as that between father and daughter in *Mathilda* —so passionate, in fact, that the daughter's love, like Mathilda's, kills her father. Like Mathilda, Clarice Eversham is as perfectly devoted to her widowed father as he is to her. As the narrator of "The Mourner" puts it, "They were never separate. . . . When a father is all that a father may be, the sentiments of filial piety, entire dependence, and perfect confidence being united, the love of a daughter is one of the deepest and strongest, as it is the purest passion of which our natures are capable. Clarice worshipped her parent" (92). Clarice and her father sail to Barbados. When their ship begins to sink in a storm, she stubbornly refuses to board a lifeboat without him. Stunned by Clarice's "woman's obstinacy," the lifeboat's captain warns Clarice that "You will cause your father's death—and be as much a parricide as if you put poison into his cup" (94). The captain's prediction proves to be correct: when a second lifeboat eventually appears, it has room for only one passenger. Clarice flees to the lifeboat; her father drowns.[2]

Consumed with guilt at having caused her father's death, and bereft of her father's affection, Clarice, like Mathilda, becomes a social outcast. She abandons her relatives, hides herself away in a forest cottage, and leads the life of a hermit. Like Mathilda—and like Frankenstein's spurned "monster"—Clarice's act of parricide makes her hunger after "self-destruction" (89). As the narrator puts it, "[W]ithout positively attempting her life, she did many things that tended to abridge it and to produce mortal disease" (91). Eventually, like Mathilda, Clarice succeeds in ending her life and achieves peace by reuniting with her father in dream. She refuses "all medical attendance" (91). In the narrator's words, after Clarice dies, "Our hearts had told us that the sufferer was at peace—the unhappy orphan with her father in the abode of spirits!" (98).

Shelley also published three novels during this middle period: *Valperga* (1823), *The Last Man* (1826), and *Perkin Warbeck* (1830). *Valperga* and *Perkin Warbeck* are historical novels; *The Last Man* is both an apocalyptic vision of the end of the world and an epitaph for Mary Shelley's husband. In these novels, as in Shelley's short fiction, the story of the father/daughter relationship appears at the periphery of the work. *Valperga*, for example, focuses on the career of Castruccio, a young Italian nobleman who schemes and fights for power in fourteenth-century Tuscany and who loves, alternately, Euthanasia and Beatrice. The character of Castruccio is the true center of *Valperga*, but Shelley devotes ample attention to delineating Euthanasia and Beatrice as daughters of a particular stamp, due to their relationships to their parents. As in the case of *Mathilda*, Shelley wrote *Valperga* to provide money for her bankrupt father—she sent William Godwin the manuscript in 1822, hoping he might turn it to his "immediate advantage."[3]

Euthanasia dei Adimari, the noblewoman who rules the castle from which *Valperga* takes its name, is the first female character in Shelley's novels who is utterly competent in worldly terms. Euthanasia possesses the intelligence and capacity for anger characteristic of Elizabeth Lavenza in the 1818 version of *Frankenstein*. As we will see, she also prefigures Fanny Derham of *Lodore*. Euthanasia ministers to the sick and poor in the manner of a truly feminine "angel" of mercy,[4] yet she is also a capable administrator, a lawmaker, and even a political conspirator. She runs the castle she has inherited from her mother in a prudent and benevolent manner. When the tyrant Castruccio—who is Euthanasia's childhood friend and erstwhile betrothed—demands she surrender Valperga, Euthanasia passionately declares that she will die before abandoning her fiefdom and the people who rely upon her for protection (2:222–24). Once Castruccio's forces have crept through Valperga's defenses, Euthanasia agrees to a surrender to avert further violence to her subjects. She leaves Valperga with her head held high, at the head of her party, astride her horse (2:274).

Like so many of Shelley's daughters, Euthanasia is utterly devoted to her father and calls her love for him the "first and the most religious" (I, 199) tie. It is the unconventional education Euthanasia's father gives her, in fact, that makes her such a capable and worldly woman. Like Mary Shelley's father, Euthanasia's father educates her in classical cultures. She learns Cicero and Virgil by reading aloud to her father after he loses his sight (1:28); she learns Roman history and philosophy in his company (1:195); above all, Euthanasia's father teaches her to worship wisdom and liberty (1:197). Gilbert and Gubar have argued that Milton's daughters, by reading to their blind father, reinforce the father's demand for slavish obedience and learn a language they can use only in secret.[5] Euthanasia, on the other hand, acquires from her father's tutelage intellectual vigor, a taste for abstract learning, and the ability to act decisively. He teaches Euthanasia that either "judgement or passions" (1:198) must rule the human spirit. Euthanasia chooses to be governed by judgment and reason. Her father's spiritual legacy guides her wise behavior as a ruler. Before she capitulates to Castruccio's forces, Euthanasia calls upon the "Spirit of thy father" to aid her (2:265). Although courted by Castruccio, Euthanasia recognizes his many flaws and refuses to marry him, thus escaping the strictures of traditional marriage. As we shall see, Euthanasia's independent mind, penchant for action, and unconventional femininity forecast the situation of Fanny Derham, the character in *Lodore* whose father refuses to give her a woman's traditional "sexual education"[6] (*Lodore*, 272).

If Euthanasia embodies Mary Shelley's affection for William Godwin and her grasp of the enabling effects for a daughter when a loving father gives her the education usually reserved for a son, Beatrice embodies Shelley's grasp of the fate of female sexuality in a culture defined by males. Beatrice is the inheritor of an exclusively female tradition: her father is unknown; she is the illegitimate daughter of a dead feminist prophet, Wilhelmina of Bohemia, a female heretic who saw herself as "the Holy Ghost incarnate upon earth for the salvation of the female sex" (2:26).[7] Orphaned at an early age and reduced to the same state of beggary as most of Shelley's emblematic daughters, Beatrice is for a time hidden with a wretched leper, who conceals her in his cave (2:35–37). When she makes her first appearance in *Valperga*, she is compared to Beatrice Cenci, the Italian daughter made monstrous by her father's incest (2:17–18). The reader soon learns that Beatrice is possessed of a vivid imagination and vast linguistic powers. She "had inherited from her mother the most ardent imagination that ever animated a human soul" (2:86); she uses this poetic gift to transport crowds whenever she preaches (2:45–46). Beatrice's ardent imagination leads her to give herself to Castruccio sexually. Mistaking her youthful passion for the "special interposition of heaven" (2:86), Beatrice submits willingly to Castruccio's seduction when she is "hardly seventeen" (2:87).

On one level, of course, Beatrice resembles Mary Shelley, who was herself the daughter of a dead feminist prophet, who was possessed of considerable verbal powers, and who gave herself sexually outside the bounds of marriage when she was barely seventeen.[8] But more important for our purposes is what happens to Beatrice as a result of her fall into sexuality. Beatrice loses her belief in her imagination[9] and her gift for language: her fall into sexuality effectively silences her. Like Mathilda after her sexual initiation, Beatrice (who is roughly Mathilda's age) turns herself into an outcast and describes herself in terms of bleak interior landscapes (3:76–77). She sets out on a pilgrimage to Rome to expiate her crimes against her divine Father. Her journey, she says, will "do homage to the divinity by some atonement for his violated laws" (3:77). Along the way, Beatrice is kidnapped, held captive in a castle for three years, raped repeatedly by a nameless tyrant, and eventually goes mad (3:74–97).[10] Boose's analysis of the daughter's position in Western marriage and kinship structures provides a useful gloss on this episode. As Boose demonstrates, male culture uses marriage as a vehicle through which the figure of the father controls and limits the daughter's autonomous sexuality.[11] Read from this perspective, Beatrice's "sin" is that she takes her sexuality into her own hands, intentionally engages in sex outside marriage, and thus circumvents the institutions through which cultural fathers control female sexuality. Having willfully fallen into illicit sexuality, Beatrice is not only silenced, but also loses male society's protection. Her imprisonment, rape, and torture are a function of her isolation from protective males; the sexual nature of her suffering also constitutes a fitting punishment for the sexual nature of her "crimes."

Beatrice dies after an ambiguous scene that conflates Castruccio with "the evil genius of her life"—a sign of the mad prophetess's recognition that her sexual relation to Castruccio is the source of her tragedy (3:154–55). But before she dies, Beatrice has internalized male culture's definition of herself and her behavior as monstrous. Beatrice becomes a "prophetess of Evil" (3:51). In historical terms, she embraces Paterinism, having become convinced that all creation is governed by "the eternal and victorious influence of evil" (3:44). More specifically, Beatrice sees herself as a living manifestation of evil "which circulates like air about us, clinging to our flesh like a poisonous garment, eating into us and destroying us" (3:44). Beatrice, in short, connects herself to the "disease, plague, famine, leprosy [and] fever" (3:45) that are evil's manifestations; this imagistic identification of female transgression with disease has been forecast much earlier in *Valperga*, when Wilhelmina's beliefs and behavior are described as "a living pestilence" (2:27). Beatrice thus becomes, like Mathilda and Frankenstein's creature, another daughter whose guilty sexuality consigns her to the realm of disease and death. To the extent that Beatrice views herself as a personification of evil and disease, she also prefigures PLAGUE, the female force that levels civilization in *The Last Man*.

Euthanasia and Beatrice, then, are daughters as different as Elizabeth Lavenza and Frankenstein's creature. One is privileged and protected; the other is disinherited, rejected, and scorned. Euthanasia and Beatrice are, to some extent, anomalies in Shelley's fiction. Euthanasia is the only female character in Shelley's novels who finds satisfaction in the world of work and government; Beatrice is the only female character who intentionally engages in sex outside of marriage. Both daughters are in this sense "unconventional" when measured against the social strictures of Shelley's own day. As Lew correctly notes, *Valperga* may be read "as a lament for a time—simultaneously 'lost' and 'imagined'—before the differentiation of 'separate spheres' of activity, a time when men and women could participate fully in both the private and public realms."[12] Having set the action of *Valperga* in the Italian city-states of the fourteenth century, Shelley could populate her pages with women whose unconventional behavior would make them unfit for the polite society of nineteenth-century England.

But Euthanasia and Beatrice are finally more similar to than different from Shelley's other fictional daughters. Both are shaped by the expectations of either literal or cultural fathers; both die before the novel closes, having failed to form a satisfactory attachment to a male that would allow them to move beyond daughterhood into another socially sanctioned female role.

In *The Last Man*, as in *Valperga*, the story of the father-daughter relationship appears at the periphery of the work. *The Last Man* is largely a memorial to Percy Bysshe Shelley and expresses Mary Shelley's intense grief and loneliness after her husband's drowning.[13] For a time, Shelley felt utterly isolated and abandoned by Percy's death, and she poured her grief into the pages of both her diary and novel. As she wrote in her journal in 1824, "The last man! Yes I may well describe that solitary being's feelings, feeling myself as the last relic of a beloved race, my companions, extinct before me" (MWS *Journals* 2:476–77). The result in *The Last Man* is a novel that, through the characterization of Adrian, idealizes Percy Shelley's youth, invokes the power of Percy Shelley's political beliefs, and elevates Percy Shelley's "active spirit of benevolence."[14] Near the end of the work, Shelley has the last man alive, Lionel Verney, describe Adrian's effect with characteristic hyperbole:

> I was an untaught shepherd-boy, when Adrian deigned to confer on me his friendship. The best years of my life had been passed with him. All I had possessed of this world's goods, of happiness, knowledge, or virtue— I owed to him. He had, in his person, his intellect, and rare qualities, given a glory to my life, which without him it had never known. Beyond all other beings he had taught me, that goodness, pure and single, can be an attribute of man. It was a sight for angels to congregate to behold, to view him lead, govern, and solace, the last days of the human race. (328)[15]

Other biographical connections are easy to find in *The Last Man*. Raymond, who abandons himself to an illicit extramarital attachment and eventually dies fighting in Greece, is obviously modeled after Lord Byron. Lionel Verney's father is obviously modeled after William Godwin: he falls repeatedly into crushing debt; he enjoys a period of public renown before falling into utter obscurity; and since Adrian reveres him, he unwittingly creates the occasion for Adrian's interest in Verney. Shelley casts herself, of course, as Lionel Verney, the last man alive on earth, who is slowly robbed of all possessions and relationships, first by political instability, and then by PLAGUE. Shelley's characterization of Lionel Verney also recalls Frankenstein's creature in at least two ways: Verney is an orphan and a beggar; Shelley uses Godwin's environmental arguments, in the manner of *Caleb Williams*, to explain Verney's initial lawlessness and violence.[16] What is most interesting about Lionel Verney, however, is the very fact that he is male. In a novel whose central purpose is to immortalize Percy Shelley's politics and personality, Mary Shelley does not cast herself as her husband's wife, but instead as the male companion to Shelley and Byron. In the midst of her grief and longing for Percy's return, Shelley also saw herself as her husband's equal and partner, and she preferred to portray herself working beside him and Byron, rather than ministering, in her wifely role, to feminine domestic tasks.

For our purposes, however, two aspects of *The Last Man* are most important: the way the novel portrays the family unit and the devastating power of PLAGUE. As Ellis correctly notes, one crucial element in the narrative of *The Last Man* is the fate of the family and domestic affections.[17] The family unit constitutes "real life" for Verney (*The Last Man*, 158); the family unit, as invoked in the idyll at Windsor (64–66), is the source of Verney's emotional stability and the chief breeding ground for domestic affection. But by the time PLAGUE completes her inexorable march across Europe, the family unit has become PLAGUE's last victim as well. Whether one reads the political narrative of *The Last Man* as Shelley's vindication of republican redemption in the future or as her warning that republicanism is bound to fail, one thing is certain: PLAGUE destroys every human institution, beginning with utterly diverse forms of government, and ending with the family unit itself.

What finally demolishes every human institution, from governments to families, is, of course, an emphatically female force. As Gilbert and Gubar have noted, Shelley uses *The Last Man* to create, after the pattern of *Frankenstein*, another monster who punishes the human race.[18] While both Mathilda and Frankenstein's "monster" associate themselves with disease and blight, PLAGUE is a living embodiment of disease—a deadly female pollution that robs man of his power over creation and insinuates herself into his very flesh. As Lionel Verney puts it: "[N]ow is man lord of the creation? Look at him—ha! I see plague! She has invested his form, is incarnate in his flesh, has entwined herself with his being, and blinds his heaven-seeking eyes" (*The Last Man*, 229). As Verney's language suggests, PLAGUE, like other manifestations of the female in Western culture, robs man of his ability to rise above the physical.

The bleak landscapes Shelley associates with PLAGUE are as telling as PLAGUE's feminine gender. The final encounter between mankind and PLAGUE plays itself out in the valley of Chamounix, the very spot where Frankenstein's "monster" confronts his maker. Verney describes mankind's futile attempts to escape PLAGUE in this way:

> We vainly sought the vast and ever moving glaciers of Chamounix, rifts of pendant ice, seas of congealed waters, the leafless groves of tempest-battered pines, dells, mere paths for the loud avalanche, and hill-tops, the resort of thunder-storms. Pestilence reigned paramount even here. By the

time that day and night, like twin sisters of equal growth, shared equally
their dominion over the hours, one by one, beneath the ice-caves, beside
the waters springing from the thawed snows of a thousand winters, another and yet another of the remnant of the race of Man, closed their eyes
for ever to the light. (309)

Shelley exiles Frankenstein's "monster" to this cold, forbidding terrain;
as we have seen, Mathilda internalizes this same landscape as an expression
of her isolation and grief after her father's confession of incest; and Beatrice
describes herself in terms of a geography equally bleak.

If, as this analysis suggests, we can read PLAGUE as another incarnation of the monstrous daughter, PLAGUE's destruction of the family unit
itself has a compelling logic: the domestic affections engendered by the
nuclear family embody within themselves, after all, the psychic mechanisms
that make the daughter "monstrous." Accordingly, PLAGUE first equal-
izes all people and institutions (230–31), and she then obliterates them.
Frankenstein's creature and Mathilda both succeed in eliminating the figure of the offending father, but PLAGUE succeeds in eliminating the very
institution that perpetuates the father's control over the daughter: the nuclear
family. And, having completed her work, PLAGUE, like both Mathilda
and Frankenstein's creature, engages in an act of self-immolation. In the
frigid and remote valley of Chamounix, PLAGUE's "barbarous tyranny came
to its close," when PLAGUE "abdicated her throne and despoiled herself of
her imperial sceptre among the ice rocks that surrounded us" (310).

II.

With *Lodore* (1835) and *Falkner* (1837), Shelley's last two novels, the story
of the daughter's conflict with the father resumes its place at the center of
Shelley's fiction. Many of the contours of the father/daughter story remain
unchanged in these last works: the passionate character of the relationship,
the daughter's struggle against the father's dominion over her, and the sheer
number of tyrannical fathers and dead or powerless mothers who populate
each novel's background. But there is an important difference. In Shelley's
last two works, the figure of the daughter finally moves beyond the range of
the father's power and desire, and simultaneously ceases to see herself as
monstrous. She subverts paternal limits and breaks the father's determining
hold on her—ironically, through the apparently conventional act of behaving like a mother.

When Shelley began *Lodore* in 1831, she was nearly thirty-four and her son Percy Florence was eleven; William Godwin was seventy-five.[19] Since the publication of *The Last Man*, Shelley had been engaged in various literary tasks: she had written and published *Perkin Warbeck*,[20] a historical novel for which Godwin provided Shelley with much background information; she reviewed Godwin's *Cloudesley* for *Blackwood's*. Shelley took up other important projects at the same time she was working on *Lodore*, such as writing an introductory memoir of William Godwin's life for a new edition of *Caleb Williams* (published 1 April 1831) and, in October 1831, writing the introduction to her much-revised version of *Frankenstein*, which was published in November of the same year. All this literary work was produced against a background of extreme personal struggle. As a mother, Shelley was in the process of sacrificing her comfort and happiness for her child. She enrolled Percy Florence in Harrow and struggled to pay his bills there; eventually she moved to Harrow herself in 1833 to reduce expenses. There, two of the most miserable years of Shelley's life followed as she battled loneliness and a devastating rejection by a suitor. Meanwhile, William Godwin was practically destitute and Shelley labored to provide him with enough financial assistance to keep him afloat. She wrote *Lodore* to meet Godwin's financial needs as well as her own, simultaneously pleading to her journal, "God grant that after these few Months are elapsed I may be able to take refuge in Nature & solitude from the feverish misery of my present existence. Here gaunt poverty & cruel privation dog my pleasures close." (MWS *Journals* 2:520).

Lodore, more overtly than Mary Shelley's other novels, analyzes the many varieties of the daughter's education at the father's hands and portrays the impact of this education on the daughter's behavior and life.[21] *Lodore* focuses on three daughters: Ethel Fitzhenry, daughter of Lord Lodore; Fanny Derham, daughter of one of Lodore's school friends; and Cornelia Santerre, the wife of Lord Lodore. Ethel Fitzhenry, like Shelley's other devoted daughters, loves her father with a combination of impassioned attachment and awestruck distance as she passes through adolescence. As the narrator puts it:

> There is perhaps in the list of human sensations, no one so pure, so perfect, and yet so impassioned, as the affection of a child for its parent, during that brief interval when they are leaving childhood, and have not yet felt love. There is something so awful in a father. His words are laws, and to obey them happiness. . . . Afterwards we may love, in spite of the faults of the object of our attachment; but during the interval alluded to, we have

not yet learned to tolerate, but also, we have not learned to detect faults. All that a parent does, appears an emanation from a diviner world; while we fear to offend, we believe we have no right to be offended; eager to please, we seek in return approval only, and are too humble to demand a reciprocity of attention; it is enough that we are permitted to demonstrate our devotion. Ethel's heart overflowed with love, reverence, worship of her father . . . she knew of nothing that might compare to him; and the world without him, was what the earth might be uninformed by light: he was its sun, its ruling luminary. (105–6)

This passage reflects the same mixture of passion, awe, and eagerness to please that Shelley felt for Godwin at Ethel's age. Interestingly, Shelley also tinges Ethel's relationship to her father with sexuality, and therefore with implications of incest, in ways that recall *Mathilda* and *Frankenstein,* and look forward to *Falkner.* As in the case of *Mathilda,* the father's love for his daughter is intensified and made conscious by the appearance of a younger rival for the daughter's hand. When Whitelock, Ethel's drawing teacher, makes advances, Lodore realizes he is vulnerable only in his daughter (25) and resolves to return to Europe to protect the exclusivity of his daughter's attachment to him (31–32). But Shelley has suggested the latent sexuality of Lodore's tie to Ethel even before Whitelock appears on the scene. The emotions that Ethel and Lodore feel for each other sound very much like those of a husband and wife:

The goodness of her heart endeared her still more; and when it was called forth by any demand made on it by him, it was attended by such a display of excessive sensibility, as at once caused him to tremble for her future happiness, and love her ten thousand times more. She grew into the image on which his eye doated, and for whose presence his heart perpetually yearned. Was he reading, or otherwise occupied, he was restless, if yet she were not in the room; and she would remain in silence for hours, occupied by some little feminine work, and all the while watching him, catching his first glance towards her, and obeying the expression of his countenance, before he could form his wish into words. When he left her for any of his longer excursions, her little heart would heave, and almost burst with sorrow. On his return, she was always on the watch to see, to fly into his arms, and to load him with infantine caresses. (18–19)

Were it not for the word "infantine" in the last line, this passage might describe the reactions of two lovers: the male's "trembling," perpetual "yearning," and "restless" discontent if the beloved should leave the room; the female's "heaving," "bursting," and anxious effort to catch her lover's every glance. Similarly, a few pages later, Shelley's language suggests that the attachment between Lodore and Ethel exceeds the conventional bounds of family affection. Ethel imagines her father's "dark, expressive eyes . . . penetrating the depths of her soul" (31). Ethel's presence has a dramatic effect on Lodore:

> [S]he inspired her father with more than a father's fondness. He lived but for her and in her. Away, she was present to his imagination, the loadstone to draw him home, and to fill that home with pleasure . . . surely he, who would stand so fast by her through all—whose nightly dream and waking thought was for her good, would even, when led to form other connexions in life, so command her affections as to be able to influence her happiness. (21).

Shelley's language is, again, laced with sexual implication: Ethel inspires "more than a father's fondness" in Lodore; the father lives "for and in" his daughter; the daughter fills the father's home with "pleasure" and inhabits his nightly dreams, so that the father trusts he can command his daughter's affections throughout her life.

The point is that Shelley uses *Lodore*, as she does her other fictions about daughters, to trace the current of the sexual attachment that exists between a father and his daughter. This theme of latent incest also shapes the relationship between Ellen Gray and her father in "The Elder Son," a short story Shelley wrote at the same time as *Lodore*.[22] Ellen Gray's relation to her father has the same contours as Ethel's. The father fixes all his passion on his daughter after his wife dies; he loves her "to idolatry" (244), but remains distant; she repays his affection "with enthusiastic fondness, notwithstanding his reserve" (244). In language that echoes Ethel's words, the protagonist says her father is "something greater, and wiser, and better, in my eyes, than any other human being" (244). Just before Ellen's father dies, he finally expresses his love. Their devotion to each other reaches a new level of intensity; as in the case of *Lodore*, Mr. Gray becomes more than a mere father to Ellen, so that the father/daughter bond endures beyond the father's death. Ellen describes her feelings for her father in language filled with sexual innuendo: "He became my father, friend, and brother, all in one; a thousand dear relationships combined in one stronger than any. This sudden melting, this divine sensibility, which expanded at once, having been so long shut up and hid, was like a miracle" (245).

This theme of latent incest is the primary device that structures the

relationship between Ellen Gray and her father; in *Lodore*, of course, incest
is only part of Ethel's story. As Shelley specifically says, Lodore gives Ethel
a "sexual education" (272); this "sexual education" grows out of their passionate attachment to each other, but finally relates more to the ways a
father acculturates his daughter into the habits of traditional womanhood
by making her dependent, passive, and submissive.

The reader is first introduced to the story of Lodore and his daughter
some twelve years before the main action of the novel begins. Lodore's
marriage to Cornelia Santerre has failed; heartbroken, he has stolen their
three-year-old daughter and exiled himself to the wilds of Illinois. Hidden
away in the Edenic surroundings of the American continent, Lodore struggles
to replace his love for his wife with the love of his daughter. Lodore raises
Ethel to be a worthy companion; specifically, he wishes his daughter to
possess "all the perfection of which the feminine character is susceptible"
(21). Accordingly, Lodore's behavior toward his daughter fosters the traits
of dependence and submission, traits the figure of the father associates with
female perfection. As the narrator observes:

> There is a peculiarity in the education of a daughter, brought up by a father
> only, which tends to develop early a thousand of those portions of mind,
> which are folded up, and often destroyed, under mere feminine tuition.
> [Lodore] made [Ethel] fearless, by making her the associate of his rides;
> yet his incessant care and watchfulness . . . tended to soften her mind, and
> make her spirit ductile and dependent. He taught her to scorn pain, but to
> shrink with excessive timidity from any thing that intrenched on the
> barrier of womanly reserve which he raised about her . . . a word or look
> from him made her, with all her childish vivacity and thoughtlessness,
> turn as with a silken string, and bend at once to his will. . . . He resolved
> to make her all that woman can be of generous, soft, and devoted . . . to
> cultivate her tastes and enlarge her mind, yet so to control her acquire-
> ments, as to render her ever pliant to his will. (18, 21)

Several observations may be made about Shelley's description of the
daughter's traditional education at the hands of the father. Lodore makes
Ethel fearless but fundamentally "ductile and dependent." More than anything, Lodore makes Ethel submissive to his desires—she bends as on a
"silken string" and is "ever pliant to his will." The narrator notes that "mere
feminine tuition" tends to destroy the very portions of the mind that the
father's education develops—that is, feminine tuition destroys the daughter's
submissive and dependent behavior. The implication, of course, is that a

mother's education makes a daughter independent and self-sufficient, an implication Shelley clearly illustrates, later in the novel, in the behavior of Cornelia Santerre. In her criticism of the daughter's typical education into dependence and submission, Shelley echoes Mary Wollstonecraft's indictment of traditional female education, a condemnation Wollstonecraft articulates most eloquently in *A Vindication of the Rights of Woman*.[23]

When a father gives a daughter a "sexual education," he accomplishes one more thing: he prepares her to enter into the power arrangements of traditional marriage, in which she submits to a husband's guidance as precisely as she has to her father's. As the narrator remarks, Lodore's education makes Ethel

> an enthusiastic being, who could give her life away for the sake of another, and who yet honoured herself as a consecrated thing reserved for one worship alone. She was taught that no misfortune should penetrate her soul, except such as visited her affections, or her sense of right; and that, set apart from the vulgar uses of the world, she was connected with the mass only through another—that other, now her father and only friend— hereafter, whosoever her heart might select as her guide and head. Fitzhenry drew his chief ideas from Milton's Eve, and adding to this the romance of chivalry, he satisfied himself that his daughter would be the embodied ideal of all that is adorable and estimable in her sex. (21)

Possessed of her father's "sexual education," his daughter will make her husband into another protective, paternal figure—her "guide and head." Significantly, the narrator describes the daughter's acts of submission in religious language—she becomes a "consecrated thing reserved for one worship alone." As we shall see, Ethel Fitzhenry's submission and dependence do lead her to marry a man who behaves toward her in a paternal way. And as we shall also see, Shelley consistently describes Ethel's submissively female behavior in language that elevates and sentimentalizes it, a stylistic decision that has important feminist implications but that nevertheless has made *Lodore* unpalatable to some modern literary tastes.

But Lord Lodore is not the only model of fatherhood that Mary Shelley portrays in *Lodore*. If Ethel Fitzhenry receives a conventional "sexual education" from Lodore, Fanny Derham receives a wholly unconventional education from her father, Francis Derham. While Ethel is educated in the orthodox mode accorded most nineteenth-century daughters, Fanny, like Mary Shelley herself, is educated in a manner utterly unorthodox for a woman—in fact, in the manner generally reserved for a son. Like Euthanasia's father in *Valperga*, Fanny's father teaches her "the dead languages, and other sorts of abstruse learning, which seldom make a part of a girl's education" (100). He teaches her to read and "converse each day with" the great authors: Plato, Cicero, Epictetus (266). He teaches her to appreciate the political power of language and to use words to fight "any battle for the miserable and oppressed" (266). The result of this unconventional paternal education is a young woman much like the adolescent Mary Shelley—a girl who, in her own words, "loves philosophy, and pants after knowledge, and indulges in a thousand Platonic dreams" (100). Fanny Derham is different from Ethel Fitzhenry in almost every respect. As the narrator puts it:

> Each had been the favourite daughter of men of superior qualities of mind. They had been educated by their several fathers with the most sedulous care, and nothing could be more opposite than the result. . . . Ethel had received, so to speak, a sexual education. Lord Lodore had formed his ideal of what a woman ought to be, of what he had wished to find his wife, and sought to mould his daughter accordingly. Mr. Derham contemplated the duties and objects befitting an immortal soul, and had educated his child for the performance of them. The one fashioned his offspring to be the wife of a frail human being and instructed her to be yielding, and to make it her duty to devote herself to his happiness, and to obey his will. The other sought to guard his from all weakness, to make her complete in herself, and to render her independent and self-sufficing. . . . While Ethel made it her happiness and duty to give herself away with unreserved prodigality to him, whom she thought had every claim to her entire devotion; Fanny zealously guarded her individuality, and would have scorned herself could she have been brought to place the treasures of her soul at the disposal of any power, except those moral laws which it was her earnest endeavour never to transgress . . . the one was guided by the tenderness of her heart, while the other consulted her understanding, and would have died rather than have acted contrary to its dictates. . . . The one brought up his child to dependence; the other taught his to disdain every support, except the applause of her own conscience. (272–73)

Mary Shelley's comparison of Ethel Fitzhenry and Fanny Derham sums up the difference between the conventional woman and the unconventional woman, between the young girl educated into the traditionally feminine ideals of submission and dependence and the young girl educated into the traditionally masculine traits of assertion and self-sufficiency. Ethel is a creature of feeling; Fanny is a creature of intellect. Ethel has learned how to be a "wife"; Fanny has learned how to be an "immortal soul." While Ethel is eager to "give herself away" to gain a man's support and protection, Fanny "zealously guards her individuality" and would "scorn herself" if she yielded her autonomy completely to another human being. Ethel has become obedient, and essentially passive; Fanny takes command of situations and is energized by her questing spirit. And both girls have their fathers to thank for the idiosyncrasies of their personalities. As Shelley implies, fathers foster either "feminine" or "masculine" traits in their daughters and thereby give them either the limited horizons of the womanly role or the broader possibilities for expression and action usually accorded to "masculine" conduct.

Shelley's attitude toward Fanny Derham is entirely positive. According to the narrator, when Fanny is only fourteen years old, her soul already reveals "an embryo of power, and a grandeur of soul, not to be mistaken" (101). Fanny and Ethel meet each other just before Ethel returns to England from America; when the two women encounter each other a second time some years later, the narrator describes Fanny as a "superior being" completely free of "the baser qualities of human beings" (260). Ethel herself looks upon Fanny "with wonder as a superior being" (266). And Shelley arranges the plot of *Lodore* to juxtapose Fanny's deep perceptions and decisive ability to act against Ethel's weakness, passivity, and dependence. When bailiffs arrive to arrest Edward Villiers, Ethel's husband, for debt, Fanny deals with them, since Ethel has no idea how to help her husband. Later, while Ethel is deciding to display her wifely devotion by cloistering herself with Edward in jail, Fanny is the character familiar with the vagaries of Edward's creditors and solicitors (298–300). Toward the end of *Lodore*, Fanny sets in motion the events that allow Ethel and Edward to leave prison and Cornelia to redeem herself. Fanny visits Cornelia, Lady Lodore, to inform her that her daughter has immured herself in a debtors' prison and to see if Lady Lodore can offer help. Shortly afterward, Cornelia gives up her fortune so that her daughter and son-in-law can be freed (310–11). And Fanny is the only character who, seeing to the bottom of Cornelia's heart, guesses the motherly devotion and generosity that lie there. After Ethel and Edward have left prison and Lady Lodore has disappeared, Ethel presumes her mother has vanished into the social whirl of life on the Continent. Even Cornelia's lover, Horatio Saville, misunderstands Cornelia, and, "since it is usually supposed that women are always under the influence of one sentiment," he assumes she has begun an affair with another man (361). Fanny is the only character who insists that Lady Lodore's disappearance "springs from the most honourable motives" and that "there was nothing personal or frivolous in the feelings that mastered her." She is the only person who guesses that, whatever Lady Lodore has done, she has chosen a path "which, while it benefited others, was injuring herself" (361). With the single exception of Cornelia, Fanny Derham is the character in *Lodore* who possesses the most discriminating understanding of human motivation and the strongest capacity to act in support of others.

Shelley's enthusiasm for Fanny no doubt stems from the fact that Shelley sees Fanny's situation as, in some ways, a reflection of her own. Fanny's relation to her father is much like the relation that Mary Shelley had to William Godwin during his later years: Fanny, like Mary, "nursed her father, watched over his health and humours, with the tenderness and indulgence of a mother" (100).[24] Mary also puts into Fanny Derham's education all the "masculine" elements of her own education in William Godwin's study: the emphasis on philosophy, on intellectual achievement, on becoming something "great and good" rather than a mere wife. In portraying two very different daughters shaped by two very different fathers, Mary Shelley continued to describe and explore her sense of the contradictory currents of her own upbringing in William Godwin's home. Fanny Derham's education into unconventional femininity, with its emphasis on the "masculine" traits of intellect, independence, and assertion, resembles the early training Mary Godwin received from her father, in which he treated her more like a son than a daughter and expanded her horizons beyond the conventionally feminine. Ethel's "sexual" education into conventional femininity, with its emphasis on submission to beloved males and self-abnegation in the service of others, is not unlike the education into traditional daughterhood that Mary Shelley received from William Godwin much later, after Fanny Imlay's death. When Shelley began *Lodore* as she approached the age of thirty-four, she was still grappling with the conflicting demands of self-assertion and self-abnegation, of autonomy and the loss of self in the service of another. In other words, she was still wrestling with the conflict between sonship and daughterhood, a dichotomy set up by William Godwin's contradictory and shifting standards for his daughter's behavior.

If Mary Shelley introduces any negative elements into her portrayal of Fanny Derham, they have to do with the author's understanding of the kinds of difficulties that such an unconventional and singular woman can expect to encounter. Fanny's problems arise not from any weaknesses in her character, but from the restrictions of a society that offers women few opportunities for self-sufficiency or meaningful work. For example, when Ethel meets Fanny for the second time, halfway through the novel, Fanny sadly tells her that "adversity and I are become very close friends since I last

saw you" (261). The reason? Fanny's father died, leaving the family penniless. Without any means of earning a livelihood, Derham's widow and two
daughters were prey to creditors until a kindly relative set them up with a
boarding house to run. Fanny hopes to work as a governess eventually, once
her mother and sister no longer need her help in running their home. In a
Wollstonecraftian observation on the limited possibilities for a woman's
professional and financial independence, the narrator comments ruefully on
Fanny's chances of fulfillment in the only work open to her: "Fanny was too
young and too wedded to her platonic notions of the supremacy of mind, to
be fully aware of the invaluable advantages of pecuniary independence for a
woman. She fancied that she could enter on the career—the only career
permitted her sex—of servitude, and yet possess her soul in freedom and
power" (359). Perhaps most crucial, Fanny's singular commitment to the
life of the intellect, combined with her frankness, means that she will not
marry. This situation is tragic because it deprives Fanny of the opportunity
to exercise her sexuality and the chance to live in conjunction with a man—
the only way for a woman to achieve social status in nineteenth-century
England. But in another sense, this aspect of Fanny's situation is liberating.
Fanny's lack of conventional femininity allows her wider possibilities for
female friendship and lets her serve as a model and source of support for
other women. As the narrator says of Fanny's relationships to both sexes:

> Such a woman as Fanny was more made to be loved by her own sex than
> by the opposite one. Superiority of intellect, joined to acquisitions beyond
> those usual even to men; and both announced with frankness, though
> without pretension, forms a kind of anomaly little in accord with mascu-
> line taste. Fanny could not be the rival of women, and, therefore, all her
> merits were appreciated by them. They love to look up to a superior being,
> to rest on a firmer support than their own minds can afford; and they are
> glad to find such in one of their own sex, and thus destitute of those
> dangers which usually attend any services conferred by men. (267)

As Mary Shelley insists, Fanny's singularity makes her both an inspiration to more ordinary women and a refuge for them, since her support is free
from the social and emotional "dangers" attached to the support provided
by men.

Fanny Derham's unique strengths—her intellect, her ability to transcend conventional feminine personality traits and roles—make her into
one of the central characters in *Lodore*. And, significantly, Fanny Derham
is the character who closes the book. After Mary Shelley has finished the

stories of Cornelia and Ethel, she turns to Fanny Derham to bring the novel to an end. The point she makes about Fanny is an important one: Fanny Derham is so unconventional, and so different from the other women of her time, that it is difficult to imagine her future:

> She [Fanny Derham] cannot be contaminated—she will turn neither to the right nor left, but pursue her way unflinching; and, in her lofty idea of the dignity of her nature, in her love of truth and in her integrity, she will find support and reward in her various fortunes. What the events are, that have already diversified her existence, cannot now be recounted; and it would require the gift of prophecy to foretell the conclusion. In after times these may be told, and the life of Fanny Derham be presented as a useful lesson, at once to teach what goodness and genius can achieve in palliating the woes of life, and to encourage those, who would in any way imitate her. (396)

In short, in the world of nineteenth-century England, Fanny Derham's story cannot yet be told. Her tale might unfold in the future of "after times," just as Euthanasia's story could unfold in the distant past of fourteenth-century Italy. When Shelley completed *Lodore,* the real world of nineteenth-century social expectation was too confining even to predict the fate of a woman as unconventional as Fanny.

But if Shelley confesses that she cannot yet imagine an ending for Fanny Derham, she imagines with certainty the fate of Ethel Fitzhenry, the daughter brought up under the father's conventional "sexual" education. Unlike Fanny, Ethel will marry. But Ethel's "sexual" education leads her to marry a man she can view as a father, thus allowing Ethel to preserve and repeat her relationship to Lodore. Shelley takes great pains to characterize Ethel's married relationship as parallel to and a reenactment of her relationship to Lodore. Lodore is killed in a duel just before he and Ethel leave America for England. As Lodore's second, Edward Villiers helps Ethel complete the journey home that her father had conceived and arranged (118–19). Ethel is initially attracted to Villiers because, as her father's friend, he provides her with a palpable link to her cherished lost love. Villiers knew and admired her father; Villiers attended the same schools; Villiers is even possessed of many of the same behavioral quirks as Lodore.[25] At first Ethel thinks she cannot "endure existence without the supporting influence of [Lodore's] affection" (121), but she eventually comes to rely upon Villiers for the kinds of emotional support Lodore had provided her. Ethel repeatedly characterizes her love for Villiers using the same terms the narrator chooses to describe Ethel's love for her father—that is, in terms of her submission to his will and her dependence on him. For example, when Villiers decides for a brief period to break off their engagement, Ethel is heartbroken, but she acquiesces without a murmur. "I am a foolish girl. . . ." she says; "I will not doubt that you decide for the best" (191). Later, Ethel's dependence and habit of submission lead her to join Villiers in debtors' prison. There, she can devote herself to her husband, the man "whom it was the sole joy of her life to wait on, to be sheltered by, to live near" (301). Ethel herself has a lively sense of the extent to which her relation to Villiers repeats her relation to Lodore and of the extent to which her devotion to her father's desires determines her choice of a mate. In fact, Ethel views herself as a precious inheritance, passed from one generation of males to the next. Ethel "call[s] upon her father's spirit to approve her attachment" and then reflects "that Edward's hand had supported [Lodore's] dying head—that to Edward Villiers's care his latest words had intrusted her,—she felt as if she were a legacy bequeathed to him, and that she fulfilled Lodore's last behests in giving herself to him" (181).[26]

   If Lodore's "sexual" education causes Ethel to enter into the power arrangements of traditional marriage by choosing a husband she can view as a father, it also makes her weak and incapable of independent action. Ethel is painfully aware of this flaw in her character. When Edward Villiers decides he must go to London to settle his financial affairs and decides to leave Ethel in the country with her aunt, Ethel reproaches him for his absence, saying, "I can ill bear it. I am impatient and weak" (240). Later, when she joins Edward in debtors' prison and her mother implores her to leave their humiliating surroundings, Ethel replies, "I cannot. It is impossible for me voluntarily to separate myself from Edward—I am too weak, too great a coward" (315). Ethel is too timid to break down the walls of mistrust between her mother and herself for most of the novel; she repeatedly characterizes herself as a "weak, foolish thing" (299). And, as we have seen, Mary Shelley organizes the plot of Lodore to emphasize Ethel's weakness and inability to act, thus highlighting the comparative strength of the other female characters, especially Fanny Derham. Ethel's dependent female behavior may elevate her to the stature of a saint, but it also imprisons her spiritually, and, in Edward's debtors' prison, quite literally. The "prison" of dependency that Ethel shares with her husband is no less confining because she takes to it voluntarily, and, in fact, utterly enthusiastically—or because Mary Shelley seems to commend Ethel for immuring herself with her husband. As we shall see, daughters who voluntarily imprison themselves with the lover/father also figure importantly in *Falkner*, Shelley's last novel.

As this discussion implies, Shelley's portrayal of Ethel Fitzhenry is suggestively ambiguous. Shelley lavishes many pages on the loving details of Lodore's relation to his daughter, but she also consistently undercuts the father's behavior. In some instances, the narrator directly criticizes Lodore's education, as in this typical passage:

> A lofty sense of independence is, in man, the best privilege of his nature. It cannot be doubted, but that it were for the happiness of the other sex that she were taught more to rely on and act for herself. But in the cultivation of this feeling, the education of Fitzhenry was lamentably deficient. Ethel was taught to know herself dependent; the support of another was to be as necessary to her as her daily food. She leant on her father as a prop that could not fail, and she was wholly satisfied with her condition . . . in mind she was too often indolent, and apt to think that while she was docile to the injunctions of her parent, all her duties were fulfilled. She seldom thought, and never acted, for herself. (22–23)

In other instances, Shelley uses carefully chosen imagery to distance herself from Lodore's "sexual" education of his daughter. On one occasion, Ethel becomes a "parasite" who cannot tell whether its host is a protector or a threat. As the narrator puts it, the father "can cultivate and direct the affections of the pupil, who puts forth, as a parasite, tendrils by which to cling, not knowing to what—to a supporter or a destroyer" (21–22).

The same narrative ambiguity surfaces in the sentimental language Shelley uses to portray Ethel's marriage to Edward Villiers. As we have seen, Shelley describes Ethel's acts of daughterly submission to her father in religious terms: Ethel is a "consecrated thing reserved for one worship alone" (21); the "celestial beauty of [Ethel's] nature" (21) is preserved by her father's fond care and protective domination. Similarly, Shelley uses religious language to characterize the relationship between Ethel and her husband, a tie based on Ethel's dependence on and deference to her husband's wishes. In a typical passage, Shelley says the following about Ethel's feelings for Villiers. Ethel has just decided to live with her husband in the humiliating surroundings of his debtors' prison:

> [A] tenderness and an elevation of feeling animated her expressive countenance. . . . She looked at him, and her eyes then glanced to the barred windows. . . . [Ethel knew] that whatever evil might attend her lot, the

good so far outweighed it, that, for his sake only, could she advert to any feeling of distress. It was a consciousness of being in her place, and of fulfilling her duty, accompanied by a sort of rapture in remembering how thrice dear and hallowed that duty was. Angels could not feel as she did, for they cannot sacrifice to those they love; yet there was in her that absence of all self-emanating pain, which is the characteristic of what we are told of the angelic essence. (301–2)

There is a certain warmth of feeling in this description. Shelley clearly finds the protective embrace of Ethel's marriage to be both comforting and attractive. Yet the sentimentality of Shelley's religious language is also, to use Mary Poovey's phrase, "excessive and compensatory."[27] The fact that the religious language of *Lodore* is usually associated, as it is here, with acts of female submission and sacrifice ("Angels could not feel as she did, for they cannot sacrifice to those they love") suggests that the sentimentality of Shelley's language might compensate for the hostility generated by the very necessity of female submission. Further, Shelley's sentimentally elevated religious language suggests and parallels a cultural truth: that society encourages women to behave in a submissive and self-sacrificing manner, and accords them, in exchange, a sentimentally overvalued cultural position. In other words, Shelley implies that the traditionally good daughter/woman becomes a "saint" or "angel," but only at the expense of sacrificing herself to the will and protection of the male.[28]

The third daughter figure in *Lodore*, and the one who can most accurately be termed the novel's protagonist, is Cornelia Santerre, the wife of Lord Lodore. Lodore is not only about the impact of fathers on their biological daughters and about the weaknesses of the father's "sexual education" of his daughter. It is also about husbands, wives, and the pernicious effects of the paternalistic arrangements between them that society condones. *Lodore* traces Cornelia's struggles, her redemption, and the reasons for the particular form that redemption takes. Cornelia first appears in *Lodore* as an apparently shallow woman who errs by refusing to submit herself to her husband's guidance and control. Lodore sees Cornelia as his recalcitrant daughter; as the novel unfolds, Cornelia evolves from a wife whose husband treats her like a daughter, into a woman who discovers her destiny by exercising the intermittent power latent in motherhood.[29]

When the reader first meets Cornelia Santerre, she seems the classic example of the vain and irresponsible woman who suffers because of her monstrous pride, stubbornness, and shallowness. Shelley carefully structures Cornelia's story to reveal her self-centered willfulness. First of all,

Cornelia is a bad wife. She refuses to learn anything from Lodore; she will not separate herself from her domineering mother to acknowledge the primacy of her tie to her husband. When Cornelia flirts with a young Polish nobleman, it infuriates Lodore. He slaps the man, who then challenges Lodore to a duel. Rather than fight, Lodore banishes himself to America, thus making Cornelia the indirect cause of her husband's exile from England. Cornelia refuses to follow her husband into the American wilderness; when he writes from the American frontier to ask for a reconciliation, she will not hear of it. Worse than Cornelia's behavior as a wife is her behavior as a mother. She does not spend any time with Ethel immediately after the baby's birth, and she tends to enjoy her parties more than the demands of motherhood. Cornelia allows Lodore to take her daughter away from her; even after Ethel returns to London as a grown woman, Cornelia is loath to see her. Cornelia's willful and selfish behavior continues to darken her life after her husband's death. She ruins her relationship to Horatio Saville, a young nobleman who adores her, when her arrogant belief in her power over him drives him to marry someone else (157). In her self-centeredness and taste for "society," Cornelia Santerre is a forerunner of Thackeray's Becky Sharp, who so scandalized Victorian audiences when *Vanity Fair* was published, twelve years after *Lodore*. Cornelia is "ignorant, accustomed to the most frivolous employments, shrinking from any mental exercise" (54). In an analysis that could come directly from the pages of *A Vindication of the Rights of Woman*, the narrator traces Cornelia's many deficiencies to a single source:

> [T]hrough the bad education she had received, and her extreme youth, elevation of feeling degenerated into mere personal pride, and heroism was turned into obstinacy . . . her mind was narrowed by the mode of her bringing up, and her loftiest ideas were centered in worldly advantages the most worthless and pitiable. (91)

But on closer inspection, Shelley's attitude toward the undomesticated Cornelia is not as totally negative as it initially seems. To begin with, Shelley goes to great pains to make clear that Cornelia's personality is, in fact, very like Lodore's. Early in the novel, the narrator describes the young Lodore in this way:

> He would not wantonly have inflicted a pang upon a human being; yet he exerted any power he might possess to quell the smallest resistance to his desires; and unless when they were manifested in the most intelligible

manner, he scarcely knew that his fellow-creatures had any feelings at all, except pride and gladness in serving him, and gratitude when he showed them kindness. (36)

A short time later, Shelley describes the young Lady Lodore in similar terms:

> Her beauty and the admiration it acquired, sate her on the throne of the world . . . her sway she had believed to be absolute; it was happiness for others to obey. . . . She had not learned to feel with or for others. To act in contradiction to her wishes was a crime beyond compare, and her soul was in arms to resent the insolence which thus assailed her majesty of will. (91)

In these passages, Shelley is careful to portray Lodore and Cornelia as mirror images of each other. Both consider themselves superior; both are accustomed to adulation and, therefore, think other people take great pleasure in serving and obeying them. Both have little capacity for grasping or responding to the feelings of other people. Most important, both Cornelia and Lodore hate any resistance to their desires that might be posed by the wishes of other people. Cornelia may be willful and self-indulgent, but her husband, apparently, is possessed of the same unpleasant traits. These shared personality traits make for a volatile and difficult marriage; they also serve to indicate that the reader should not blame Cornelia alone for the failure of her marriage.

Shelley shapes the reader's sympathies in favor of Cornelia in a second way. Shelley roundly criticizes Cornelia for failing to exhibit the conventional feminine virtues; yet she continually softens the impact of Cornelia's actions and creates empathy for her, even in her unregenerate state, by explaining her motivations or the extenuating circumstances of her situation. For example, Shelley portrays Cornelia as a bad mother by having her "peevishly" insist that newborn Ethel be removed from her presence. But Shelley just as quickly insists that Cornelia's ill-humor is perfectly understandable, since "her confinement was followed by a long illness," and "she was reduced to the lowest ebb of weakness; but Lodore, as men are apt to do, was slow to discern her physical suffering . . . as she peevishly repeated the command that his child should go" (58–59). Similarly, Cornelia avoids her daughter when Ethel returns to London many years later, but Shelley immediately gives her a praiseworthy reason for doing so: Cornelia sees that Ethel is old enough to enter polite society and does not want to spoil her reputation by "making her the public talk" (165). Shelley also carefully qualifies the extent to which Cornelia can be considered a bad wife. When Cornelia is attentive to Casmir Lyzinski, for example—whom she does not realize is her husband's illegitimate son—the narrator ascribes her actions to a genuine "desire of pleasing" (64) rather than a petty flirtatious impulse. Cornelia does refuse to follow Lodore and baby Ethel into the American wilderness, but Shelley notes that Cornelia never really imagines Lodore will leave her behind in England. When she realizes how serious he is about the plan, she follows Lodore and Ethel to LeHavre, but their ship has sailed and she is too late to stop or join them (90). And Cornelia may be a bad wife when she refuses to learn anything from her husband or to separate herself from her domineering mother. But her behavior is certainly understandable enough to elicit sympathy from the reader: Cornelia is very young, very inexperienced, and has never been separated from her mother before. She has difficulty allowing her devotion to her remaining female parent to be replaced by devotion to a strange and domineering husband. Besides, there may be something questionable in the sorts of things that Lodore wants Cornelia to learn about wifeliness and the way he proposes to teach them to her. As Shelley makes clear, Lodore desires a wife who embodies the conventional female virtues and who will submit, in a daughterly fashion, to his guidance and care.

Cornelia Santerre hardly inclines, in a spontaneous way, toward either virtuous domesticity or feminine submission. She is completely unintellectual, but she is courageous and determined not to depend on her husband's protection. Cornelia is happiest in the company of admiring males, but she is also determined to resist what she sees as her husband's tyrannical behavior. Above all, Cornelia Santerre possesses an uncommon amount of what is commonly seen as a male virtue: pride. Having been educated by an imperfect mother, Cornelia does not possess a shred of attractive feminine submissiveness. Shelley often portrays Cornelia's pride as a flaw in her character, but she equally often depicts it as one proper response of an autonomous personality. For example, Cornelia eventually decides she has paid too much attention to Casmir Lyzinski and "inwardly resolved to do so no more." Her pride makes her resent what she anticipates as Lodore's remonstrance against flirting: "It was particularly disagreeable . . . that her husband should use authority, as she feared that he was about to do, and exact from his wife's obedience, what she was willing to concede to her own sense of propriety" (67). In most instances, Cornelia's "willfulness" with respect to Lodore is an expression of her desire for autonomy in her marriage and her desire not to be dominated by her older husband. In short, her "willfulness" toward Lodore is indeed willful, but it is also portrayed as the defiant—and necessary—self-preservation of a resolute spirit. As the narrator approvingly notes, Cornelia "was a woman who in Sparta had formed a heroine; who in periods of war and revolution, would unflinchingly have met calamity, sustaining and leading her own sex" (91).

Given Lodore's desire for a woman he can guide and shelter, Cornelia's pride and her distance from the conventionally ideal female virtues can only exacerbate their marital difficulties. Lodore's expectations for Cornelia are both unrealistic and debilitating. The chief problem is that they grow out of Lodore's sense of what he wants Cornelia to be rather than what she naturally is. When Lodore first meets Cornelia, for example, he finds her cowering beneath a rocky ledge during a thunderstorm; in a passage related from Lodore's point of view, Shelley describes his first impression of her:

> There was a radiance, a softness, an angel look, that rendered her countenance singular in its fascination; an expression of innocence and sweetness; a pleading gentleness that desired protection; a glance that subdued, because it renounced all victory . . . he was fully repaid when he saw her, who hailed with gladness a protector. (48)

When Lodore first sees Cornelia, he makes her into the very embodiment of the ideal woman who fulfills his desire for power and control: she is soft and innocent; she wants protection and "wins" him by allowing him to be the victor. Significantly, Lodore interprets Cornelia's submissive appearance in religious language—he sees "a radiance, a softness, an angel look." The difficulty is that Cornelia is not like Lodore's vision of her in the least. She is more a Spartan heroine than a gentle, retiring flower of young womanhood.

Nevertheless, Lodore marries Cornelia and, once married, sets about making her into his vision of the kind of woman he thinks she is and still wants her to be. He is not as satisfied by her natural qualities of vivacity, good humor, and wit, as he is "by the promise which they gave for the future" (52), once he has properly shaped them. He sees himself as Cornelia's teacher, a role made easier by the disparity in their ages: Cornelia is sixteen when they marry, the same age as Mathilda upon her father's return; Lodore is approximately thirty-three, about the same age as Mathilda's father. Lodore's attitude toward his wife is decidedly paternal—she is, after all, just the age of Lodore's illegitimate son, Casmir Lyzinski. As Mary Shelley makes clear, Lodore seeks to assert a power over his wife that is both husbandly and paternal, but fails because he is too imperious and because he expects too much submission from her:

> And here his error began. . . . During the days of courtship he had looked forward with pleasure to playing the tutor to his fair mistress: but a tutor can do nothing without authority, either open or concealed—a tutor must sacrifice his own pursuits and immediate pleasures, to study and adapt himself to the disposition of his pupil. As has been said of those who would acquire power in the state—they must in some degree follow, if they would lead, and it is by adapting themselves to the humour of those they would command, that they establish the law of their own will, or of an apparent necessity. But Lodore understood nothing of all this . . . he was imperious: opposition startled and disconcerted him, and he saw heartlessness in the want of accommodation and compliance he met at home. He had expected from Cornelia a girl's clinging fondness . . . nor did she feel the womanly tenderness, which sees in her husband the safe-guard from the ills of life, the shield to stand between her and the world . . . a shelter from adversity, a refuge when tempests were abroad . . . she displayed toward him none of that deference, and yielding submission, which might reasonably have been expected from her youth. . . . He had expected devotion, attention, love. (56–57)

And what Lodore finds in Cornelia instead is defiance, pride, and resistance. Cornelia refuses to display any of the dependent tenderness her daughter Ethel eventually gives to her husband. Lodore's major failure in his marriage is a failure in flexibility and accommodation. Because he cannot "study and adapt himself to the disposition of his pupil," it is perhaps not surprising that the "pupil" so little adapts herself to the desires of her "tutor." His other major failure, of course, is embedded in his insistence on being his wife's "tutor" in the first place. By insisting on "teaching" his wife, Lodore assumes a paternal role: he refuses to recognize Cornelia's autonomy and seeks to make her a dependent child. When Lodore sees only "heart-lessness in the want of accommodation and compliance he met at home," he fails to understand that Cornelia would rather not become an obedient daughter to him. When Lodore expects "a girl's clinging fondness" from his wife and her "deference, and yielding submission," he fails to grasp that Cornelia does not want her husband to have the expectations of a father for her, in which the prerogatives of male power and control are paramount. In short, when Lodore tries to make his wife into a childlike and protected creature, he not only tries to make her into a daughter, but also into something for which she has no natural inclination.

The image of ideal wifeliness into which Lodore tries to mold Cornelia is, of course, simply the conventional one, which values female humility and dependence. Part of Mary Shelley's point is that this socially sanctioned pattern of husbandly behavior, paternalistic in all its aspects, expresses male needs and desires while it limits female autonomy and authenticity. But Mary Shelley also suggests a very immediate and obvious human truth: If a wife is not naturally inclined to docility, this pattern of paternalistic/husbandly behavior can create tragedy for a married pair.

Cornelia Santerre's marriage to Lord Lodore certainly has elements of the tragic about it. Cornelia and Lodore are generously disposed to each other early in their relationship, though they misunderstand and misread each other from the beginning. Almost immediately after their wedding, they begin to behave according to the pattern that eventually separates them entirely: Lodore attempts to enforce his will too imperiously; Cornelia resists and defiantly labels Lodore a "tyrant" or "despot." Lodore's first action in their marriage, for example, is to attempt to separate Cornelia from her mother, whom he finds "worldly" and altogether too "selfish and artful" (53, 55). Cornelia, in response, "looked on his conduct as tyrannical and cruel. She retreated from his manly guidance, to the pernicious guardianship of Lady Santerre, and she sheltered herself at her side, from any effort Lodore might make for her improvement" (54–55). After Ethel is born, the disappointed Lodore focuses all his affection on his daughter, excluding and ignoring his defiant wife; as the narrator puts it, "whatever whim, or whatever plan, he formed with regard to his daughter, he abided by unmoved, and took pleasure in manifesting his partiality for her" (59). Cornelia, in response, rails against his lack of feeling for her:

> She looked on her husband as a man essentially selfish—one who, worn out by passion, had married her to beguile his hours during a visitation of *ennui*, and incapable of the softness of love or the kindness of friendship. ... she believed that his object was to deprive her of the consolation of her daughter's love, and that his chief aim was to annoy and insult her. (60)

Cornelia soon finds some comfort in her affection for Casmir Lyzinski, an affection that the narrator pointedly and repeatedly describes as totally innocent (64, 65). Since no one yet realizes that Casmir is Lodore's illegitimate son, the narrator also insists that Lodore's behavior about Casmir is marked by what everyone around him sees as "a caprice perfectly unintelligible" (63). So when Lodore demands, "with pointed sarcasm of manner" (65), that Cornelia cease her attentions to Casmir, Cornelia is again wounded and defiant:

The unfounded suspicions of a lover may please as a proof of love, but those of a husband, who thus claims affections which he has ceased to endeavour to win, are never received except as an impertinence and an insult. Those of Lord Lodore appeared to his haughty wife but a new form of cold-hearted despotism, checking her pleasures whencesoever they might arise. (65)

The pattern of Cornelia's marriage to Lodore continues in this way until they are separated by his flight to the wilds of America. He attempts to reform and domesticate Cornelia by exerting his authority over her in an imperious manner; she resists, decrying his "tyranny." Eventually, as we have seen, Lodore simply gives up on Cornelia and transfers his attention to more malleable clay—unable to shape his defiant wife to his vision of ideal femininity, he decides to shape his daughter instead. As the narrator puts it, "Lord Lodore had formed his ideal of what a woman ought to be, of what he wished to find his wife, and sought to mold his daughter accordingly" (272).

There is, of course, a second difficulty in Cornelia's marriage, aside from her husband's determination to shape her to his desires and her determination to resist. Both Cornelia and her husband have to deal with the interfering presence of her mother, Lady Santerre, who demands her daughter's unrelenting devotion, and teaches her entirely the wrong values when she directs her to "view society as the glass by which she was to set her feelings, and to which to adapt her conduct" (54). Lady Santerre—whose name, as William Veeder has observed, suggests a distance from the natural, a determined insistence to be "without earth"[30]—is important both for her effect on her daughter's behavior and for what she represents as a teacher. Lady Santerre symbolizes, first of all, an inversion of natural maternal feelings for a child: rather than devoting herself to her daughter's welfare, she manipulates her daughter to be certain that Cornelia will devote herself to her mother's well-being. In this respect, Lady Santerre dominates Cornelia as much as Lodore tries to; the narrator describes her actions and motivation in consistently negative terms:

> She was a clever though uneducated woman: perfectly selfish, soured with the world, yet clinging to it. To make good her second entrance on its stage, she believed it necessary to preserve unlimited sway over the plastic mind of her daughter. If she had acted with integrity, her end had been equally well secured; but unfortunately, she was by nature framed to prefer the zig-zag to the straight line; added to which, she was imperious, and could not bear a rival near her throne. From the first, therefore, she

exerted herself to secure her empire over Cornelia; she spared neither
flattery nor artifice; and, well acquainted as she was with every habit and
turn of her daughter's mind, her task was comparatively easy. (54)

Lady Santerre thus not only craves total power and control over her
daughter; she lacks all integrity and stoops to flattery and deceit. She is a
worse influence on Cornelia as a mother than Lodore is as a quasi-father.
Lodore, it would seem, is totally right to regard Lady Santerre as "pernicious" and a mere "oily flatterer" (53).

But if Mary Shelley castigates Lady Santerre for her desire to dominate
her daughter, she also insists that social arrangements have made Lady
Santerre what she is. Lady Santerre was humbly born. She was, like most
girls, given little education, but she had the good fortune to possess a good
face and was thus lucky enough to marry a young nobleman who stood to
inherit money (49). So Lady Santerre entered into the way of life reserved
for women of means in the nineteenth century: the social world of visits,
balls, and trips to spas. When her husband died she was ill-equipped to
maintain her style of life in the "world"; her daughter became her ticket for
reentry into polite society. Mary Shelley certainly portrays Lady Santerre's
social aspirations as empty and pathetic—in fact, as the source of the most
wrongheaded decisions that Cornelia makes—but, given women's limited
options in the nineteenth century, Lady Santerre has few other possibilities.
She is inclined to domestic retirement even less than Cornelia; the social
world is the only arena in which she can field her ambition. From this
perspective, Lady Santerre is a living embodiment of Mary Wollstonecraft's
warning in *A Vindication of the Rights of Woman:* women educated only in
the arts of pleasing men and landing husbands are doomed to lead empty
lives and to exert a pernicious effect on their children.[31]

Educated as she has been to make "society" a career and her saving
milieu, Lady Santerre teaches Cornelia the same thing. Given Cornelia's
extremely close tie to her mother and the early age at which she marries
Lodore, Cornelia Santerre is thus provided with only two options for her
future by her closest relations: to make herself into the domestic creature
Lodore desires or to engage in the social life of the "world," which, though
frivolous and empty, at least allows her some scope for independence and
autonomy. Cornelia's options are, of course, better than Fanny Derham's—
though Fanny has been educated to independence and the life of the intellect, she can hope for nothing better than what the narrator calls the "servitude" of a governess's job. Cornelia's options—dependent wifeliness or
social frivolity—are precisely the options available to most women married

to men of substance in the middle of the nineteenth century. Until she is reunited with her daughter, Cornelia has nothing better.

Cornelia's escape into the life of the fashionable world, then, is at first an escape from Lodore's demands on her. After Lodore takes Ethel to America, life in society becomes both her only available milieu and a distraction from the loss of her beloved child, a loss so sharp that Cornelia dreams obsessively of being reunited with Ethel: "In her dreams she often beheld, instead of the image of the gay saloons in which she spent her evenings, a desert wild—a solitary home—and tiny footsteps on the dewy grass guiding her to her baby daughter, whose soft cooings, remembered during absence, were agonizing to her" (93). Shelley paints Cornelia's life for the next fifteen years, until she is thirty-four-years old, in broad strokes, concentrating on two major emotional issues in Cornelia's life: the fact that her life in society seems increasingly meaningless and trivial to her and the fact that she is tortured by the absence of her child. Cornelia finds that society, although her only occupation, "palls" (143) for her as she learns how truly empty and pointless it is. As she grows older, Cornelia realizes more and more "that her life was aimless, unprofitable, blank" (303). At the same time, Cornelia nurses her longing for her daughter as her deepest sorrow, a sorrow she hides carefully from the prying eyes of her curious acquaintances in polite society (146). When Horatio Saville realizes how deeply Cornelia grieves for Ethel, he travels to America to convince Lodore to return Cornelia's "babe" to her (151). After Lodore dies and Saville leaves Cornelia for a Neapolitan bride, Cornelia longs yet more acutely for the sustenance of a tie to her daughter (1600).

Cornelia's sense of the meaninglessness of her life and her longing for her daughter come together dramatically during the scene in which Cornelia visits Ethel and Edward Villiers in debtors' prison. The affection that Ethel and Edward share makes Cornelia's life seem yet blanker; she resolves to find a sense of purpose in sacrificing herself on behalf of her daughter (315–18). To this end, Cornelia secretly sells her inheritance to pay Edward's debts and remove the young couple from prison. She even gives Ethel and Edward her house, saying that she wants to travel on the Continent, when in fact she plans to retire into poverty and seclusion in some rural area. The plot of *Lodore* then unfolds swiftly, and with some surprising twists. During her journey into retirement, Cornelia suffers a transforming illness. She is ill for a long period of time. During her delirium she has an obsessive dream, in which Ethel sits beside Lodore's tomb and earnestly calls her mother to "Come! Come!" (387).

When Cornelia recovers, she has changed significantly. Her pride has ebbed; her illness has produced "a disposition attuned to content and a wish for tranquillity" (386). Essentially, Cornelia has lost her desire to struggle against the ghosts of Lodore's lingering influence. She is even more committed to finding purpose in her life through self-sacrifice and, for the first time, Cornelia castigates herself for being a bad wife. In fulfillment of her dream, she visits Lodore's grave, where she grasps fully how she has failed at the feminine virtues of wifeliness and devotion:

> Cornelia had never before felt so sensibly that she had been a wife neglecting her duties, despising a vow she had solemnly pledged, estranging herself from him, who by religious ordinance, and the laws of society, alone had privilege to protect and love her. (388)

Cornelia's sense of guilt is genuine, but there is an irony embedded in her conclusion that "religious ordinance, and the laws of society alone" give Lodore the power to protect her. "Alone" is syntactically ambiguous. Does it suggest that Lodore alone has the power to protect Cornelia? Or does it suggest something quite different: that "religious ordinance and the laws of society alone" give him this protective power—that is, that religion and custom are the only things that create Lodore's mandate to protect Cornelia? Shelley herself, of course, never entirely accepted the moral force of either religious law or social custom.

After her visit to Lodore's tomb, Cornelia settles in a poor peasant cottage buried deep in the Vale of Bewling. There she communes with nature, cares for an elderly peasant woman and advises the woman's lovesick daughter. Eventually, Cornelia is reunited with Ethel, who has learned of her mother's sacrifice and comes to take her into her own home. Saville is gratified by Cornelia's self-sacrifice and her total dedication to the "genuine affections of the heart." Since his Italian wife has conveniently died, he proposes to Cornelia. Cornelia's supreme sacrifice and devotion earn her religious epithets. The peasant women call Cornelia an "angel" sent to them by God (378); Horatio Saville sees that Cornelia has managed to "embody in [her] actions all that can be imagined of glorious and angelic" (363). The narrator also seems to concur heartily in the judgment of these characters, saying of Cornelia that "she had risen to a sphere above, beyond the ordinary soarings of mortals—a world without a cloud, without one ungenial breath" (321). Yet there seems to be an irony embedded in this narrative rumination as well, since the "sphere" it invokes is so patently unreal.

Thus, on one level, Shelley clearly endorses and celebrates the salvation that Cornelia finds when she finally embraces the limits of conventional femininity. For Cornelia, as for Ethel, the traditional feminine virtues come to embody a woman's natural "goodness"—the "goodness" the narrator describes as woman's transcendent duty. Shelley is also careful to portray Cornelia's maternity as in some sense liberating. For one thing, Cornelia's new life as a devoted mother, even within—or perhaps because of—its limits of voluntary renunciation, has much more meaning and purpose than her old life of social frivolity, even with the autonomy it offered.[32] And, significantly, Cornelia's new life of devotion to her daughter, for all its conventionality, allows her to escape some of the configurations of traditional marriage—in particular the patterns of dominance and dependence involved in her relationship to Lodore. For Cornelia, devotion to her child rather than her husband becomes the ruling emotion in her life. The new Cornelia defines herself by her sacrifices as a mother rather than her dependence as a wife, so that the duties of motherhood supersede and transcend the requirements of wifeliness. While Shelley rewards Cornelia's conventional femininity with a good husband, that husband is a distinctly secondary figure in Cornelia's emotional life. As the narrator says of Cornelia's marriage to Saville:

> [Cornelia] respects, admires, in some sense it may be said, that she adores her husband; but even while consenting to be his, and thus securing her own happiness, she told him that her first duties were towards Ethel—and that he took a divided heart, over the better part of which reined maternal love. (395)

By consecrating herself to the sacrifices of motherhood, Cornelia knows she is doing the "natural" thing. If Lady Santerre's selfish manipulation of her daughter was monstrous because it was "unnatural," then Cornelia's self-sacrifice on behalf of her daughter is holy because it is so unreservedly "natural." Shelley implies, among other things, that women are naturally inclined to sacrifice themselves for their children, while not instinctively inclined to submit themselves to the authority society vests in their husbands. Indeed, Mary Shelley arranges the plot of *Lodore* so that Cornelia is reunited with Ethel in a setting of natural fecundity, away from the strictures of social arrangements. Cornelia is in retirement at her peasant cottage; as she stoops to catch the fragrance of "fresh violets" and jonquils "heavy with [their] burthen of sweet blooms" (391), Cornelia thinks:

Yes . . . nature is the refuge and home for women: they have no public career—no aim nor end beyond their domestic circle; but they can extend that, and make all the creations of nature their own, to foster and do good to. We complain, when shut up in cities of the niggard rules of society, which gives us only the drawing-room or ballroom in which to display our talents, and which, for ever turning the sympathy of those around us into envy on the part of women, or what is called love on that of men, besets our path with dangers or sorrows. But throw aside all vanity, no longer seek to surpass your own sex, nor to inspire the other with feelings which are pregnant with disquiet or misery, and which seldom end in mutual benevolence, turn your steps to the habitation which God has given as befitting his creatures, contemplate the lovely ornaments with which he has blessed the earth;—here is no heart-burning nor calumny; it is better to love, to be of use to one of these flowers, than to be the admired of the many—the mere puppet of one's own vanity. (391–92)

William Veeder has interpreted this passage as Mary Shelley's insistence that "woman's highest office is to be the mother or wife of a great man"[33]—that is, that Mary Shelley believes women, because of their "natures," are not fit for any "public career" nor any "aim nor end beyond their domestic circle." But given the context of the whole of *Lodore*—and the context of Mary Shelley's other statements about the confining nature of feminine roles—this passage in fact insists upon something quite different. When Cornelia observes that women have "no public career—no aim nor end beyond their domestic circle," she makes a factual statement about nineteenth-century society rather than a philosophical evaluation of women's inherent talents. She merely indicates that its social arrangements do not permit women any meaningful possibilities for work or autonomy outside of the family. This is precisely the same point that Mary Shelley makes in her own voice when she writes James Robins in 1828 that "my sex has precluded all idea of my fulfilling public employments" (MWS *Letters*, 2:22). For Cornelia, and for Mary Shelley, "nature" is an alternative to the emptiness of the fashionable life that convention allows Cornelia to participate in, and that she flees—a "refuge" from "the niggard rules of society, which gives us [women] only the drawing-room or ballroom in which to display our talents." And "nature" in this passage is also a substitute for traditional relations between men and women, a "home for women" away from "what is called love on [the part] of men." Nature—and "nature" includes maternity, the most fundamentally "natural" of female possibilities—gives women a more transcendent career than they can find in either

the life of polite society or the conventional patterns of male-female relationships. For Cornelia, mothering Ethel represents a withdrawal from and
self-chosen replacement for the traditional relations between men and
women.

Ironically, of course, embracing motherhood by embracing nature means
opting for many of the limits associated with conventional notions of femininity: devoting oneself to children means adopting in particular the traditional female habits of selflessness and self-sacrifice in support of others.[34]
But Cornelia's choice is a deliberate one. Her accommodation may be inevitable, but it is also freely chosen. Further, when Cornelia devotes herself to
the sacrifices of motherhood, she transcends precisely that characteristic of
conventional femininity that flaws Ethel: dependent weakness. Cornelia
always remains strong; when she sacrifices herself for her daughter, she
draws on an impressive capacity to support and maintain others. Finally,
one can argue—as Mary Poovey has in the case of Shelley's last novel,
Falkner—that Shelley uses Cornelia's decision to embrace conventional
femininity to explore some of that femininity's hidden and subversive power
over men. After all, when Cornelia sacrifices everything for Ethel and Edward, the latter of whom she dislikes intensely, she gains a significant
amount of control over her despised son-in-law. As the narrator points out,
Edward is humiliated by the news that his mother-in-law has saved him
and his wife; his "cheeks glowed with shame . . . at being the object of so
much sacrifice and beneficence on the part of his mother in-law" (365).
And, in a symbolic sense, Cornelia's maternal renunciation establishes her
control of events at the novel's close. It is the figure of the mother, after all,
who asserts her power by rescuing her daughter from her symbolic prison of
dependence on a husband, after the interfering father figures have been
neutralized or eliminated.

In the closing pages of *Lodore,* then, Mary Shelley endorses and celebrates her formerly defiant heroine's redemption into conventional femininity—a domesticity that elevates the self-sacrifice and self-abnegation of
motherhood and commends the woman who can exhibit great strength in
the support of others. Yet, notwithstanding Shelley's exploration of the
power latent in motherhood, Shelley remains acutely aware of the restrictions imposed by the maternal role. While Shelley extols an accommodation to the conventional limits of femininity, she simultaneously underscores the personal toll those limits exact. Shelley's ambivalence surfaces in
some of the images and settings she uses to depict Cornelia's transformation
from a spirited social butterfly into a self-effacing angel of a mother. For

example, just after Cornelia pledges to sacrifice all her worldly goods for her daughter and son-in-law, the narrator first praises Cornelia's sacred elevation "beyond the ordinary soarings of mortals" (321). But in the next paragraph, the narrator is decidedly less certain about whether Cornelia's sacrifice will canonize her or kill her:

> As before, when she cast off Lodore, she had never admitted a doubt that she was justified before God and her conscience for refusing to submit to the most insulting tyranny; so now, believing that she had acted ill in not demanding the guardianship of her daughter, and resolving to atone for the evils which were the consequence of this neglect of duty on her part, she had no misgivings as to the future, but rushed precipitately onwards. As a racer at the Olympic games, she panted to arrive at the goal, though it were only to expire at the moment of its attainment. (320–21)

By describing Cornelia as an Olympian athlete, Shelley underscores her heroism. But if Cornelia expires at the moment she attains her goal, her heroism has decidedly murderous overtones.

And, in a sense, Cornelia's heroic sacrifice does kill her—or at least eliminates the defining characteristic of her rebellious personality, her defiant pride. Before her transforming illness, Cornelia feels more kindly disposed to the memory of her husband and considers visiting his tomb. But she is certain her defiance of Lodore was not a mistake: "[My visit] is not to atone—for surely I was not guilty towards him" (339). After she recovers from her illness, this proud conviction is gone. The turning point seems to occur in the recurrent dream she has during her fever and delirium, a dream in which Ethel sits at the side of Lodore's tomb and beckons her mother to "Come! Come!" (387). The imagery of this prophetic dream is decidedly ambiguous: Cornelia's loss of her defining pride, represented by her visit to her husband's tomb, is both a redemptive submission to Lodore's ideas and a way for Cornelia, like Antigone, to bury herself alive. The imagery of Cornelia's recurrent dream makes her daughter ambiguous in precisely the same way. Ethel calls Cornelia to the salvation of sacrifice; she also calls Cornelia to her grave. Cornelia's return to her child, in short, is both a moment of liberation and a moment of entombment. As such, Cornelia's decision to embrace maternity looks backward to Mathilda's maternal behavior toward her father and, as we shall see, forward to the maternal behavior of a very different sort of daughter in *Falkner*.

Most of the female characters of *Lodore*, both major and minor, end the novel by devoting themselves to conventional femininity and someone other than a husband. Cornelia consecrates herself to Ethel; Ethel, though married blissfully to Edward Villiers, locates her primary emotional tie in her father. As the narrator puts it, Ethel "might be said to live perpetually in thought beside her father's grave . . . she placed the home of her happy married life close to [its] sacred earth" (205). Fanny Derham, of course, does not turn into a traditionally feminine type, but she cherishes her father's memory and yearns to be reunited with him. Even the young wife of Captain Villiers, Edward's dissolute father, rejects him. When Captain Villiers's dissipation increases, the wife "in a fit of remorse left him, and returned to nurse her father during a lingering illness, which is likely to continue to the end of his life, though he shows no symptoms of immediate decay" (395).

Lodore is the first of Mary Shelley's major works in which a daughterly protagonist, after struggling against the father's dominion over her, evades his power and lives long enough to become an actual mother. Unlike Mathilda and Frankenstein's "monster," who both die, Cornelia outlives Lodore and reclaims her tie to Ethel. *Lodore* is also the only work of Shelley's career that portrays a successful relationship between a mother and a daughter. As we have seen, mother/daughter relationships in Shelley's fiction are usually truncated—or never begin—due to the mother's death. Though Cornelia's relationship to Ethel is similarly ruptured at *Lodore*'s opening when Lodore kidnaps Ethel, the entire novel works toward the reunion of mother and daughter. As Shelley described the novel's situation to her publisher, Charles Ollier,

> A Mother & Daughter are the heroines—The Mother who after sacrifising *all* to the world at first—afterwards makes sacrifises not less entire, for her child—finding all to be Vanity, except the genuine affections of the heart. In the daughter I have tried to pourtray in its simplicity, & all the beauty I could muster, the *devotion* of a young wife for the husband of her choice— The disasters she goes through being described—& their result in awakening her Mother's affection, bringing about the conclusion of the tale— Perhaps a fitting motto would be Sir Walter Scot's well known lines beginning "O woman in our hours of ease &c." (31 January 1833 MWS *Letters*, 2:185)[35]

As we shall see, the devotion between mother and daughter that Shelley emphasizes in *Lodore* looks forward to the fidelity between a mother figure and a very different type of child in *Falkner*.

It is not surprising that, in 1831, Mary Shelley would begin a novel that celebrates the womanly virtues of devotion, self-sacrifice, and maternity, and that simultaneously expresses hostility toward the figure of the father. Essentially, Shelley gave her heroine her own options, and she used her heroine to express her sense of the simultaneously redemptive and restrictive accommodations society—and fathers—demand of their daughters. When Shelley began *Lodore*, she was thirty-four, Cornelia's age at the end of the novel. Like Cornelia, Shelley sacrificed her comfort and happiness for her child and found that sacrifice gave meaning to her life. But simultaneously, Shelley fought to support and cheer a dependent figure of a very different sort: her father. Godwin's health was failing; he was penniless; at the age of seventy-five he still worked unsuccessfully to earn enough money from his pen to live. Shelley wrote *Lodore* to provide for her father's care (MWS *Letters*, 2:183), orchestrated other projects on his behalf, and meanwhile wished "for nothing but an exemption from pecuniary annoyances, both for myself & my father" (2:170–71). Her poverty, as she put it, was "as the bars of a prison" (MWS *Journals*, 2:516). If Shelley found meaning and emotional sustenance in the personal sacrifices she made for her child, she found similar meaning in her devotion to her aging father. But she must have felt an equal portion of anger at a father who continued to ask so much of his daughter and who continued to return so little. As we shall see, Shelley's last novel, *Falkner*, again orchestrates these twin themes of daughterly devotion and hostility toward the figure of the father. But in Shelley's final novel, the daughter's victory over the father's demands is more complete.

5

Falkner

Lodore proved to be Shelley's most popular novel since *Frankenstein*. When reviewers commended *Lodore* for its "exceeding gracefulness" and "touching eloquence,"[1] Shelley was quickly commissioned to write *Falkner*. *Falkner* succeeded equally well and was described by a reviewer at the *Monthly Repository* as Mary Shelley's "finest work."[2] Yet even Shelley's contemporary critics noted *Falkner*'s "trite conventionalisms, in the shape of moral reflections,"[3] a charge often leveled by twentieth-century commentators. As in the case of *Lodore*, the sentimentality of *Falkner* has often presented an obstacle to modern readers. And as in the case of *Lodore*, the figure of the monstrous daughter has disappeared from *Falkner*, to be replaced by a daughter who is both passionately devoted to and maternally protective of the figure of the father.

In *Falkner*, Shelley sets herself many of the same novelistic tasks as in *Lodore*: to depict and endorse the limits of conventional womanhood; to celebrate the renunciations of motherhood; and to elevate, above all, the womanly virtue of fidelity. But in the examination of these themes, Shelley embarks on other tasks. As Mary Poovey has shown, *Falkner* is structured by evasionary tactics that express its author's anger and frustration. Equally important for our purposes, *Falkner* pursues some of the matters Shelley opened in *Mathilda* and elaborated in *Lodore*. In her last novel, written half before her father's death and half after it, Shelley again examines the duties of the daughter, the failures of the father, and the inescapable sexuality of their tie to each other. Responding to William Godwin's *Deloraine*—a novel that praises a daughter's selfless devotion to her father's needs—*Falkner* portrays a daughter who unselfishly submits herself to her father's desires and, by doing so, paradoxically gains control over him.

Mary Shelley conceived of *Falkner* late in 1835; the novel was published by Saunders and Otley in January of 1837, nine months after William Godwin died as Mary Shelley watched at his bedside. Two years before Mary Shelley began work on *Falkner*, William Godwin published his last

novel, *Deloraine* (1833). As we have seen, the relations between Godwin
and his daughter were intensely close during the last years of his life. He
relied on her increasingly for all forms of support, both emotional and
financial; she felt burdened by his needs, but struggled to meet them with
protestations of support and infusions of cash. William Godwin's vision of
his complex relationship to his daughter during these years found its most
complete literary expression in the pages of *Deloraine*, in his description of
the intimate bond between the titular character and his beloved only daughter. *Deloraine* may be read as Godwin's fullest evocation of the perfections
of the father-daughter relationship; *Falkner* may be read as Shelley's response.

   Deloraine is, in many ways, a novel written in typical Godwinian style.
Like Falkland in *Caleb Williams*, Deloraine is wracked by a guilty secret; like
Caleb himself, Deloraine is hunted by an uncompromising adversary, so
that pursuit becomes the major structuring device of the work. In *Deloraine*,
Godwin continues to display his lifelong disdain for the conventional instruments of English justice, in particular the courts of law; as in *Caleb
Williams*, Godwin repeatedly focuses on the psychological workings of the
human mind as it attempts to come to terms with the emotions of love and
loss. But for all these predictable Godwinian resonances, his last novel has
a very different emotional center. *Deloraine* concerns itself primarily with
the relations between parents and children; unlike Godwin's earlier novels,
it centers its attention on the varieties of filial duty and filial piety's rewards
and difficulties.

   Since *Deloraine* is seldom read today, some plot summary is necessary
to clarify the novel's chief events and themes. The central characters of
Deloraine are the titular hero and Catherine Deloraine, his daughter by his
first wife. Though Godwin does not begin their story until late in the novel's
second volume, he sets the stage for their relationship by using the first half
of his book to examine the filial devotion of other children for their parents.
Specifically, Godwin describes the love of a simple villager named William
for his mother, and the submissive tenderness that Margaret Borradale,
William's first love and Deloraine's second wife, displays toward her beloved but imperfect father. Godwin portrays William, a man who eventually becomes Deloraine's rival, as a son who commendably puts filial duty
before all his other inclinations. When his father dies, William returns to
live with his widowed mother, where he takes his father's place as her
protector and chief "domestic friend."[4] Later in the novel, when Margaret
Borradale tells William that her father wants her to break their engagement,

William wholeheartedly endorses her decision to abide by her father's wishes (1:189–90). William is a man who believes that a child's devotion to his parents surpasses all other relationships. After Deloraine murders William in a fit of passion, part of Deloraine's grief derives from his belief that William was a good man who grasped the correct hierarchy of human affections.

Margaret Borradale is as devoted to her father as William is to his mother. Margaret's father begs her to provide for his old age, specifically by marrying a distant cousin, the young Lord Borradale. Young Borradale is "empty and conceited" (1:154); Margaret is deeply in love with William. But she relents and agrees to the marriage, insisting to William that it is her responsibility to "sacrifice her own preferences on the altar of filial duty" (1:167). William agrees and withdraws his suit; Deloraine subsequently applauds her decision, saying it made her a "spotless monument of filial submission and obedience" (1:273). Later in the story, the tensions of Margaret's engagement to Lord Borradale ruin her health and nearly kill her. Margaret's father relents and gives her permission to marry William. William's ship sinks within sight of land as he is returning to claim her hand, and he is presumed dead; Margaret falls into a gloom from which she never recovers. Margaret and her parents eventually meet Deloraine, who proposes marriage. Margaret does not love Deloraine but agrees to the match, again to please her father. She feels guilty that her "obstinacy and self-will" (1:278) wrecked her father's hopes for a secure old age. She concludes that her "submission" to her father's desire will "prove the best expiation she could make for that scene, in which she had so unwillingly been the cause of his griefs" (1:279).

As this plot summary suggests, Godwin portrays Margaret Borradale, Deloraine's second wife, as a daughter who places devotion to her father above all other virtues and relationships. Godwin's characterizations and imagery consistently commend Margaret for her unwavering filial piety. Godwin does depict the violence sometimes visited on a daughter by the imperatives of filial affection—the narrator admits that, in acceding to her father's wishes, "the virtue of Margaret destroyed her" (1:198). But the occasional passing observation about Margaret's suffering notwithstanding, Godwin sees the daughter's self-sacrifice as entirely positive. Neither Godwin's narrator nor any of his characters ever suggests that Margaret should temper the filial devotion that triggers her near self-destruction.

In the same manner, Godwin emphatically refuses to imply that Margaret's father is selfish or domineering. Margaret's father is sometimes peremptory; he is perhaps excessively concerned about procuring financial resources for his old age. But Godwin portrays Mr. Borradale's expectations for his daughter as entirely reasonable and benevolent. When Mr. Borradale asks Margaret to marry the suitor he prefers, he recalls the way he cared for her as a child, and "he intreated, he adjured her to have compassion upon him" (1:159; 162). Further, Godwin points out that Mr. Borradale "was not without his compunctions and his tenderness" (1:166) for his daughter. When he realizes how close to death his demands have brought Margaret, he repents entirely, admitting that he was "dazzled" by the "noble and generous propositions" (1:221) offered to him by Lord Borradale, and offers to redeem himself by becoming Margaret's "indentured servant" (1:223). In short, William Godwin portrays Mr. Borradale as a loving father who justifiably thinks his daughter should put his needs before her own. In Godwin's eyes, Borradale merely miscalculates by asking a sacrifice that lies beyond the power of his daughter's physical constitution.

Godwin's portraits of William, Margaret, and Mr. Borradale communicate *Deloraine*'s primary messages before the main characters take the action's center stage: that relationships between children and parents are sacred; that duty often calls a child to sacrifice other inclinations for the parent's sake; and that filial self-sacrifice is blessed and ennobling. Godwin's portrayal of the relationship between Deloraine and his beloved daughter, Catherine, carries these convictions even further. In his depiction of Catherine and Deloraine, Godwin draws heavily from autobiographical material, evoking his vision of his complex relationship to Mary Shelley. He portrays a father-daughter relationship that is preternaturally intense, predicated on the daughter's self-sacrifice, and in which the daughter elevates her father's needs above her own. In doing so, Godwin articulates his image of the perfect daughter and of the ideal relation between a father and his female child. Godwin's last novel may be read as an expression of the powerful needs of a father; it may also be read as an expression of Godwin's hopeful conviction that his own daughter would continue to fill them.

As William Godwin composed *Deloraine*, his autobiographical material aroused feelings so intense that his writing stalled. Godwin wrote the first two volumes of the novel easily. In them, he sketches not only the story of William and Margaret, but the broad outlines of his marriage to Mary Wollstonecraft and the basic events of Mary Godwin's childhood and adolescence. Godwin tells the tale of Deloraine, an English gentleman whose beloved first wife, Emilia, dies, leaving him with a daughter named Catherine. Deloraine comes to regard Catherine as the "living representative" (1:91) of her mother and struggles to raise Catherine in Emilia's image. Like Mary Godwin, Catherine develops into an accomplished writer who describes scenes with exquisite taste and "impressive sensibility" (1:106). In an act reminiscent of Godwin's decision to send his daughter to Scotland, Deloraine sends thirteen-year-old Catherine to another country to complete her education and broaden her horizons. When Catherine returns to England, she is a young woman.

Deloraine, in the meantime, enters into an unsatisfactory second marriage with Margaret Borradale, whose emotions have atrophied after the loss of William. Margaret cannot return Deloraine's passionate attachment. When William unexpectedly reappears in the second volume, very much alive, Deloraine kills him in a jealous fit. Margaret dies of grief and shock; Deloraine immediately replaces his attachment to his wife with his passion for his daughter. He prepares to flee his crime by exiling himself from England, but he vows to see Catherine one last time. During the visit, Catherine insists on fleeing with Deloraine because it is her duty as a daughter, because she loves him so passionately, and because caring for him will give her "an object for which to live, a principle that shall direct my smallest actions" (2:198). As Catherine puts it, in a cry charged with sexual innuendo:

> Take me, my father! . . . Mould me at your pleasure! Henceforth I have no destination in life, no office concentrating all the powers of my nature, but that of being devoted to your service and advantage. In this service there is perfect freedom; in this religion there is pure felicity. (2:198)

Soon after this point in the composition of *Deloraine*, Godwin's imagination faltered. As Godwin began the last volume—in which Deloraine and his daughter cement a bond that supersedes his two marriages and then leave England to wander over Europe in isolated intimacy—he found his pen strangely blocked. He wrote to Mary, imploring her to "spark" his imagination:

> I am still in the same dismaying predicament in which I have been for weeks past, at a loss for materials to make up my third volume. This is by no means what I expected. . . . [I]t unfortunately happens that I cannot lay my present disappointment to the charge of advancing age. I find all my faculties and all my strength in full bloom about me. My disappointment has put that to a sharp trial. I thought that the severe stretch of my faculties would cause them to yield, and subside into feebleness and torpor. No

such thing. . . . I am afraid you will think I am useless, by teazing you with "conceptions only proper to myself." But it is not altogether so. A by-stander may see a point of game which a player overlooks. Though I cannot furnish myself with satisfactory incidents, I have disciplined my mind into a tone that would enable me to improve them, if offered to me. My mind is like a train of gunpowder, and a single spark, now happily communicated, might set the whole in motion and activity.[5]

Godwin himself saw that his inability to write incidents for the last third of his novel was not an ordinary case of creative lapse—he insisted that his imaginative faculties were in "full bloom," that his mind was like a "train of gunpowder" ready to explode into creative expression. At some level, Godwin may have grasped that, in writing about the passionate mutual attachment between a father and his daughter, in which both exile themselves from social norms to live together in secluded intimacy, he was treading on forbidden ground. Mary Shelley's reply to her father's letter is lost, so we cannot know precisely how her participation "sparked" the completion of *Deloraine* or what specific events she might have suggested to release Godwin from his creative impasse. It is tempting to speculate, however, that Mary Shelley provided Godwin with the broad outlines of a plot she soon turned to her own purposes: a plot in which a daughter devotes herself to exile with her father, is instrumental in saving him from a legal prosecution that might result in his execution, and eventually ends up living with her father forever, having secured a husband who will consent to such an arrangement. As we shall see, these events constitute the broad outlines of the plot of Shelley's final novel, *Falkner*.

As Godwin sketches his vision of the personality and behavior of the perfect daughter, familiar lineaments emerge. Catherine Deloraine is in many ways a younger version of Marguerite de Damville in *St. Leon*, Godwin's first fictional revision of his dead wife, Mary Wollstonecraft. Catherine, like Marguerite, is amiable, accomplished, and possessed of innate feminine innocence and delicacy. Like Marguerite, Catherine has no taste for a worldly career, preferring to devote herself to feminine domestic duties. Like Marguerite, Catherine is self-silencing. When Deloraine reveals his murderous actions to her, Catherine stands still and mute, knowing "she must in no way betray what she suffered" (2:189). After Catherine and her father have settled into their first home abroad, she steadfastly refuses to express guilt or fear. As Deloraine puts it, "[W]hatever were her thoughts in this respect, she kept them sacredly in the chamber of her own bosom" (3:46). And when Deloraine entrusts their safety to a cynical Frenchman,

Catherine at first protests, but then "felt it her duty to acquiesce and be silent" (3:142).

Catherine's silent, submissive behavior causes Deloraine to bestow on her precisely the same set of images St. Leon used to describe his wife, Marguerite. Catherine becomes an apotheosis of feminine duty and self-sacrifice; as a result, she is consistently represented in religious terms. (See 2:97–98; 2:201; 3:77; 3:82; 3:300; 3:154.) Godwin portrays Catherine Deloraine in the language of veneration and saintliness because, for all her feminine delicacy and habits of submission, she exhibits remarkable strength: her ability to endure self-sacrifice, and by enduring self-sacrifice to support and console her father. In this respect, Catherine's daughterly behavior is remarkably similar to Marguerite de Damville's wifely behavior: although both women seem to be frail domestic angels, they marshall extraordinary resources of strength in the service of the men central to their lives. That is, Catherine and Marguerite are both fundamentally maternal in their ability to support and console; Catherine and Marguerite both define themselves by renouncing their own inclinations to the needs of a powerfully demanding male. Catherine declares her determination to sacrifice herself in order to support and console her father near the end of volume 2, as soon as he reveals he committed murder:

> [S]he roused herself, and subdued the weakness of her frame to an emphatic steadiness. . . . Father, replied Catherine, you do but shew me the more your need of a companion, such as I will be to you. Oh, you do not know with what art and unwearied skill I will medicine your griefs. My patience shall conquer your moroseness. I will prove so considerate and kind, that I will defy you not to smile upon me. You cannot be without a companion; and no companion will be so suitable for you as I am determined to be found. . . . I will be at hand to smooth your pillow, when you most need a friend. I will pour the balm of consolation into your wounds, when the world most combines to destroy you. If you go to prison, I will go with you. If you are arraigned in a court of justice, I will be near you. If you mount the scaffold, I will ascend with you. (2:190, 2:192–93, 2:196)

In the last volume of *Deloraine*, Catherine fulfills this promise to renounce all to her father's care. Playing Antigone to Deloraine's latter day Oedipus, Catherine shares her father's exile and humiliation, and becomes his comfort and guide. Catherine and Deloraine leave England and settle in Bruges; Catherine makes a home there for her father, assuages his suffering, and even rekindles his spirits by entertaining him with her stories (3:45–50; 3:77–82). When father and daughter are forced to flee deeper into the Continent, Catherine transforms the isolated castle in which they hide into another home, where she watches jealously over Deloraine's welfare and passes intimate hours reading and talking with him (3:148–56). Catherine and Deloraine are ultimately chased back to England. When Deloraine decides to give himself up, Catherine intercedes with his pursuer, who is "melted" by her filial devotion. He gives up the chase because Catherine "came instinct with the holiest of causes, that of a father" (3:299). At the close of the novel, Catherine and Deloraine are reunited with one of Deloraine's passionate admirers, a doctor named Thornton, whom she marries:

> Between him [Thornton] and Catherine there rose a softer passion. He admired in her the invincible filial affection with which she had followed me in all my misfortunes and disgrace; and he adored her for the boldness of undertaking, and the more than human eloquence, with which she had finally subdued and disarmed my seemingly inveterate persecutor. They married. Catherine was the illustrious personage that gave radiance to the scene of our domestic life; for we all lived together. But Thornton and I felt no uneasiness at her superiority. We were satisfied that every thing was in its due order, and willingly submitted ourselves to her benignant sway. (3:305–66)

Godwin closes *Deloraine* with a revealing deployment of his characters. In the father's version of the perfect resolution to life with his beloved daughter, the father becomes the center of a triangular relationship. The daughter and son-in-law both count the father as their primary attachment; the daughter and her husband feel a significantly "softer passion" for each other; the son-in-law admires his wife above all for her devotion to her father. Situated forcefully at the center of this emotional triangle, the father grants the daughter apotheosis for her moral "superiority" and the power of her "benignant sway," both of which grow out of her thorough willingness to suffer and sacrifice herself for her father's sake.

As Godwin's portrayal of Catherine Deloraine amply illustrates, she is a daughter who "regarded filial duty and affection as paramount to all other ties" (3:55). Given the intensity of Catherine's self-sacrificing devotion to her father, it is little wonder that Deloraine concludes "there was something in the love of my daughter, that surpassed every thing that I had before witnessed in a human creature" (2:202). When Mary Shelley read *Deloraine*, she must have responded deeply to the powerful message about daughterhood her father embodied in the novel. After all, *Deloraine* evokes in literary form the woman Godwin so often asked Shelley to be in life: the daughter who silences herself in her father's service, puts her father's needs before all other inclinations and duties, and devotes herself to her father's support and comfort. At the same time, of course, Godwin's portrayal of Catherine and her father is an expression of his own powerful need for the emotional comforts provided by a daughter who consents to play a maternal role. When Godwin wrote *St. Leon* many years earlier, he portrayed Mary Wollstonecraft as a maternal type; in *Deloraine,* Godwin places Mary Wollstonecraft's daughter in the same role, thus expressing what Boose has identified as the father's desire to use his daughter to recreate his lost oedipal tie to the mother.[6] As he wrote the last volume of his last novel, Godwin cast himself in the role of Oedipus at Colonus, racked with guilt, excluded from human society, wandering in exile toward a merciful death. Simultaneously, Godwin cast Mary Godwin Shelley as his Antigone, the daughter who sacrifices everything to minister to her father's needs, cures his isolation with her maternal ministrations, and guides him toward a peaceful end.

Deloraine appeared in print on 12 February 1833, as Mary Shelley was writing *Lodore;* by late 1835, Shelley had planned and begun *Falkner,* her own last novel. Like *Deloraine,* and like Mary Shelley's other novels, *Falkner* studies parents and children, and centers itself on the portrayal of a demanding father and his passionately devoted daughter. Like *Deloraine, Falkner* elevates the bond between parent and child above all other human relationships and makes feminine fidelity the central human virtue. As Mary Shelley told Maria Gisborne, "[A]s I grow older I look upon fidelity as the first of human virtues—& am going to write a novel to display my opinion" (MWS *Letters*, 2:260). Shelley was aware that her canonization of feminine fidelity in *Falkner* might seem too conservative to some. She even warned Trelawny not to read the novel, insisting that "you will not approve of much of what I deem natural feeling because it is not founded on the New light" (MWS *Letters*, 2:282).

Falkner resembles *Deloraine* in at least one other significant way: completing the book proved difficult for its author. *Falkner* at first wrote itself (MWS *Letters*, 2:264)—Shelley finished the first volume in a few months. She wrote rapidly over the summer of 1836, coming close to the conclusion of her work. But William Godwin died in April 1836. Shelley nursed him tirelessly through his last illness; she began collecting his papers and writing his life immediately after his death. By October 1836, the strain of Godwin's death, combined with the emotional pressure of grappling with his image in two different genres—fiction and biography—took its toll. Shelley broke down; she retired to Brighton with Julia Robinson to recuperate. In Brighton, she was able to complete the last chapters of *Falkner*, though she could not at first face the revisions.[7] Shortly afterward, Shelley decided not to finish her account of Godwin's life, telling Trelawny that she could not risk ruining Percy's reputation by raking up old controversies (MWS *Letters*, 2:280–81). Powerful emotional forces were no doubt at work both in Shelley's difficulty in completing *Falkner* and in her decision to stop writing Godwin's biography. Like Shelley's other novels, *Falkner* takes up the intimidating task of exploring the sexual tension inherent in the father-daughter relationship. But once Godwin died, this theme may have begun to lose its obsessional quality for Shelley. And, having used the pages of *Falkner* to explore the totality of her feelings for her dead father once again, Shelley may have had neither the desire nor the interest to complete a hagiographic biography of him that began as an attempt to canonize his memory and preserve his reputation.

Upon first inspection, the major female characters of *Falkner* seem to celebrate the traditional womanly virtues embodied by Ethel Fitzhenry in *Lodore*, by Elizabeth Lavenza in *Frankenstein*, and by William Godwin's Catherine Deloraine. Alithea Rivers Neville, for example, is the very model of conventional feminine propriety and perfection. Alithea is the mother of Gerard Neville and murdered lover of the titular character, Rupert Falkner. Though Alithea dies before the novel begins, her influence is felt throughout the book: she is the source of Falkner's guilt, the inspiration for Neville's quest, and the model for Elizabeth Raby's adult behavior. Alithea's personality is sketched in a series of narrations imbedded in the text and provided, in turn, by Neville, Neville's stepsister, Rupert Falkner, and Elizabeth Raby. As seen through the eyes of the other major characters in *Falkner*, Alithea is acutely sensitive and sympathizes instinctively with the feelings of others.[8] She is humble and self-effacing. She lives silently within the limitations imposed by a tyrannical husband (1:293); she never shows a ruffled temper or an angry mood (2:182). Alithea is, of course, spotlessly pure. Although a woman of "tremblingly alive" sensibilities, she is guided "by excellent principles, and a truth never shadowed by a cloud" (1:288). Above all, Alithea is distinguished by her ability to sacrifice herself in the service of others. Alithea comforts Falkner when he runs away from school as a youth (2:196–98). Later, while married to Sir Boyville Neville, Alithea ministers to the needs of the rural folk who live around his country seat (1:295). Most significant, Alithea sacrifices first her happiness and then her very life to the care of her child. When Falkner returns from a long stay in India to find Alithea unhappily married to Boyville Neville, Falkner begs Alithea to run away with him. She refuses, saying that "we do not live to be happy, but to perform our duties" (2:243). And as Alithea sees it, her foremost and most cherished duty lies in protecting and caring for her son, Gerard. When Falkner kidnaps Alithea, she screams in agony at being separated from her child; later, Alithea runs away from Falkner and tries to cross a swollen river to find her way back to the boy. She drowns in the course of her escape attempt, with her dead body becoming a striking symbol of maternal sacrifice.

Since Alithea incarnates all the traditional feminine virtues, and in particular the virtue of domestic self-sacrifice, Mary Shelley describes her in the language the culture assigns to female selflessness: the language of religious veneration. All the characters, and especially the males closest to her, refer to Alithea in divine terms. To her son, Alithea is an "angel mother" (1:271) who makes the domestic circle into a "Paradise" (1:272). To Rupert Falkner, Alithea possesses an "angelic essence" highlighted by "the angelic softness of [her] disposition" (2:204–5). It is Falkner, Alithea's "murderer," who sums up the response to Alithea shared by all the characters in the novel: "[O]ne glance at the only daughter of Mrs. Rivers, served to disclose that an angel dwelt in the paradise" (2:181).

If Mary Shelley celebrates Alithea Neville as the perfect emblem of womanly, maternal behavior, she apparently celebrates Elizabeth Raby, the heroine of *Falkner*, as the perfect daughter. As Elizabeth Raby grows up, she develops into a character who not only embodies all the virtues of conventional feminine behavior but who, like Godwin's Catherine Deloraine, puts those virtues to work in the service of a beloved father figure. Like Catherine Deloraine, Elizabeth Raby is amiable and innocent; like Catherine Deloraine, Elizabeth is accomplished yet domestic. Most important, like Catherine Deloraine, Elizabeth behaves toward her father with habits marked chiefly by submission and silence. Elizabeth swears at an early age to obey her father and never to set her will above his (1:198); late in the novel, she describes herself as "his servant," dedicated to the "sacred duty" of protecting his interests (3:97–98). As a child, Elizabeth refuses to complain about the rigors of their vagabond life together (1:100). Later, when Falkner ignores her pleas and goes to fight in the Greek war for independence, Elizabeth weeps mutely (1:178). When Elizabeth's father forbids her to mention Alithea's son, Gerard, in whom she has begun to develop an interest, Elizabeth "mentally resolved never to mention the name of Neville again" (1:226). She thereafter becomes "accustomed . . . to preserve silence on a subject deeply interesting to her" (1:260). Elizabeth Raby comes to embody the daughter who consistently does her father's bidding while silencing her own voice. As the narrator approvingly sums it up, Elizabeth's father's "slightest wish was with her a law, and she submitted without a murmur." (1:225)

But Elizabeth Raby is perhaps most like Godwin's Catherine Deloraine in the particular type of strength she possesses: her ability to support and console her father and to sacrifice her own inclinations in the process. For all Elizabeth's submission and delicacy, she exhibits remarkable stamina in fulfilling what she sees as the sacred calling of her life: caring for her adopted father. Elizabeth begins to support Falkner at a tender age. Grateful that Falkner has rescued her from an uncaring guardian, Elizabeth repays him even as a small child by smoothing his temper and cheering his spirits. As the narrator puts it, "[C]hanging places, even at that early age, she soothed his impatience, while he was beguiled of his irritability by her cheerful voice and smiling face" (1:95). As Elizabeth grows older, she devotes herself to her father's care and consolation in more concrete ways. When she is sixteen, Elizabeth again consecrates herself "to the task, first of saving [Falkner's] life, if it should be in danger; and, secondly, of reconciling him in the end to prolonged existence (1:167–68). When Falkner is wounded in battle in Greece, Elizabeth rescues Falkner from a squalid Greek village, nurses him back to health, and spends many hours at his bedside cajoling him into better spirits. Near the end of the novel, Falkner is imprisoned in Carlisle, to await trial for Alithea's murder. Recognizing that "to preserve her faithful attachment to him amidst dire adversity, was her sacred duty" (3:99), Elizabeth joins Falkner in jail to tend his health and banish his depression.

Of course, such unremitting devotion to her father's needs demands continual sacrifice. Elizabeth learned early in life, from her mother, that "there is nothing so beautiful and praiseworthy as the sacrifice of life to the good and happiness of one beloved" (1:166). Accordingly, Elizabeth's daughterly behavior is marked by the renunciation of her own desires to Falkner's. As Elizabeth and Falkner roam the European continent, she suffers cold, fear, and hunger. Later, Elizabeth ruptures her relation to one companion after another to remain by Falkner's side. She leaves behind a favorite governess so she can follow Falkner unfettered; she forsakes her Raby relatives, who threaten to disown her if she associates with Falkner after his indictment for murder (3:95–98). Most significant, Elizabeth willingly severs her attachment to Gerard Neville, whom she has come to love, rather

than be parted from Falkner in his distress (3:61–65). In her unremitting
determination to renounce her own needs for the sake of her father's, Elizabeth Raby is clearly a daughter cast from the same mold as Godwin's
Catherine Deloraine. Just as it is possible that Shelley provided Godwin
with the broad outlines of a plot for his last volume of *Deloraine,* so it is
highly likely that Mary Shelley, in turn, had Godwin's portrait of the perfect
father-daughter relationship specifically in mind as she wrote *Falkner.* In
both novels, devoted daughters follow their beloved fathers into a difficult
and protracted European exile, for the express purpose of caring for and
consoling them; in both novels, the daughters create a supportive and intimate home for their fathers wherever they temporarily settle. At the climax
of both novels, the daughters are instrumental in preserving their fathers
from unjust legal proceedings—Catherine Deloraine by persuading Travers
to quit pursuing Deloraine, and Elizabeth Raby by declaring her resolve to
locate Osborne in America and bring him back to England to testify on
Falkner's behalf. Finally, both novels end with what is apparently an emotionally satisfying conclusion for each author: an arrangement whereby the
daughter marries a younger man, but remains by her father's side forever, in
a complex emotional triangle that elevates the daughter's virtue and self-
sacrifice.

When Mary Shelley portrayed Elizabeth Raby as a paragon of filial
duty, eager to support and care for her father in every conceivable fashion,
she clearly endorsed many aspects of Elizabeth's behavior. Part of Shelley's
novelistic purpose in writing *Falkner* was, as she specifically stated, to depict
and celebrate the virtues of feminine fidelity. On one level, Mary Shelley
viewed Elizabeth's sacrifices and self-abnegation on behalf of her father as
positive and ennobling. The narrator of *Falkner,* after all, praises Elizabeth's
behavior without irony and consistently describes her in elevated terms such
as the following:

> Elizabeth . . . had something holy and solemn kneaded into the very
> elements of her mind, that gave sublimity to her thoughts, resignation to
> her disposition, and a stirring inquiring spirit to her conversation. (1:240–
> 41)

> To behold this young and lovely girl wandering by the lonely shore, her
> thoughts her only companions; love for her benefactor her only passion,
> no touch of earth and its sordid woes about her, it was as if a new Eve,
> watched over by angels, had been placed in the desecrated land, and the
> very ground she trod grew into paradise. (1:173)

Falkner is clearly a paean to the "divine fire" (2:73) of devoted daughterly behavior and a fond evocation of the transcendent beauties of father-daughter relationships. In many respects, Shelley uses her last novel to vindicate her own choices and sacrifices on behalf of William Godwin in his last days.

But to say all this is to tell only half the story imbedded in the pages of *Falkner. Falkner* is, like *Frankenstein, Mathilda,* and *Lodore,* a deeply ambivalent and subversive work. *Falkner* clearly elevates the conventional daughterly virtues of submission and self-sacrifice to a father's needs; it just as clearly undercuts the system of power relationships that produces those values. *Falkner* is clearly a celebration of feminine fidelity; it is just as clearly an exploration of the subversive powers of that same fidelity. As Shelley wrote *Falkner,* she created a daughter who silenced her own voice to do her father's bidding, but she simultaneously gave voice in other ways to a characteristic range of her own daughterly discontents.

Falkner ostensibly presents itself as a sustained tale of the sacred tie between parent and child—especially between a father and his daughter—and the many enduring joys derived from that tie. But, on close inspection, quite another story emerges. If we scrutinize the web of family relations that Mary Shelley creates as a background for the action of *Falkner,* we find that all the major characters in the novel are orphans, literally or emotionally, and all the fathers are tyrants. The family history of the titular character serves as a paradigm. Rupert Falkner's mother dies when he is four years old; Falkner's father beats the boy and drinks himself to death, dying just as Rupert enters adolescence (2:166–73). Rupert is taken into the home of a paternal uncle, but the loss of his mother and the assaults of his father have already shaped his character: he regards himself as a "monster" (2:157) who, neglected as a child, never succeeded in governing his passions.

Gerard Neville is similarly orphaned of a mother and then mistreated by a despotic father. Alithea Neville disappears when Gerard is seven (1:299–301). When Sir Boyville Neville cannot force Gerard to do his bidding, he imprisons him in a barricaded room until Gerard promises to cooperate (2:53–54). The "memory of intolerable tyranny" makes Gerard feel "friendless; still orphaned in his affections" (2:55). The women in *Falkner* fare little better in their relations with their parents. Alithea Rivers Neville loses her mother as she is leaving adolescence (2:202–7); her father, a "rude tyrant" (2:210), prevents her from marrying her beloved Rupert Falkner (2:209–12). Elizabeth Raby loses both parents when she is only four (1:9); as we shall see, her relationship to her adopted father, Falkner, is often marked by

his selfishly dominating behavior. This pattern of absent mothers and tyrannical fathers even extends to the minor characters who populate the
background of *Falkner*. We learn, for example, that Elizabeth's biological
father, Edwin Raby, lost his mother at an early age (2:107). His father,
Oswi Raby, disowns his son for making a bad marriage and then abandons
his son's tiny child—Elizabeth—rather than encumber his fortune with
another dependent (2:108).

This prevalence of absent mothers in *Falkner*—and in all of Mary
Shelley's fiction except *Lodore*—certainly reflects Mary Shelley's personal
sense of the deprivations of growing up without a mother. But what is more
significant for our purposes is the way that *Falkner* portrays what happens
to children, and especially girls, after their mothers disappear. In Shelley's
fictional world, sons are beaten into submission to paternal authority in a
literal manner; daughters are coerced into doing the father's bidding in less
physical but equally forceful ways. These difficult and often brutal relationships between children and their fathers make a stark backdrop for the
action of a novel whose ostensible subject is the sacred delight of the father-
daughter tie.

Shelley's portrayal of Rupert Falkner as a father is revealing in several
other ways. Rupert Falkner is in many respects an attractive and compelling
fatherly presence. He is energized by Byronic vitality;[9] his passionate love
for Alithea Neville is drawn in larger-than-life proportions. Once Falkner
decides to adopt the orphaned Elizabeth, his devotion to her is preternaturally intense. Falkner watches over Elizabeth with passionate solicitude; his
love for his adopted daughter becomes the emotional center of his life.

Yet Rupert Falkner is far from the perfect paternal figure, and Shelley
uses his flaws to criticize the failings of the figure of the father. For all his
attractiveness, Shelley makes it clear that Falkner is an outlaw. He is "restless, and even fierce," with a face full of "passionate and unquiet thoughts"
(1:37–38). He kidnaps Alithea Neville and indirectly causes her death.
When he "adopts" Elizabeth Raby, Shelley describes his decision as essentially a second kidnapping, since Falkner decides to do "rather what he
wished, than what was strictly just" (1:78). Later in the novel, when Falkner
is beset by remorse over the miserable conditions in which Gerard Neville
lives—a misery for which Falkner is responsible, having caused the death of
Gerard's mother—Falkner decides to expiate his guilt by fighting in the
Greek war of independence. But, as Shelley emphasizes, Falkner's decision
to fight in Greece is more masochistic, willful, and self-centered than con-
trite: it imposes a terrible hardship upon Elizabeth, who refuses to let Falkner

abandon her and instead accompanies him to the Balkan Peninsula. Falkner's behavior makes it clear that paternal figures freely impose their will upon those who love them; Shelley's narrator comments upon the impact of this imposition of paternal will repeatedly. As the narrator puts it in a typical passage, Elizabeth shudders

> to think of the scene of desolation and suffering in which she felt that she should soon be called upon to take a part. There was no hope or help, and she must early learn the woman's first and hardest lesson, to bear in silence the advance of an evil, which might be avoided, but for the unconquerable will of another. Almost she could have called her father cruel. (1:177–78)

From Mary Shelley's perspective, the father's behavior is indeed "cruel." He possesses the power to exert his "unconquerable will"; he does so without scruple. As Shelley's narrator makes clear, the father's "unconquerable will" teaches his daughter—and by extension every woman—her "first and hardest lesson": that she is powerless to oppose him, and that she must "bear in silence" whatever evils are brought about by the dominating will of powerful male figures.

Shelley uses her depiction of Rupert Falkner to portray and criticize a second paternal inclination: the tendency of the father to use his daughter to meet his own often unacknowledged emotional needs. As we have seen, Lord Lodore molded his daughter, Ethel, into his image of the perfect wife; this "sexual education" resulted in a woman who was conventionally submissive, silent, and entirely dependent upon her father. Like Lodore, Falkner decides to make Elizabeth Raby into the image of a lost lover. Like Lodore, Falkner also insures the success of his venture by isolating his daughter from society and other influences, in a foreign country. Lodore takes Ethel to the wilds of the American frontier; Falkner travels with Elizabeth in the opposite direction, reaching as far as Moscow and Odessa. For each father, the sexual education of his daughter is both a species of control and a way of satisfying his own unmet emotional requirements. In the case of Falkner,

> To arrive unwelcomed at an inn—to wander through unknown streets and cities, without any stimulus of interest or curiosity—to traverse vast tracts of country, useless to others, a burthen to himself—alone, this would have been intolerable. But Elizabeth was the cure; she was the animating soul of his project: her smiles—her caresses—the knowledge that he benefited her, was the life-blood of his design. He indulged with a sort of rapture in the feeling, that he loved, and was beloved by an angel

of innocence, who grew, each day, into a creature endowed with intelligence, sympathies, hopes, fears, and affections—all individually her own, and yet all modelled by him—centred in him—to whom he was necessary—who would be his: not like the vain love of his youth, only in imagination, but in every thought and sensation, to the end of time (1: 89–90).

In this passage, Mary Shelley captures some of the hidden motivation that shapes the way fathers treat their daughters. When Falkner ventures to educate Elizabeth into womanhood, he wants to control and possess the malleable clay of a young woman. This wish is evident in the language Falkner uses to describe his hopes to himself: Falkner wants Elizabeth to be "modelled by him—centred in him"; he must be absolutely "necessary" to her; Elizabeth "would *be* his" (italics mine). Further, as this passage makes clear, Falkner adopts Elizabeth for essentially self-serving reasons: if he attaches her fate to his, Elizabeth can be the "cure" for his loneliness and emotional desolation. It warms Falkner to have "the knowledge that he benefited her"; but the weight of the passage rests on Falkner's analysis of the way that adopting Elizabeth will soothe his own emotional devastation.

Significantly, the closing words of this passage focus on one of the currents of the father-daughter relationship central to the meaning of *Falkner*: the intense sexuality of the father-daughter tie. As we shall see, much of the latent power of *Falkner* derives from the way Shelley reveals and explores the hidden dynamics of father-daughter relationships; the most important of these patterns resides in the incestuous nature of the mutual affection of father and daughter. As Falkner puts it to himself in this passage, he yearns for his adopted daughter to succeed and replace his lover, Alithea Neville; he wants Elizabeth to be his, "not like the vain love of his youth, only in imagination, but in every thought and sensation, to the end of time." A few pages later in the novel, Falkner contemplates the delights of his life with Elizabeth in similarly sexual terms. Their life together makes Falkner feel "a half remorse at the too great pleasure he derived from her society" (1:101–2). When he is separated from Elizabeth, Falkner thinks "how passionately he loved her" (2:124). He receives a packet of letters from Elizabeth which, like a lover, he kisses fervently, all the while feeling his heart "bursting" within him (2:125, 2:131). Shelley repeatedly describes Falkner's feelings for Elizabeth in language replete with sexual overtones: Falkner is "ardent" (1:97; 3:127); he experiences "eager longings" (3:128) for his daughter; his feelings for her "tremble," "burst," and "swell" (2:130; 3:275). Elizabeth herself frequently refers to Falkner as "my more than father" (1:152, 1:180;

3:113); and the narrator pointedly notes that Falkner's feelings for Elizabeth are "not paternal" (3:127).

Many of the visual images that Mary Shelley uses to evoke the love of Falkner and Elizabeth are equally sexual in their implication. For example, while Falkner and Elizabeth discuss his plan to fight in Greece, he sits her on his lap and, "clasping her to his heart, he showered kisses on her head and neck" (1:155). Later, after Falkner is wounded in battle, Elizabeth rests on a pillow next to him, while his bony fingers play with the ringlets of her hair (1:193). Toward the end of the novel, the night before Falkner faces trial for Alithea's murder, he has a suggestive dream that, paralleling Victor Frankenstein's dream in *Frankenstein*, highlights the incestuous currents of his love for Elizabeth. Earlier that day, Elizabeth had insisted she would live with Falkner after his trial, regardless of its outcome. Elizabeth had asserted she could not "be to you what [Alithea] was," but had gone on "playfully" to remind Falkner that "We are not parent and child" (3:246–47). In Falkner's dream, the climactic moments of his connection to Elizabeth and his connection to Alithea merge; a "fair lingering shape" beckons to him to join her in life; Falkner wakens and cannot tell if the beckoning shape belongs to his lover, Alithea, or his daughter, Elizabeth (3:252–53).

If Rupert Falkner's feelings for his daughter are charged with sexual overtones, Elizabeth's feelings for her father are equally tinged with sexual implication. For example, when Falkner wants to leave Elizabeth to fight in Greece, she insists on following him because it is her daughterly duty. But she has a second and equally compelling reason. As she puts it, she does not want to be abandoned like a sailor's wife:

> Am I to be left, like a poor sailor's wife—to get a shocking, black-sealed letter, to tell me that, while I was enjoying myself, and hoping that you had long been———? It is wicked to speak of these things. (1:158)

As this passage suggests, Elizabeth sees herself as more than her father's daughter: she also plays the role of his wife. Elizabeth's language for her devotion to her father is repeatedly characterized by the same sexual overtones. Elizabeth tells Falkner that "you have made me yours for ever" (1:199); when Elizabeth reflects on her feelings for Falkner, she realizes she is "bound to him by stronger than filial ties" (1:166). The narrator's descriptions of Elizabeth's response to Falkner are similarly replete with sexual suggestion. Just after the narrator notes that Falkner feels "a half remorse at the too great pleasure" he derives from Elizabeth, she goes on to describe the way Elizabeth reciprocates: "[H]ers was a sort of rapturous, thrilling adoration, that dreamt not of the necessity of a check, and luxuriated in its boundless excess" (1:102). Later, when Elizabeth is reunited with Falkner after a long absence, the narrator remarks that Elizabeth "saw him, she flew to his arms, she dissolved in tears, and became all woman in her tender fears" (3:139–40). As Shelley makes clear, Elizabeth is filled with "an ardent desire" (1:172) for Falkner; Elizabeth's love for her father is "her only passion" (1:173). Accordingly, Shelley continually describes Elizabeth's response to Falkner in language that involves "throbbing" (1:204), "trembling" (3:139; 3:275), "swelling" (1:125), and "bursting" (3:250).

The sexual suggestiveness of the language Shelley uses to portray the tie between Elizabeth Raby and her adopted father is heightened by one fundamental fact: Rupert Falkner is not really Elizabeth's father at all. All the language just examined is sexually suggestive when we think of Falkner and Elizabeth as father and daughter; it becomes even more sexually charged when we remember that Falkner and Elizabeth are not related to each other biologically. The same may be said of the various plot situations into which Shelley casts Falkner and Elizabeth. For example, we have seen the sexual innuendo latent in Elizabeth's decision to follow Falkner to Greece, thereby avoiding the fate of the "sailor's wife." But the sexual tension of this situation is intensified when readers remind themselves that Falkner and Elizabeth are in fact not father and daughter at all, so that Elizabeth follows a man to whom she is entirely unrelated by birth or any other recognized social tie. This tension does not arise when Elizabeth is a small child, since there is little sexual tension generated by a situation in which a single man decides to protect and raise a small girl as she passes through the asexual period of childhood. But as Elizabeth reaches adolescence and beyond, the ambiguities of her peculiar position increase. The innocence of their relationship is predicated only on what Elizabeth repeatedly calls their sense of "fidelity" and "duty" to each other (3:245–47).

The unlawful nature of the mutual attachment between Falkner and Elizabeth becomes most clear in the last volume of the novel. In fact, much of the action of the novel's third volume explores the sexual ambiguities of their relation and behavior, along with the complications posed by Elizabeth's competing tie to Gerard Neville. As the third volume of *Falkner* opens, Gerard's father sees to it that Falkner is jailed for the murder of Alithea Neville; Falkner must remain in prison until the next assizes and until various witnesses can be located. Simultaneously, all the major characters learn that Elizabeth is not Falkner's actual daughter, but a girl he has raised without the benefit of a legitimate social tie (3:82–85). When Elizabeth discovers that Falkner has been jailed in Carlisle, she vows to join and live with him there. All the characters are horrified by what they see as Elizabeth's social transgression—even her license—in maintaining such an intimate tie to a man to whom she is not related by birth. Her aunt, Mrs. Raby, and Gerard Neville's sister, Lady Cecil, beg Elizabeth to abandon her plan; they criticize the "foolish romance of her notions" (3:98) and point out that staying in jail with Falkner would be improper even if Elizabeth were his actual daughter. Since she is not Falkner's real daughter, her idea is utter "madness" (3:95); Mrs. Raby later half thinks to herself that Elizabeth's tie to Falkner is "wild and dangerous" (3:270). Gerard Neville is equally repelled by Elizabeth's plan and argues the same point:

> Were you his daughter, my heart would not rebel—blood calls to blood, and a child's duty is paramount. But you are no child of his; you spring from another race—honour, affection, prosperity await you in your proper sphere. What have you to do with that unhappy man? (3:111–12)

Even Elizabeth acknowledges the latent lawlessness of her intimacy with Falkner and the extent to which her affection for him is a social transgression. She fears that, in rebelling against "such submission to society," she "sought a bold and dangerous freedom" (3:99). Later, she characterizes herself to Gerard Neville as a "savage" for her unwillingness to give up her tie to Falkner: "I suppose indeed that I am something of a savage," Elizabeth says, "unable to bend to the laws of civilization. I did not know this—I thought I was much like other girls" (3:112–13).

In the context of this concurrence over the unlawfulness of Elizabeth's relationship to Falkner, several of the major scenes that make up the closing volume of the novel become even more charged with sexual innuendo and ambiguity. As Falkner sits in prison, he dreams of Elizabeth, "his sweet household companion, his familiar friend, his patient nurse" (3:127-28). As the narrator puts it, "His passions were ardent, and . . . were centred in his adopted child" (3:127); he "long[s]" for her "inexpressibly" (3:131). As Elizabeth hurries to Falkner's cell after his indictment has been announced, "her heart beat as if it would burst her bosom" (3:138); she trembles and loses all self-command as she enters his cell, where she becomes "all woman" as she dissolves in his arms (3:139). Falkner asks Elizabeth if she can still "cling" to him; she answers him in the accents of a lover, murmuring to him that he is "Dearer, more beloved than ever!" (3:140). Then Elizabeth and Falkner spend several months together in prison, engaged in the mundane intimacies of a loving couple, just like the young lovers Ethel and Edward in *Lodore*. Elizabeth sews while Falkner reads aloud; their hearth glows cheerfully, despite the bars that checker the sunlight on the cell's floor. As the narrator observes, in language more appropriate to describing mates than a father and his daughter, or an older man and a young woman unrelated to him:

> In this position, they each grew unutterably dear to the other—every moment, every thought, was full to both of the image of either. . . it is a sweet blessing when our household companion charms our senses by the loveliness of her person, and makes the eye gladly turn to her, to be gratified by such a form and look. (3:146)

Later, after Falkner has been acquitted, he returns to the room where Elizabeth waits for him:

> Falkner entered—she flew to his arms, and he pressed her to his bosom, wrapping her in a fond, long embrace, while neither uttered a word. A few moments of trembling almost to agony, a few agitated tears, and the natural gladness of the hour assumed its genuine aspect. . . . Falkner and his beloved companion were left alone, and for a few short hours enjoyed a satisfaction so perfect that angels might have envied them. (3:275–77)

These kinds of scenes, with their sexually charged language, are significant in a number of ways. Shelley is clearly exploring the sexual ambiguities of Elizabeth Raby's relationship to Rupert Falkner. Her sexually charged language draws some of its power from the fact that, in the relation between Elizabeth and Falkner, so many roles overlap. Falkner is Elizabeth's father, yet he is not her father; he is her protector, yet he is her ardent lover. Elizabeth, for her part, is Falkner's daughter, yet most emphatically not his daughter. The signs of affection between Elizabeth and Falkner—the caresses, the kisses, the longings, the tremblings, swellings and burstings—are always subliminally sexual. Since Falkner both is and is not Elizabeth's father, this sexuality is always illicit. When the reader conceives of Elizabeth Raby as the actual daughter of Falkner, the sexuality of their relationship is disquieting because Shelley has focused and described what is typically unrecognized and repressed: that fathers and daughters desire each other physically. And when the reader remembers that Elizabeth is completely unrelated to Falkner, the texture of their mutual desire shifts: their mutual sexual attraction seems more potent and capable of fulfillment, since it is not restrained by cultural taboos against incest.

Part of the peculiar power of *Falkner*, then, derives from its submerged sexuality, with its exploration of the incestuous currents of the father-daughter relationship. On this score, *Falkner* may be compared to Shelley's much earlier novel *Mathilda*. *Falkner* is, in fact, the most sexually driven of all Shelley's novels except *Mathilda;* upon rereading it, the reader is struck by the sheer pervasiveness of the sexually suggestive language Shelley uses to connect Falkner to Elizabeth. In this context, it is little wonder that Shelley employs a resonant pattern of imagery to describe the link between the father and his adopted daughter. Falkner is habitually cast as Satan, the ruined tempter; Elizabeth is compared to Eve, the archetypal daughter turned temptress (3:16, 65, 115 and others; 1:173, and others).[10]

But if *Falkner* is one of the most sexual of Shelley's novels, it is also the most sentimental. "Sentimentality"—that is, Shelley's apparent obsession with praising Elizabeth's virtuous daughterliness in excessive and elevated language—is just the charge that has condemned *Falkner* with critics and spoiled the novel for modern readers.[11] But the sentimentality of *Falkner* can be read as a deliberate artistic strategy. As Lynda Zwinger notes, the appeal of the sentimental has always been its "erotic coloration":[12] that is, the ability of sentimentality simultaneously to express and conceal sexual desire. In the case of *Falkner*, Shelley's sentimentality conceals or deflects the reader's attention away from the novel's submerged sexuality. Shelley's narrative reflections about the ideal and elevated nature of Elizabeth Raby's daughterhood often occur immediately after Shelley has used sexually suggestive language to describe the connection between Falkner and Elizabeth. For example, just after Shelley has described the way in which Elizabeth's "fond heart swelled with rapture" at the thought of Falkner, she describes Elizabeth's motivation using language of a decidedly different—and elevated—cast: Elizabeth is happy and innocent, she says, and has stepped "pure and free into life, innocent as an angel—animated only by the most disinterested feelings" (1:125).[13] The effect, of course, is to obscure the suggestive sexuality Shelley has embedded in the language describing Elizabeth's feelings for Falkner. Thus, the sentimentality of *Falkner*, especially in its ringing evocations of the perfect purity of Elizabeth's daughterly behavior, can often be read as a deliberate defensive strategy designed to screen the shocking admission of the father and daughter's mutual desire. In this context, the sentimentality of *Falkner* becomes more than an expression of what Mary Poovey calls the "excessive and compensatory fidelity" of the daughter who feels powerful hostility toward her father.[14] The sentimentality of *Falkner* is also analogous to the "automatic writing" to which the narrator of *Mathilda* resorts. It is in this context that we can best understand Shelley's odd and ambiguous description of Elizabeth as "the type . . . of ideal and almost unnatural perfection" (1:165). Elizabeth's saintliness and sentimental devotion to Falkner are, quite precisely, "unnatural": they are a way of hiding the inevitable—and utterly natural—sexual energies that inform all relationships between daughters and their fathers.

When Mary Shelley wrote *Falkner*, she completed her exploration of an idea that first surfaced in *Frankenstein*, was addressed most overtly in *Mathilda*, and appeared in some form in nearly every one of her other published novels: that parents and their children are incestuously attached to each other. Shelley's handling of the incest theme in her last novel allowed her to accomplish several purposes. Artistically, the incest theme allowed Shelley to produce a novel that was subliminally titillating to its audience. Beneath the surface of daughterly rectitude and high moral devotion, Shelley sketched a father-daughter relationship fraught with mutual sexual passion. Further, Shelley's depiction of Rupert Falkner, like her portrayals of the insistently devoted fathers in *Mathilda* and *Lodore*, allowed her to express her sense of the power conferred upon the father by his passionate and controlling attachment to his daughter. Most important, the incest theme gave Shelley a vehicle for coming to terms with the full ramifications of her feelings for her own father after his death.

Parallel to Shelley's exploration of father-daughter incest in *Falkner* lies a second portrayal of the way women relate to men: as mothers. The issue of motherhood is crucial to *Falkner*; as in *Lodore*, motherhood is the female role Shelley elevates above all others. The character who initially most embodies the contradictions and consolations of maternity is, of course, Alithea Neville. Alithea comes by her maternal personality naturally. As she tells Falkner, her mother brought her up to a higher purpose than pleasing a man: "She brought me up to fulfil my duties, to be a mother in my turn. I do not deny . . . that I share in some sort my mother's fate, and am more maternal than wife-like" (2:249). Accordingly, all Alithea's actions are motivated by her strict fidelity to her children, especially her son, Gerard. Alithea at first refuses to see Falkner when he returns after many years to find her. When she realizes Falkner hints at elopement, she draws back horrified and says, "Never, dear Rupert, speak thus to me again, or we must again part—I have a son" (2:246). After Falkner kidnaps Alithea, she awakens from a faint and murmurs Gerard's name (2:270). Later, she runs away from Falkner to return to her son, drowning in the escape attempt with her son's name on her lips (2:293). In short, all Alithea's behavior is driven by the conviction she asserts so emphatically to Falkner: "A mother is, in my eyes, a more sacred name than wife" (2:251).

Shelley displays her concurrence with this view by placing the fidelity of mothers to their children at the very heart of the plot of *Falkner*. Gerard's quest to clear his mother's name is motivated by his belief that Alithea would not have abandoned her son willingly. Alithea's faithfulness to Gerard is the virtue that turns Rupert Falkner from a passionate fiend into a grieving man who tries to make restitution for his crime of desire (2:264–72). And Elizabeth Raby's behavior is shaped indelibly by Alithea's fidelity to her son. The first time Elizabeth hears Alithea's story, she is convinced that Alithea would never have left her child willingly:

> She believed, that in a nature as finely formed as hers was described to have been, maternal love, and love for such a child as Gerard, must have risen paramount to every other feeling. . . . Perhaps Mrs. Neville had loved—though, even that seemed strange—but her devoted affection to her child must have been more powerful. (2:63)

Later in the novel, after Elizabeth reads Falkner's version of the kidnapping and imagines the moment of Alithea's death, her identification with Alithea becomes complete. She vows to model herself after Alithea and reconsecrates herself to the womanly virtue of fidelity. It is precisely this reverence for feminine fidelity that motivates Elizabeth to trespass against social codes and remain at Falkner's side.

Thus the author of *Falkner*, with all the novel's major characters, agrees heartily with Gerard Neville's assertion that "the divine stamp on woman is her maternal character" (3:57). Shelley also sees motherhood as the most natural of female roles. Her characters often assert that maternal fidelity is a natural feminine instinct. And, as she did in *Lodore*, Shelley sets scenes symbolic of maternal sacrifice in consonant natural settings. For example, after a long description of the verdancy of the Cornwall countryside, the action of *Falkner* opens with the orphaned Elizabeth playing at her mother's grave—a scene that not only recalls Mary Shelley's own habit of visiting Mary Wollstonecraft's grave but that also associates Elizabeth's dead mother with the fertility of nature. Later, Shelley sets the novel's climactic moment of maternal sacrifice—Alithea's death by drowning—while the natural elements rage (2:275ff.)

Shelley's text also makes clear that, as in *Lodore*, motherhood can answer female desires left unsatisfied by conventional marital arrangements. Shelley shows how Alithea devotes herself to motherhood as a replacement for the joys of a good marriage. When Alithea's marriage to Sir Boyville Neville sours, she loses herself in devotion to her child (1:296–300). When Rupert Falkner begs Alithea to elope with him, she refuses because she would rather "devote my existence to my children than to be that most blessed creature, a happy wife" (2:251). Shelley's attitude toward this displacement of affection away from husbands and onto children is entirely positive. For Alithea Neville, as for Cornelia Fitzhenry, maternity provides an alternative to emotional dependence on and subservience to a demanding male.

Clearly, then, Shelley uses the pages of *Falkner* to portray the powerful tie between a mother and her child as one legitimate form of feminine creativity and fulfillment. Less obviously but just as forcefully, Shelley uses her depiction of motherhood in *Falkner* to explore the father-daughter relationship. It is at this point that Shelley's treatment of maternity intersects with her treatment of father-daughter incest; it is also at this point that the peculiar potency of motherhood becomes clear. As we shall see, Shelley uses *Falkner* to show how the daughter's maternal nature gives her intermittent power over her father. In this respect, *Falkner* inverts the power relationships portrayed in *Deloraine*. Elizabeth Raby punishes her father for his misdeeds, while Catherine Deloraine cannot. And, significantly, much of Elizabeth's ability to punish Falkner is lodged specifically in the maternal power she wields over him.

The power of maternity—and specifically the way in which a daughter's maternal nature gives her an equivocal power over her father—becomes most clear in Shelley's portrayal of Elizabeth Raby. As the novel progresses, Elizabeth identifies more and more with Alithea. In a scene close to the center of the novel, Elizabeth finishes reading Falkner's account of the day he kidnapped Alithea. Falkner tells the story, of course, from his point of view. In the next chapter, Elizabeth imagines the climax of the same tale—Alithea's death—from Alithea's point of view. This episode constitutes the only spot in the novel where the reader sees directly into Alithea's consciousness; significantly, the reader knows Alithea directly only at the moment of her death and only through the imaginative intervention of a daughter. As Elizabeth imagines Alithea's feelings, her identification with Alithea becomes complete. Elizabeth's fantasy slips from the past into the present tense (2:291–93); as soon as Alithea sinks under the waves, thinking of her son, this passage occurs:

> But she is innocent. The last word murmured in her last sleep—the last word human ears heard her utter, was her son's name. To the last she was

all mother; her heart filled with that deep yearning, which a young mother feels to be the very essence of her life, for the presence of her child. There is something so beautiful in a young mother's feelings. Usually a creature to be fostered and protected—taught to look to another for aid and safety; yet a woman is the undaunted guardian of her little child. She will expose herself to a thousand dangers to shield his fragile being from harm. . . . The world is a hideous desert when she is threatened to be deprived of him; and when he is near, and she takes him to the shelter of her bosom, and wraps him in her soft, warm embrace, she cares for nothing beyond that circle; and his smiles and infantine caresses are the life of her life. (2:293–94)

Mary Poovey has remarked upon the division of imaginative sympathy in this passage and the pages immediately preceding it—that Elizabeth begins by identifying with the dead mother, but, as the passage progresses, shifts her identification to the child. For Poovey, this shift suggests "the extent to which the narrative consciousness . . . longs for entry into just such a domain of maternal love."[15] One cannot argue with Poovey's observation that the latter half of this passage expresses a longing to be a child wrapped in the bliss of the maternal embrace. This passage is crucial precisely because it suggests more: it also evokes the multiple perspectives implicit in the way women experience mothering.

As Nancy Chodorow explains it, the heart of the maternal experience lies in the mother's simultaneous imaginative identification with the experiences of both her own mother and her child. Drawing on the work of Melanie Klein, Chodorow observes:

Klein discusses the dynamics of maternal regression and the identifications and interactions it entails. She speaks of the mother's multiple identifications and the variety of internal object-relationships which go into her mothering. A mother identifies with her own mother (or with the mother she wishes she had) and tries to provide nurturant care for the child. At the same time, she reexperiences herself as a cared-for child, thus sharing with her child the possession of a good mother.[16]

As Chodorow sees it, this simultaneous dual identification—with the experience of the mother and the experience of the mothered child—lies at the crux of the way that motherhood is "reproduced" in Western culture. This dual identification is precisely what Elizabeth Raby experiences in the passage above. Elizabeth first imagines the "deep yearning" the young mother feels for her child; this feeling blends imperceptibly into an identification with the child's hunger for his mother's "soft, warm embrace." By identifying simultaneously with the experience of Alithea Neville's child and Alithea Neville herself—who, after all, was the surrogate mother designated for Elizabeth by her actual mother—Elizabeth, in effect, experiences the feelings of a mother for the first time. She identifies with the multiple perspectives that women feel as they mother. Essentially, Elizabeth makes herself into a mother. And, as we shall see, Elizabeth soon assumes a maternal stance toward someone Alithea has mothered, but who otherwise seems an unlikely candidate for maternal affection from Elizabeth herself: her father, Rupert Falkner.

This passage serves as an emotional crux in *Falkner,* then, because it marks a critical transition in Elizabeth's development as a woman. Through her complex identification with Alithea, Elizabeth becomes capable of mothering. This passage is also significant because in it Shelley focuses on a disjunction inherent in maternal experience: the fact that women are seen as the weaker sex, in need of male protection, yet are simultaneously regarded as mythically powerful—as the natural caretakers of those least able to care for themselves.

The whole episode in which Elizabeth imagines Alithea's story is, finally, simply odd. It occurs as a strange disruption at the center of a long story about a father and his daughter. And, for all the importance of the idea of motherhood to the meaning of *Falkner,* Alithea Neville's story, as seen from her point of view, takes up very little space at the novel's heart. It is only a few pages long; it is framed by Falkner's account of the kidnapping on one side and Elizabeth's letter to Gerard Neville, in which she reaffirms her fidelity to her father, on the other (2:298). The story of the dead mother, indeed, lies submerged at the heart of *Falkner* just as the story of the lost mother lies hidden at the heart of *Frankenstein,* Wollstonecraft's *Wrongs of Woman,* and other significant texts dealing with female development. Late in his career, Freud discovered the girl's pre-oedipal attachment to her mother lying behind her intense attachment to her father and all her other attachments, in the manner "of the Minoan-Mycenean civilization behind the civilization of Greece."[17] Similarly, Sandra Gilbert, studying several texts dealing with fathers and daughters as narratives of female development, finds that the story of the dead mother is imbedded, nearly hidden, at their center. The same point may be made about the relationship of Alithea Neville's story to the rest of the novel: it lies buried at the work's emotional center.[18] Alithea's story is simultaneously enabling and cautionary, since it prepares Elizabeth to relate to her father in a newly powerful way, yet warns her of the mother's deadly fate. Shelley's *Falkner*, in fact, bears two other revealing resemblances to Gilbert's paradigmatic texts of female development, George Eliot's *Silas Marner* and Edith Wharton's *Summer*. In all three works, the plot revolves around the relation of an adoptive father to his adopted daughter, with the father redeemed at story's end by the girl's love; in all three works, the daughter ends up with the father through the agency of a brother figure, in an incestuously charged situation. But the resolution of *Falkner* does not necessarily suggest the daughter's total "acquiescence" to the father, as Gilbert suggests is the case with *Silas Marner* and *Summer*.[19] Instead, in the way *Falkner* punishes the father and explores the power of the mother, it may be read as an evocation of the daughter's final, if equivocal, ascendancy over her father. Seen from this perspective, Shelley's last novel becomes not only a telling revision of *Deloraine*, William Godwin's last novel, but also a map that traces the daughter's escape from the father's domination.

In the first two As Mary Poovey has shown, *Falkner* not only expresses the daughter's hostility toward her father, but allows the daughter to punish the father for his many misdeeds.[20] Elizabeth's repeated insistence on saving Falkner's life may be read as a form of veiled aggression. When Elizabeth pushes Falkner's gun away from his temple early in the story, she saves his life, but forces him into an agonized existence where he struggles unsuccessfully to escape the consequences of his guilt. Similarly, when Elizabeth rescues Falkner from death in a Greek village, she not only prolongs his misery, but she immediately takes him aboard an English ship where they meet Gerard Neville, so that Falkner once again confronts the horror of his guilty secret. Most important, Elizabeth continually encourages Gerard Neville in his quest to find Alithea's kidnapper and clear his mother's name. Thus, in the first two volumes of *Falkner*, Elizabeth acts in the name of the mother by inexorably, if unwittingly, shaping the events that force Falkner to confess his guilt and face the son of the woman he killed.

In the closing volume of *Falkner*, Elizabeth's utter fidelity to her father, which expresses itself as a maternal desire to support and comfort him, punishes him as surely as her earlier expressions of veiled hostility. Shelley inverts the structure of the father-daughter relationship by portraying Elizabeth's daughterly fidelity to Falkner as a form of maternal affection. As we have seen, this pattern first became apparent in the opening two volumes of the novel. During her childhood and adolescent years, Elizabeth cared for and consoled Falkner throughout their wanderings, often acting with a maturity that belied her years. But at the beginning of the third volume of

Falkner, with Elizabeth now a mature young woman and having specifically reclaimed the role of the lost mother through her identification with Alithea Neville, Shelley makes Elizabeth conscious of the maternal nature of her feelings for her father:

> She loved Falkner . . . yet she intimately felt the difference that existed between her deep-rooted attachment for him she named and looked on as her father, and the spring of playful, happy, absorbing emotions that animated her intercourse with Neville. To the one she dedicated her life and services; she watched him as a mother may a child; a smile or cheerful tone of voice were warmth and gladness to her anxious bosom, and she wept over his misfortunes with the truest grief. But there was more of the genuine attachment of mind for mind in her sentiment for Neville (3:62).

As the remainder of *Falkner* unfolds, Elizabeth continues to watch over Falkner "as a mother may a child," and she specifically dedicates "her life and services" to Falkner's care. Knowing that she can "be all in all of happiness and comfort to him" (3:93), Elizabeth stays by his side in jail, and after the jury acquits Falkner of Alithea's murder, Elizabeth's maternal fidelity makes her refuse to leave Falkner, though he begs her to.

When Elizabeth remains staunchly by her father's side throughout the last volume of *Falkner,* she is doing exactly what William Godwin's perfect daughter did for her father in *Deloraine:* supporting and consoling him. By taking up her father's care, Elizabeth is also living up to traditional expectations for daughterly behavior: in the absence of a wife, the support and consolation of the father conventionally fall to an unmarried daughter. But there is a difference. Shelley makes Elizabeth acutely aware of the maternal character of her behavior toward her father. By doing so, Shelley allows Elizabeth to subordinate and infantilize Falkner, something Godwin never permitted Catherine to do in *Deloraine.* Since Elizabeth is conscious of the maternal nature of her tie to Falkner, she can also be aware of the extent to which she prefers "the genuine attachment of mind for mind in her sentiment for Neville." That is, Elizabeth can entertain the notion of a relationship to a man who does not require mothering, a relationship that can meet her needs more completely, thereby potentially supplanting her tie to her father.

By highlighting the maternalism of Elizabeth's tie to Falkner, Shelley illustrates, as she did in *Mathilda,* the pervasiveness of the social pattern in which fathers rely on their daughters for the comforts of maternal support and consolation. And, as in *Mathilda,* the daughter's maternalism suggests what modern commentators have recently described as a psychoanalytic truth. We have discussed, both in Godwin's expectations for Mary Shelley's support and in Mathilda's maternal behavior toward her father, Boose's analysis of the father's "seduction" of his daughter—that is, that the father's seduction of his daughter is embedded within his attempt to reconstruct his lost tie to the pre-oedipal mother. The same point may be made about *Falkner:* in it, father-daughter incest and the maternal behavior of the daughter intersect in the same way they do in Shelley's life, in *Mathilda,* and in *Oedipus at Colonus.* Falkner's relationship to Elizabeth is sexually charged because it repeats his relationship to Alithea Neville and, lying prior to that, his relationship to the pre-oedipal mother. Conversely, whenever Elizabeth behaves in a maternal way toward Falkner, her acts of motherly support and consolation inspire Falkner to experience emotions tinged with sexual energy.

Shelley's portrayal of the growth of Falkner's affection for Alithea Neville lends support to this psychoanalytic interpretation. As she did in the case of Mathilda's father and his wife, Diana, Shelley emphasizes the way that Falkner's love for Alithea develops out of his love for the central mother figure in his life. Falkner loses his mother at the age of four. As an adolescent, he is befriended by Alithea's mother, Mrs. Rivers, who was a close friend of Falkner's actual mother and who takes her place as a surrogate, supplying Falkner with all the maternal affection for which he has yearned. Shelley's language stresses that Falkner sees Mrs. Rivers as the crucial mother figure in his life and that her supportive presence becomes essential to him. As Falkner puts it, the sound of his name on Mrs. Rivers's lips "breathed of a dear home, and my mother's kiss" (2:177). Falkner is thrilled that Mrs. Rivers calls him her son (2:185); sharing her "maternal tenderness" with Alithea becomes Falkner's chief joy (2:189). In a description prescient of psychoanalytic discourse, Shelley portrays the way that, when Mrs. Rivers dies, Falkner transfers the weight of his childlike feelings for her onto his beloved. Falkner has always loved Alithea; but after her mother's death, his affection for his companion and lover becomes weighted with and colored by his emotions for her mother, the surrogate mother Falkner has just lost. As Falkner puts it:

> [Alithea] had sprung into womanhood. . . . Before I loved—now I revered her—her mother's angelic essence seemed united to hers, forming two in one. The sentiments these beings had divided, were now concentrated in her; and added to this, a breathless adoration, a heart's devotion. (2:205–66)

Falkner had seen Alithea as a lover and Mrs. Rivers as his mother, but, on Mrs. Rivers's death, "the sentiments these beings had divided, were now concentrated in [Alithea]." In short, Falkner's intense attachment to the mother transforms itself and lives on as a passionate, childlike devotion to Alithea Neville. Falkner continues to view himself as Alithea's "protector" (2:189), but he yearns even more fundamentally for Alithea to wrap him in a consoling maternal embrace. Thus, when Falkner is separated from Alithea, the sight of a woman and her baby thrills him into simultaneous identification with both the mother's lover and her infant: it makes his soul dissolve "in tender fancies of domestic union and bliss with Alithea" (2:220). And, as we have seen, this quasi-maternal tie to Alithea resurfaces in Falkner's relationship to Elizabeth, both when Falkner feels sexual longing for Elizabeth and when he encourages Elizabeth to support and console him, which she does in the manner of a mother watching jealously over her child. In its careful portrayal of the centrality of motherhood—and in particular the way the father's desire to retrieve his tie to the long-lost mother re-expresses itself first in his relation to a lover and finally in his relationship to his daughter—*Falkner* anticipates the speculations of contemporary feminist psychoanalysis in a remarkable manner.

Whenever a father impels his daughter to play the role of his mother, of course, he runs a risk—the danger of reversion to infantility and, with it, the loss of power. As Boose has suggested, this risk is implicit in Lear's decision to make his daughter his mother and "to set my rest / On [Cordelia's] kind nursery" (*King Lear* 1.1.123–24). When Lear chooses to rely on his daughters for comfort in his old age, he symbolically divides his kingdom and hands his power over to them. In this context, "the lurking presence of the father's infantility is a truth so bitter that Lear threatens to whip the Fool for speaking it."[21] A similar point may be made about the father in *Falkner*. When Falkner craves emotional support and consolation from Elizabeth, and drives her to play a maternal role in caring for him, she meets his every desire, and she infantilizes and gains power over him in the process. Shelley is careful to reveal the extent to which Elizabeth's maternal behavior toward Falkner both exerts power over him and punishes him. It is in this sense that Elizabeth's obsessive fidelity to Falkner becomes a weapon in the hands of the daughter. She uses its maternal aspects to control and subordinate the father, and, in doing so, to humiliate him.

In the third volume of *Falkner*, after Elizabeth has become conscious of the maternal nature of her feelings for her father, her unremitting fidelity to him does, indeed, infantilize and subordinate him. Shelley chooses her language carefully to highlight the power Elizabeth has gained over Falkner. For example, when Elizabeth defies all social codes to join her father in prison and take care of him there, her feeling is one of triumph: "[H]er eyes glistened with a feeling at once triumphant and tender, while reflecting on the comfort she was bringing to her unfortunate benefactor" (3:102–3). Elizabeth no doubt feels some sense of triumph at the idea of transcending social conventions, but her "triumphant and tender" feelings derive more specifically in this sentence from the thought of supporting and comforting a helpless father. Similarly, Elizabeth's attempts to care for her father by clearing his name serve to humiliate him. Elizabeth learns that a man named Osborne can be a decisive witness in her father's favor; she vows to save Falkner by traveling to America to locate Osborne, but Gerard Neville insists on going in Elizabeth's stead. When Falkner learns of the scheme, the necessity of relying upon Elizabeth and Gerard disturbs Falkner deeply: "[H]e felt humiliated by the very generosity that filled him with admiration" (3:193). As the novel draws to a close, Falkner continues to experience humiliation (3:215), mortification (3:226), and ignominy (3:260), all of which ultimately derive from the maternal fidelity that motivates Elizabeth to assist Falkner in clearing his name so that he can be released from jail.

In these specific ways, Shelley's *Falkner* differs from her father's *Deloraine*. Both novels portray and celebrate the daughter who displays her strength by sacrificing all other inclinations to care for, console, and support her father. But Godwin never permits the daughter to humiliate or gain power over the father. Shelley's portrayal of Elizabeth's strength in watching over Falkner, and all that strength's subversive aspects, may also be read as a direct repudiation of what Godwin has to say about feminine weakness in *Deloraine*. In the first volume of the novel, Deloraine makes this speech to his wife:

> Man is the substantive thing in the terrestrial creation: woman is but the adjective, that cannot stand by itself. A sweet thing she is; I grant it: no one has a greater right to say this than I have. But she is a frail flower; she wants a shelter, a protector, a pioneer. . . . Sometimes she is in intellect the rival of her father, her husband, or her brother; sometimes, but rarely, she outstrips him—to remind us, if I may so express it, what the Creator could have done, if that had been reconcileable to the great plan of the whole. (1:70–71)

It is ironic, of course, that Godwin would place this rumination about women's inherent weaknesses in a novel whose last volume focuses on the strength a daughter ought to display in supporting and caring for her father.

Shelley's portrayal of Elizabeth's maternal strength effectively reverses the terms of Godwin's description. When Elizabeth mothers and supports Falkner, the male becomes the "adjective" that "cannot stand by itself," while the daughter becomes "a shelter, a protector, a pioneer."

In the last volume of *Falkner*, Shelley even rewrites the plot of Godwin's *Deloraine* to allow the daughter's maternal behavior toward the father to subordinate and punish him. In *Deloraine*, as we have seen, the daughter's incessant care for her father not only supports him in his exile, but thoroughly preserves his public reputation. When Catherine Deloraine intercedes with Travers, the avenger who strives to bring Deloraine to trial for William's murder, Travers is "melted" by Catherine's filial devotion and gives up his pursuit entirely. Thus, the daughter's agitation for justice averts the public spectacle of a trial; she saves her father from public humiliation and allows him to preserve his reputation intact. Something very different happens in *Falkner*. As we have seen, Elizabeth continually encourages Gerard to seek out his mother's killer and clear Alithea's name. Thus, as Elizabeth strives for justice she inexorably—if unwittingly—becomes an active participant in the events that land her father in jail. Far from averting her father's public humiliation in a court of law, Elizabeth provokes it. Thus, though both Godwin and Shelley tell a tale in which the daughter acts as the agency through which justice is achieved, the consequences for the father are very different. In Godwin's version of this exemplary tale, the daughter's quest for justice preserves both her father's life and his public reputation. But in Shelley's rewriting of her father's story, the daughter's pursuit of justice forces the father into public admission of his guilt and into public remorse for his crimes of passion.

The closing pages of *Falkner* also constitute a telling revision of Godwin's *Deloraine*. As we have seen, each novel ends in a triangular relationship that seems to satisfy the emotional needs of its author. The daughter weds a character who is more brother than husband to her, and the daughter, her father, and her husband live out their lives together in an isolated country setting. In Godwin's version of the perfect resolution to a father's relation to his daughter, the father is at the emotional center of the triangle. Further, the triangular relationship is achieved easily and naturally; it spontaneously appeals to all three characters, so that no single figure is pulled into the triangle unwillingly.

Shelley's version of the closing triangle in *Falkner* has a very different emotional resonance.[22] Most obviously, the figure at the center of Shelley's triangle is the daughter rather than the father. Far from seeing the father figure as his primary attachment, as in *Deloraine*, the son-in-law in *Falkner* has counted the father as his chief enemy and must overcome serious misgivings about the acceptability of living with his mother's murderer. It is attachment to Elizabeth that draws both men together, and the novel ends with the daughter enjoying the love and adoration of two very different male figures. Further, unlike the father in *Deloraine*, the father in *Falkner* is initially humiliated by the triangular relationship and must eradicate his defining pride before he can enter into the triangle. As Shelley tells us, Elizabeth has long disapproved of "the present state of [Falkner's] mind; there was too much of pride" (2:303). When Neville agrees to enter the triangular relationship and live with Falkner "despite the world's censure" (3:304), Falkner at first feels debased by the arrangement. "Falkner's heart swelled within him as he read. He could not but admire Neville's candour . . . but pride was stronger than regret, and prompted an instant and decisive reply" (3:304): Falkner's emphatic refusal. Falkner refuses to live with Elizabeth if she marries Neville; he says he prefers to travel alone on the Continent. Elizabeth, for her part, is firmly set on keeping her father by her. Falkner eventually proposes that he and Neville trick Elizabeth into being separated from Falkner. But Gerard will have none of this ruse. He arrives at Falkner's house and insists that Elizabeth must take control of all their fates.

As this account suggests, Shelley revises the details of Godwin's plot to tell a different story about the resolution of the father-daughter relationship. In Shelley's version, the daughter humbles the father. Elizabeth has always disapproved of Falkner's excessive pride; it is exactly this paternal pride that the daughter mortifies when she insists that father, daughter, and son-in-law live together. Falkner's pride rebels at the triangular relationship because he deplores the social disapproval Neville must overcome to live with him—a social disapproval directed at Falkner for his responsibility in Gerard's mother's death. But Falkner's pride is mortified by the triangular relationship for a more fundamental reason, too. Neville has been Falkner's enemy and his competitor for Elizabeth's affections throughout the entire novel. Now that Elizabeth clearly yearns for "the genuine attachment of mind for mind in her sentiment for Neville," Falkner would rather lose himself on the European continent than watch a younger man displace him in Elizabeth's life. By insisting that Falkner remain with her, and that their relationship be expanded to include a new husband who was Falkner's former antagonist, Elizabeth punishes the father both by stripping him of his power as head of the family and by forcing him to recognize the centrality of a younger man in the daughter's life.

In a very real sense, then, Elizabeth controls her father's fate at the close of *Falkner*. By insisting on a triangular relationship that is initially distasteful to the father, Elizabeth displays a power over her father that Catherine in *Deloraine* does not possess. As Gerard Neville puts it, speaking of the daughter in *Falkner*, "[S]he alone can decide for us all, and teach us the right path to take"—a statement that reverses the dynamics of power, control, and emotional attachment with which William Godwin charges the triangular relationship that ends *Deloraine*. It is significant, in fact, that Gerard Neville is the male character who displaces Falkner and who effectively hands control of events over to Elizabeth. For when Elizabeth marries Neville, she gets a man who refuses to replicate the dynamics of Elizabeth's relationship to her father. Neville refuses to participate in Falkner's ruse to deprive Elizabeth of control over her future. He also refuses when Falkner insists, in a letter, that Neville "must be father as well as husband" to Elizabeth, that Neville "must compensate to my dear child for my loss" (3:305). Specifically, Gerard Neville refuses to exert any species of paternal authority over Elizabeth, preferring to let her direct events. Shelley has carefully prepared the reader for Neville's behavior. For one thing, Shelley has consistently described Neville's relation to Elizabeth as that of a brother to a sister, so that Neville has always related to Elizabeth more as an equal than as a representative of the prerogatives of male authority (1:216-217; 1:231; 3:117). Further, Shelley has even been careful to highlight the feminine aspects of Neville's personality, portraying him as a man who combines the best qualities of the male and female. Neville possesses an "almost feminine delicacy of attention, joined to all a man's activity and readiness to do the thing that was necessary to be done" (1:217). Elsewhere, Shelley notes that Neville is "full of sentiment, and poetry—kind and tender as a woman— resolute and independent as a man" (2:100; see also 1:214). In short, at the end of *Falkner*, Gerard Neville appears to be a husband very much like Horatio Saville in *Lodore:* a gentle, almost womanly husband who does not care to assert fatherly authority over his wife. Neville serves the same function for Elizabeth as Saville does for Cornelia: both unconventional husbands allow their wives to escape the power alignments of traditional marriage, where husbands exercise paternal control over wives.

Yet, for all her exploration of the power inherent in the act of mothering, Shelley remains acutely aware of the restrictions of the maternal role. In the final analysis, Shelley's attitude toward mothering in *Falkner* is as ambiguous as it was in *Lodore*. Shelley's ambivalence surfaces most clearly in some of the settings and images she uses to frame Elizabeth's accession to maternal power over her father. As we have seen, one of these moments occurs in the last volume of the novel, when Elizabeth, having subordinated Falkner by devoting herself to his support and care, enters his cell in Carlisle feeling "triumphant" over him. Yet the setting in which this act of subordination takes place is symbolically significant. The daughter, after all, locks herself up in prison when she dedicates herself to nurturing her father's spirits and prospects. The ambiguities of this prison scene are directly analogous to the ambiguities of the tomb scene in *Lodore*. In both cases, a woman devotes herself to maternal fidelity, thereby redeeming herself and laying claim to the power latent in maternity. But in both scenes, the woman simultaneously walls herself up—in *Falkner* through deliberate self-imprisonment, and in *Lodore* through symbolic self-entombment. Motherhood, it would seem, is a feminine role with decidedly confining implications.

It is thus entirely appropriate that Mary Shelley casts Elizabeth as Antigone, the daughter eventually walled up for her rebellion against a tyrannical father figure. Shelley draws her pattern of imagery not only from the final play of the Oedipus cycle, in which Antigone is immured for disobeying Creon, but also from *Oedipus at Colonus*, in which Antigone, the favorite daughter, sacrifices her life to care for her guilty father. The structure of the relationship between Elizabeth and Falkner repeats the structure of the relationship between Antigone and Oedipus; Elizabeth, like Antigone, sacrifices her life to wander with her tormented father in foreign exile, devoting herself to his support and consolation. Both father-daughter relationships are fraught with suggestions of incest—in *Oedipus at Colonus* because Oedipus's daughter is also his sister, and in *Falkner* because an undercurrent of sexual desire charges the relationship between the father and the daughter. Falkner, whom Shelley associates with the Eumenides (2:301), even describes his relationship to Elizabeth in language that recalls Oedipus's blindness and suffering, and the way Antigone shares it. He says to Elizabeth:

> Have I preserved you, dearest? . . . In making you mine, and linking you to my blighted fortunes, I may have prepared unnumbered ills for you. Oh, how sad a riddle is life! . . . now would I were sitting among the nameless crowd on the common roadside, instead of wandering blindly in this dark desolation; and you—I have brought you with me into the wilderness of error and suffering. (1:198)

As Lynda Boose has pointed out, it is finally the daughter's "sacrificial maternalism" that buries her alive in the two plays that conclude the Oedipus cycle: "[W]hat entombs the daughter's future is not so much the original sin of the mother and son that preexisted her but the regression back to it that the daughter and father have played out."[23] The same may be said of the father and daughter, and the murderous nature of maternity, in *Falkner*. Described from the daughter's point of view, the maternal role she plays toward her father has a dark underside. Though maternalism gives the daughter power over her father, a power Shelley invokes and celebrates, the daughter's power over her father is, ultimately, intermittent and equivocal. Given the confines of the patriarchal society in which it operates, the daughter's maternal power is limited to the confines of domestic space. As in *Lodore*, the maternal power portrayed in *Falkner* is a form of voluntary renunciation. As such, the self-sacrifice of the daughter has a markedly ambiguous force. It empowers Elizabeth—and it simultaneously entombs Elizabeth as surely as it entombed Antigone.[24]

Falkner may be read as the literary culmination of Mary Shelley's response to the complicated demands William Godwin made on his favorite daughter. In its intertwining themes of incest and motherhood, Shelley used *Falkner* to explore the full range of her feelings for her father and to excavate the psychological dynamics underpinning his need for her maternal support and consolation. In its radical rewriting of *Deloraine*, Shelley used *Falkner* to assert a temporary ascendancy over her father and to punish all fathers for their many misdeeds against the person of the daughter. In *Falkner*, as in *Lodore*, the figure of the daughter temporarily triumphs over the father's desire and domination. The father's "hideous progeny" assumes a devoted mien—and in the act of doing so both controls and transcends him.

Conclusion

Falkner was Mary Shelley's last major work of fiction. She wrote several short stories during and just after its composition: "The Parvenue" (1836); "The Pilgrims" (1837); and "Euphrasia: A Tale of Greece" (1838). Shelley produced short biographies for Lardner's *Cabinet Cyclopaedia* from 1835 to 1839: the lives of Petrarch, Boccaccio, Madame de Sévigné, Madame Roland, and a host of others. She published *Rambles in Germany and Italy in 1840, 1842, and 1843,* a travel book recounting her European tours with Percy Florence and his friends. Most important, Shelley edited Percy Bysshe's poetry and prose, a monumental endeavor that established her reputation as a literary editor. Shelley also struggled to write—but shelved as too emotionally draining—biographies of both her father and her husband. But from 1837, when she was forty, until her death in 1851 at age fifty-three, Mary Shelley wrote no more novels. Indeed, from 1841 until 1844, she wrote nothing at all. Dispirited by loss and loneliness, wracked by blistering headaches that attacked her whenever she took up a pen, Shelley gave up the craft upon which she had relied for a lifetime, and that, as she had put it in times past, "was sufficient to quell my wretchedness temporarily" (MWS *Journals*, 2:442).[1]

Although Mary Shelley suddenly stopped writing fiction at age forty, she left behind her an impressive roster of novels, works that are important for what they tell us about the daughter's destiny in patriarchal society and about the way one woman came to terms with that destiny. From *Frankenstein* to *Falkner*, Shelley's fiction explores the tensions inherent in the daughter's ambiguous position in the family romance and expresses the daughter's resentment at the disappointing lot the father finally bequeaths her. In exploring the intersecting themes of incest and maternity, Shelley's first two novels portray the daughter as doomed by the father's guilty attraction to her, condemned to view herself as sinful and filthy, and fated to die as her father's devoted and resentful lover, rather than escaping their mutual desire's grasp over her. Shelley's last two novels deploy the themes of incest and maternity to a different effect: while charting the incestuous currents latent in the father/daughter relationship and thus suggesting the power the father exerts over his daughter, *Lodore* and *Falkner* also chart the daughter's movement beyond the father's orbit, into the liberating but equivocal power of motherhood. The figure of the monstrous daughter virtually disappears from Shelley's late work, having been subsumed and transformed into the figure of the protective and punishing daughter.

In embracing the equivocal power latent in the maternal role, Mary Shelley certainly proves herself to be a feminist, as well as her mother's daughter. All of Mary Wollstonecraft's works, from *Thoughts on the Education of Daughters*, through *A Vindication of the Rights of Woman*, to *The Wrongs of Woman*, place the mother as the controlling power at the family's moral center, but simultaneously depict the way society disempowers the mother in all other respects. While Shelley's feminism is different from her mother's—among other things, Shelley refuses to embody her cultural criticism in discursive analysis, insisting that she feels uncomfortable with her "argumentative powers" (MWS *Journals*, 2:554)—Mary Shelley, like Mary Wollstonecraft, consistently portrays and criticizes male domination, the sexual education of daughters, and the monstrous effects of the social disenfranchisement of a single sex.[2]

In the final analysis, Mary Shelley's feminism, including many of the obsessive themes that characterize her fiction, also derives largely from her father's influence in both its positive and negative incarnations. Godwin trained his daughter to write, taught her to anticipate the rewards of literary sonship, and then both withdrew his affection and insisted that she behave like a dutiful daughter. In response, Mary Shelley became a cultural critic who rebelled against paternal authority. She used her fiction to depict and explore the daughter's baffled disappointment, suppressed anger, and passionate attachment to the father who both shaped and shunned her. Eventually, Shelley was able to use her fiction to tell the story of the daughter's escape from the realm of her father's power and desire. Her fictions, in fact, constitute the very tools through which she mapped that escape. By imagining heroines who learn to subvert the father's domination and who make themselves into figures who dominate the father, Shelley both reflected and scripted the story of her own movement beyond the sphere of William Godwin's influence.

After William Godwin died, Mary Shelley abandoned the craft of fiction entirely. From the time Sir Timothy Shelley died in 1844, Shelley had no need to support herself with writing at all. Shelley certainly had numerous practical reasons for turning away from fiction: the time had come to produce a complete edition of Percy Shelley's works, since several pirated editions had already appeared; her writing for Lardner was steady work; her travel books allowed her to pay tribute to her affection for Italy. But one suspects more fundamental forces at work, too. Perhaps, with William Godwin dead, Shelley lost her obsession with the father-daughter relationship that drives so much of her fiction. Perhaps, with her father physically gone, Shelley no longer had access to her old recurrent themes of daughterly passion and paternal desire, no longer felt the need to reenact the dynamics of her struggle with her father on paper. Perhaps, having moved beyond the ghost of her father's influence in her life and in her last novels, Shelley no longer felt compelled to use her fiction to articulate her present and shape her future. But whatever Shelley's reasons for giving up fiction after her father's death, one thing is clear: with William Godwin gone, his daughter no longer needed to remake the face of her father's "hideous progeny" every time she picked up a pen.

Notes

Introduction

1. To date, the only other extended study of William Godwin and Mary Shelley is Katherine Richardson Powers's *Influence of William Godwin on the Novels of Mary Shelley* (New York: Arno Press, 1980). While Powers's analysis makes many interesting connections between Mary Shelley's ideas and those of William Godwin, it does not sufficiently take into account the psychological dynamics of the father-daughter relationship. Other short studies of Mary Shelley and William Godwin are Gay Clifford, "*Caleb Williams* and *Frankenstein:* First-Person Narrative and 'Things As They Are,'" *Genre* 10 (1977): 601–17; A. D. Harvey, "*Frankenstein* and *Caleb Williams,*" *Keats-Shelley Journal* 29 (1980): 21–27; U. C. Knoepflmacher, "Thoughts on the Aggression of Daughters," in *The Endurance of Frankenstein*, ed. George Levine and U. C. Knoepflmacher (Berkeley: University of California Press, 1979), 88–119; Marilyn May, "Publish and Perish: William Godwin, Mary Shelley, and the Public Appetite for Scandal," *Papers on Language and Literature: A Journal for Scholars and Critics* 26:4 (Fall 1990): 489–512; Burton Pollin, "Philosophical and Literary Sources of *Frankenstein,*" *Comparative Literature* 17 (1965): 97–108. While this book was in the final stages of preparation for publication, Pamela Clemit's *Godwinian Novel: The Rational Fictions of Godwin, Brockden Brown, Mary Shelley* (Oxford: Oxford University Press, 1993) appeared in print. My work was therefore not able to profit from Clemit's sharp insight into the "Godwinian novel," a genre she persuasively argues was adopted and reshaped by both Brockden Brown and Shelley.

2. Jean de Palacio's book was the exception, because it studies the broad range of Mary Shelley's life and work [Jean de Palacio, *Mary Shelley dans son oeuvre* (Paris: Klincksieck, 1969)]. Since I began this study, several books have focused more attention on Mary Shelley's other novels. The two best are Anne K. Mellor's *Mary Shelley: Her Life, Her Fiction, Her Monsters* (New York: Methuen, 1988) and Mary Poovey's *Proper Lady and the Woman Writer* (Chicago: University of Chicago Press, 1984). See also William Veeder's *Mary Shelley and Frankenstein: The Fate of Androgyny* (Chicago: University of Chicago Press, 1986).

3. Carolyn Heilbrun, afterword to *Daughters and Fathers*, ed. Lynda Boose and Betty Flowers (Baltimore: Johns Hopkins University Press, 1989), 419.

4. See, in particular, Jane Gallop, *The Daughter's Seduction: Feminism and Psychoanalysis* (Ithaca: Cornell University Press, 1982); Judith Lewis Herman, with Lisa Hirschman, *Father-Daughter Incest* (Cambridge: Harvard University Press, 1981). See also numerous essays in *Daughters and Fathers* and in Patricia Yaeger and Beth Kowalski-Wallace, *Refiguring the Father: New Feminist Readings of Patriarchy* (Carbondale and Edwardsville: Southern Illinois University Press, 1989).

5. This description sums up the traditional Freudian portrait of the boy's resolution of the oedipal complex. As Nancy Chodorow points out, the oedipal resolution is much more complicated—and perhaps never completely achieved—in the case of the girl (Nancy Chodorow, *The Reproduction of Mothering: Psychoanalysis and the Sociology of Gender* [Berkeley: University of California Press, 1978], 111–40).

6. Anne K. Mellor, *Mary Shelley: Her Life Her Fiction, Her Monsters* (New York: Methuen, 1988), 213–18; Kate Ellis, "Subversive Surfaces," in *The Other Mary Shelley*, ed. Audrey Fisch, Anne K. Mellor, and Esther H. Schor (New York: Oxford University Press, 1993).

7. Mellor's *Mary Shelley: Her Life, Her Fiction, Her Monsters* is particularly powerful in this respect.

Chapter 1. Mary Shelley and William Godwin

1. Mary Shelley to Francis Wright, 12 September 1827, *The Letters of Mary Wollstonecraft Shelley*, 3 vols., ed. Betty T. Bennett (Baltimore: Johns Hopkins University Press, 1980–88), 2:4. References to Shelley's letters are taken from this edition; subsequent citations will be noted parenthetically.

2. William Godwin to Mary Wollstonecraft, 5 June 1797, *William Godwin: His Friends and Contemporaries*, 2 vols., by C. Kegan Paul (London: Henry S. King, 1876), 1:249–50. Paul collects many of Godwin's letters and journal entries; subsequent citations of Paul's text will be indicated parenthetically. Godwin and Wollstonecraft both anticipated a son throughout her pregnancy, and planned to name him after his father. See also *Godwin and Mary: Letters of William Godwin and Mary Wollstonecraft*, ed. Ralph M. Wardle (Lincoln: University of Nebraska Press, 1966), 80, 82, 88, 92, 94, 102.

3. *Shelley and his Circle*, 8 vols., ed. Kenneth Neill Cameron (vols. 1–4) and Donald H. Reiman (vols. 5–8) (Cambridge: Harvard University Press, 1961–86), 1:186–87, plate 8.

4. Ibid., 1:200-201 n. 54.

5. Mary Shelley, *Valperga; or, The Life and Adventures of Castruccio, Prince of Lucca*, 3 vols. (London: G. and W. B. Whittaker, 1823), 1:199. Subsequent citations of *Valperga* will be indicated parenthetically.

6. As Don Locke, author of the most discriminating biography of Godwin available, points out, this anecdote cannot be traced to a reliable origin. See Don Locke, *A Fantasy of Reason* (London: Routledge & Kegan Paul, 1980), 205. But the story is too celebrated—and too likely—to be entirely discounted.

7. William Godwin, *An Enquiry Concerning Political Justice and Its Influence on Morals and Happiness*, 3 vols., ed. F. E. L. Priestley (Toronto: University of Toronto Press, 1946), 2:508.

8. Robert Southey, *The Life and Correspondence of Robert Southey*, 6 vols., ed. C. C. Southey (London: Longman, 1850), 2:268.

9. Charles Lamb, *The Letters of Charles and Mary Lamb*, 3 vols., ed. Edwin W. Marrs, Jr. (Ithaca: Cornell University Press, 1975), 2:70.

10. Ibid., 55.

11. James Marshall, quoted in Locke, *Fantasy of Reason*, 206. William St. Clair has located at least one contemporary writer who found Mary Jane Godwin to be "an elegant and accomplished woman" (242).

12. Mary Shelley, quoted in Paul, *William Godwin*, 1:298. Paul prints large sections of Mary Shelley's unfinished biography of her father. The manuscript draft of her biography is in the Abinger Collection at the Bodleian Library, Oxford.

13. Florence Marshall, *The Life and Letters of Mary Wollstonecraft Shelley*, 2 vols. (London: Bentley, 1889), 1:40.

14. Betty Bennett, introduction to her *Letters of Mary Wollstonecraft Shelley*, 1:xiv.

15. Mary Shelley, *The Journals of Mary Shelley*, 2 vols., ed. Paula R. Feldman and Diana Scott-Kilvert (Oxford: Oxford University Press, 1987), 2:554. Subsequent references to Shelley's *Journals* will be indicated parenthetically in the text.

16. See Paul, *William Godwin*, 2:108: "That Mary Shelley was afterwards a worthy intellectual companion to Shelley is in no degree due to Mrs. Godwin, and little to her father's direct teaching. All the education she had up to the time when she linked her fate with Shelley's was self-gained." Following in this line of analysis, Anne K. Mellor argues that Godwin recognized Mary's considerable intellectual potential, but "agreed with his wife that she required no formal education" (*Mary Shelley: Her Life, Her Fiction, Her Monsters, 8*). While it is true that Godwin did not send Mary to a school outside the home, as he did Charles and William, Jr., this fact does not mean that Mary Godwin was given no systematic education. As Emily Sunstein has persuasively argued, the schools available to girls at the time were not of the same caliber as schools available to boys (Emily W. Sunstein, *Mary Shelley: Romance and Reality* [Boston: Little, Brown, 1989], 40). Since he had set himself up as an author of educational books for children, Godwin thought he could himself educate his daughters better at home. Mary Godwin's systematic preparation for a career in letters is evident in her most famous novel, *Frankenstein*, begun when she was only eighteen. It is extremely unlikely that Mary could have gathered all the background necessary for this work under the sole tutelage of Percy Bysshe Shelley, as some critics have argued, since by the time she began *Frankenstein* in 1818, she had lived with Shelley only two years. Emily Sunstein also persuasively traces the original source of the judgment that Mary Godwin was given little systematic education in the Godwin home, locating its origins in the attitudes and comments of Lady Jane Shelley. Lady Jane hated the Clairmonts and, wishing to portray her mother-in-law as a Cinderella figure, insisted that Mary Godwin was relegated to drudgery at home, while Claire Clairmont was given all the material and educational advantages (Sunstein, *Mary Shelley*, 392).

17. See Mary Wollstonecraft, *A Vindication of the Rights of Woman*, ed. Carol H. Poston (New York: W. W. Norton, 1975), especially chapters 2, 3 and 12 (19–52; 157–78). See also Mary Wollstonecraft, *Thoughts on the Education of Daughters: With Reflections on Female Conduct in the More Important Duties of Life* (London: J. Johnson, 1787), 25–29; 48–56, passim. William St. Clair provides an excellent overview of the extent to which an emphasis on female "accomplishments" dominated women's education during the era of Wollstonecraft and Godwin (William St. Clair, *The Godwins and the Shelleys: A Biography of a Family* [Baltimore: Johns Hopkins University Press, 1989], 504–11). As St. Clair explains, female advice books of the period assumed that women were intellectually weaker than men, that women should hide any intelligence they found themselves burdened with, and that novels in particular were to be avoided, since novels inflamed the emotions and imagination to a dangerous degree. The whole weight of Wollstonecraft's educational theory, of course, opposes these assumptions. In this context, when Godwin set up the Juvenile Library, whose main purpose was to produce children's educational books, and when he wrote for it educational books emphasizing reason, imagination, literature and history for both girls and boys, Godwin departed radically from the mainstream of educational practice in his day.

18. Cameron, *Shelley and His Circle,* 3:102.

19. See St. Clair, *The Godwins and the Shelleys,* 279–82, for an excellent discussion of the extent to which Godwin's specific emphasis on the faculty of imagination in children's education departed from the norm.

20. William Godwin to Percy Shelley, 10 December 1812, *The Letters of Percy Bysshe Shelley,* 2 vols., ed. Frederick L. Jones (Oxford: Oxford University Press, 1964), 1:340 n. 3.

21. For his children's educational books, Godwin used the pseudonyms Edward Baldwin, Theophilus Marcliffe, and W. F. Mylius. These are the works he published in the Juvenile Library series under these names: *Fables, Ancient and Modern, Adapted for the Use of Children* (1805); *The Life of Lady Jane Grey, and of Lord Guildford Dudley, her Husband* (1806); *The History of England, For the Use of Schools and Young Persons* (1806); *The Pantheon; or, Ancient History of the Gods of Greece and Rome. Intended to Facilitate the Understanding of the Classical Authors, and of the Poets in General* (1806); *Scripture Histories, Given in the Words of the Original* (1806; lost); *The History of Rome: From the Building of the City to the Ruin of the Republic* (1809); *Mylius's School Dictionary of the English Language. To Which is Prefixed A New Guide to the English Tongue by Edward Baldwin* (1809); *The Junior Class-Book; or, Reading Lessons for Every Day in the Year* (1809); *Outlines of English Grammar, partly abridged from Hazlitt's New and Improved Grammar of the English Tongue* (1810); *The Poetical Class-Book; or, Reading Lessons for Every Day of the Year, Selected from the Most Popular English Poets, Ancient and Modern* (1810); *The First Book of Poetry. For the Use of Schools. Intended as Reading Lessons for the Younger Classes* (1811); *Lives of Edward and John Philips, Nephews and Pupils of Milton. Including Various Particulars of the Literary and Political History of their Times* (1815); *History of Greece: From the Earliest Records of that Country to the Time in Which it Was reduced into a Roman Province* (1821). Peter Marshall's bibliography in his *William Godwin* is an excellent source for Godwin's publications under the Juvenile Library imprint. See also St. Clair, *The Godwins and the Shelleys,* 283–87, for an excellent discussion of some of these volumes.

22. William Godwin [Edward Baldwin, pseud.], *The History of England. For the Use of Schools and Young Persons* (London: T. Hodgkins, 1806; rpt., London: M. J. Godwin, 1812), vi–vii.

23. Mellor gives the date of this incident as Sunday, 24 August 1806 (Mellor, *Mary Shelley,* 11). Sunstein's account of Mary Godwin's education is the most complete and concrete of those offered by the major biographies. Sunstein concludes that Mary also studied Latin with Godwin, learned some etymology, natural history, geometry, and geography, and had tutors for French, Italian, and art (*Mary Shelley: Romance and Reality,* 49–50).

24. Extract from unpublished letters to Trelawny. Appendix C in R. Glynn Grylls, *Claire Clairmont, Mother of Byron's Allegra* (London: John Murray, 1939), 274.

25. Claire Clairmont to Mrs. Thomas Jefferson Hogg, 1 February 1833, *Shelley and Mary,* 4 vols., ed. Lady Jane Shelley (privately printed, 1882), 1175. Also quoted by Grylls in *Claire Clairmont,* 193.

26. Mary Shelley, *Frankenstein; or, The Modern Prometheus: The 1818 Text,* ed. James Rieger (Chicago: University of Chicago Press, 1982), 222. Unless otherwise noted, subsequent references to *Frankenstein* will be taken from this edition, with page numbers indicated parenthetically.

27. Locke, *Fantasy of Reason,* 215.

28. Sunstein, *Mary Shelley: Romance and Reality,* 42; Mellor, *Mary Shelley,* 10.

29. WG to unknown correspondent, 2 January 1808, in *A Nursery Companion,* ed. Iona

Opie and Peter Opie (Oxford: Oxford University Press, 1980), 128. Iona and Peter Opie discovered that Mary Godwin was the author of *Mounseer Nongtongpaw,* and they quote from Godwin's letter in the course of their discussion.

30. Cameron, *Shelley and His Circle,* 3:76. As St. Clair tells us, Burr brought up his daughter Theodosia in accordance with Wollstonecraft's principles in *A Vindication of the Rights of Woman* (St. Clair, *The Godwins and the Shelleys,* 300).

31. Sunstein, *Mary Shelley: Romance and Reality,* 424 n. 29. In the Abinger papers, Sunstein also located what might be Mary Godwin's drafts for her brother's lecture entitled "The Influence of Governments on the Character of the People." See ibid., 424 n. 21.

32. Quoted in ibid., 36. This passage is from Mary Shelley's unfinished and unpublished biography of her father, in the Abinger papers.

33. Cameron, *Shelley and His Circle,* 3:101.

34. Nancy Chodorow, *The Reproduction of Mothering: Psychoanalysis and the Sociology of Gender* (Berkeley: University of California Press, 1978), 139.

35. Ibid., 195.

36. Lynda Boose, "The Father's House and the Daughter in It: Structures of Western Culture's Daughter-Father Relationship," in *Daughters and Fathers,* ed. Lynda Boose and Betty Flowers (Baltimore: Johns Hopkins University Press, 1989), 36.

37. Ibid., 35–36.

38. Margaret Hennig, *The Managerial Woman* (New York: Doubleday, 1977), 100.

39. Muriel Spark, *Mary Shelley: A Biography* (New York: E. P. Dutton, 1987), 14. Sunstein gives the most thorough account of Mary Godwin's arm ailment, noting that it involved a skin eruption for which pustules had to be lanced and poultices applied. The ailment first appeared on Mary's hand, but then spread to the entire arm, which had to be put in a sling. As Sunstein correctly notes, if the affected arm was Mary's right arm, the illness and its attendant remedy meant she couldn't write (*Mary Shelley: Romance and Reality,* 55–57). From this perspective, Mary's adolescent illness takes on interesting psychological dimensions: Did her physical condition come to symbolize the potential effect of her father's rejection—that is, the silencing of Mary's voice as a writer?

40. Cameron, *Shelley and His Circle,* 3:102.

41. Ibid., 101.

42. Percy Bysshe Shelley, quoted in Thomas Jefferson Hogg, *The Life of Percy Bysshe Shelley,* with an introduction by Edward Dowden (London: Routledge, 1906), 567.

43. Percy Bysshe Shelley, "Revolt of Islam," in *Shelley: Poetical Works,* ed. Thomas Hutchinson (London: Oxford University Press, 1970), 39–40.

44. MWS *Journals,* 2:554. See also her letter to Frances Wright of 12 September 1827, in which Mary says: "Her [Mary Wollstonecraft's] greatness of soul & my father [*sic*] high talents have perpetually reminded me that I ought to degenerate as little as I could from those from whom I derived my being. For several years with Mr Shelley I was blessed with the companionship of one, who fostered this ambition & inspired that of being worthy of him" (MWS *Letters,* 2:4).

45. MWS *Journal,* 2:467. Knoepflmacher remarks on one other way in which Mary Shelley may have seen a parallel between William Godwin and Percy Shelley. Each man "had been betrayed, Mary was willing to believe, into a marriage with one inferior and unsympathetic to his genius." Mary Shelley may have seen her relationship with Shelley as a way to revive or resurrect the short-lived union between her own parents. In marrying Percy Shelley, Mary could rescue him from her father's fate, thus symbolically undoing the damage

done by her own birth. U. C. Knoepflmacher, "Thoughts on the Aggression of Daughters," in *The Endurance of Frankenstein,* ed. George Levine and U. C. Knoepflmacher (Berkeley: University of California Press, 1979), 96.

46. William Godwin, *The Elopement of Percy Bysshe Shelley and Mary Wollstonecraft Godwin. As narrated by William Godwin.* (London: Privately printed, 1911), 10.

47. Spark, *Mary Shelley: A Biography,* 23. William St. Clair adopts the same view of Percy Shelley's personality and behavior.

48. Harriet Shelley to Catherine Nugent, 20 November 1814, *The Letters of Percy Bysshe Shelley,* 1:421 n. 2.

49. As William St. Clair points out, by August of 1814 the joke was circulating the London money markets that Godwin had sold his two daughters to Shelley, one for £800 and the other for £700 (St. Clair, *The Godwins and the Shelleys,* 363).

50. Godwin, *The Elopement,* 11.

51. Percy Shelley, quoting Godwin in PBS *Letters,* 2:109.

52. Godwin, *The Elopement,* 16.

53. Percy Shelley to Mary W. Shelley, 24 October 1814, PBS *Letters,* 1:408.

54. Fanny Imlay's letters in *Shelley and Mary* support this contention. On 29 July 1816, Fanny wrote to the Shelleys and apologized for not being able to mail more books and clothing to Mary, due to the fact that she was a dependent in every way, especially when it came to money. The letter also contains a long plea in which Fanny describes Godwin's desperate financial state and implies that Mary should intercede with Percy Shelley on Godwin's behalf for money. In this letter and in Fanny's letters to Mary of 26 September 1816 and 3 October 1816, it is clear that Fanny is acting as an intermediary, conveying Godwin's requests and worries about money, as well as her own anxieties about Godwin's health and spirits. The letters of 26 September and 3 October contain Fanny's long, anxious descriptions of Godwin's financial woes, depression, inability to write, and sense of being overburdened. On 9 October, Fanny committed suicide. See also William St. Clair's excellent discussion of Fanny's death (*The Godwins and the Shelleys,* 398–413). As St. Clair correctly notes, Fanny, like Mary Wollstonecraft, tended toward the extremes of depression. During the period just prior to her death, Fanny's Wollstonecraft aunts, Everina and Eliza, decided they could not invite her to teach at their school in Ireland, a job Fanny had always assumed would be open to her and would provide her with some vestige of financial independence. Everina and Eliza feared that Fanny's association with Claire, Mary, and Percy had damaged her reputation and would ruin their school's ability to attract respectable female students. As St. Clair puts it, when Percy took Claire along on his elopement with Mary to France, he "not only ruined Claire but . . . deprived Fanny of a future" (399).

55. William Godwin to Mary Shelley, 13 October 1816, in Lady Jane Shelley, *Shelley and Mary,* 148.

56. Locke, *Fantasy of Reason,* 275.

57. See William Godwin's letter to his brother of 21 Feb.1817, in which he announces the marriage (Paul, *William Godwin,* 2:246).

58. Mellor, *Mary Shelley,* 14.

59. Christy Baxter, quoted by Florence Marshall in *The Life and Letters of Mary Wollstonecraft Shelley,* 1:34.

60. Mellor quotes a letter in which Godwin describes Fanny's intense desire to remain at home rather than go on a family trip, so that she can tend to Godwin's domestic needs: "Fanny is quite ferocious & impassioned against the journey to Margate. Her motive is a

kind one. She says, This cook is very silly, but very willing; you cannot imagine how many things I have to do. She adds, Mamma talks of going to Ramsgate in the autumn: why cannot I go then?" (Mellor, *Mary Shelley*, 14).

61. Lady Jane Shelley, *Shelley and Mary*, 734

62. 12 May 1817, in ibid., 201 B.

63. For example, on 26 September 1817, Mary Shelley wrote to Percy Shelley: "By the bye talking of authorship do get a sketch of Godwin's plan from him—I do not think that I ought to get out of the habit of writing and I think that the thing he talked of would just suit me" (MWS *Letters*, 1:43). It is not clear precisely what project Godwin had suggested for Mary, but it would be her first project since submitting *Frankenstein* to the publisher in May of the same year.

64. Percy Shelley to William Godwin, 9 March 1817, PBS *Letters*, 1:536.

65. William Godwin to Percy Shelley, 15 April 1817, in Lady Jane Shelley, *Shelley and Mary*, 201A.

66. Don Locke gives a good account of the legal maneuverings over the Skinner Street property and Godwin's presence there. Godwin moved to 41 Skinner Street in 1807 and paid rent for two quarters. But the legal ownership of the house was unclear, and a lottery was established to determine it. The lucky ticket-holders were a pair of stockbrokers named Walsh and Nesbitt, but their partnership went bankrupt before the formalities were completed, and it then became entirely unclear to whom the house belonged. Godwin stopped paying rent, since it would have been foolhardy to give money to any of the contending parties, and, besides, Godwin simply did not have the money. In August 1817, Read finally established his ownership of the house. He began legal proceedings against Godwin, the first of which came before the courts in February 1819. Read sued Godwin for £2000 pounds in damages for unpaid rent and filed a second suit to evict Godwin from the premises. These suits dragged on for another three years; Godwin and his family were finally evicted from Skinner Street on 4 May 1822. Percy Shelley drowned shortly thereafter, on 8 July 1822. Godwin's court battles with Read over back rent and costs continued until March 1825, when Godwin was forced to declare himself bankrupt.

67. Newman Ivey White, *Shelley*, 2 vols. (New York: Alfred A. Knopf, 1947), 1:542.

68. William Godwin to Percy Shelley, 31 January 1818, PBS *Letters*, 1:597 n. 3.

69. 31 January 1818. This letter is printed in Lady Jane Shelley, *Shelley and Mary*, 1:258–59. It also appears in Jones's edition of PBS *Letters*, 1:597 n. 3.

70. For example, see Mary's letter to Shelley of 24 September 1817 (MWS *Letters*, 1:42).

71. Only two letters from Percy Shelly to William Godwin written after March 1818 are printed in Jones's definitive edition. The first—25 July 1818—is pleasant and chatty. The second—7 August 1820—is an angry ultimatum about William Godwin's dealings with Mary Shelley.

72. Very little of the correspondence between Godwin and his daughter during her Italian sojourn has been preserved. *Shelley and Mary* prints seventeen letters written by Godwin to Mary Shelley between March 1818 and August 1822, the period encompassing her departure for Italy to a few weeks after Percy Shelley's death. Some of these letters were edited by Lady Jane Shelley to prune away Godwin's unflattering comments to his daughter about her husband. *Shelley and His Circle* also prints the full text of an additional letter from Godwin to his daughter during this period and a fragment of second. Dated 13 June 1820, the complete letter consists of a long and insistent plea for money (Cameron, *Shelley and His*

Circle, 8:1069–72). The fragment dates to March 1819 (8:1073). Godwin's diaries, when collated with the letters he mentions sending Mary in his published letters to her, indicate he wrote to her during this period at least fifty-one times. Of Mary's correspondence with Godwin, only one letter survives from this period (14 March 1820). William St. Clair suggests that Mary Shelley's letters to her father may have been destroyed later by members of the family who were embarrassed by the strength of love they revealed (*The Godwins and the Shelleys*, 467, 494); Emily Sunstein speculates that Shelley herself burned her father's crueler letters to her (Sunstein, *Mary Shelley: Romance and Reality*, 377). Betty T. Bennett, editor of Mary Shelley's letters, wrote this author in 1988 that she thinks it highly unlikely Mary Shelley herself destroyed the correspondence, and would assign probable blame to Lady Jane Shelley.

Shelley and Mary contains a total of thirty-three letters from William Godwin to Mary Shelley. The originals of most of these letters, as well as a few more unpublished pieces of correspondence, are to be found in the Abinger papers at the Bodleian Library, largely in Dep C524. See also Jones's edition of Percy Shelley's *Letters* for the text of a few important pieces of correspondence from Godwin to Mary Shelley. Jones prints Godwin's letters of 5 January 1818 (1:592); 27 October 1818 (2:41); 19 April 1822 (2:423); 3 May 1822 (2:423–24); 6 August 1822 (2:459–61). Of these letters, all except the letter of 5 January 1818 were previously printed in *Shelley and Mary*. *Shelley and His Circle* contains an admirable discussion of the correspondence between Godwin and his daughter during her Italian sojourn (8:1072–78).

73. William Godwin to Mary Shelley, 1 June 1818, in Lady Jane Shelley, *Shelley and Mary*, 1:280.

74. Sunstein, *Mary Shelley: Romance and Reality*, 428 n. 5.

75. Maria Gisborne, *Maria Gisborne and Edward E. Williams, Shelley's Friends: Their Journals and Letters*, ed. Frederick L. Jones (Norman: University of Oklahoma Press, 1951), 43–44.

76. Lady Jane Shelley, *Shelley and Mary*, 734.

77. See chapter 4, note 3, for a discussion of Godwin's work on *Valperga*.

78. Lady Jane Shelley, *Shelley and Mary*, 698C–698D.

79. Sunstein, *Mary Shelley: Romance and Reality*, 433 n. 12. The full title of the book is *The Fisher-Boy of Weymouth; to which are added The Pet-Donkey, and The Sisters*. As Sunstein points out, the title story is reminiscent of Godwin's *Caleb Williams*.

80. Percy Shelley to Claire Clairmont, 25 September 1818, PBS *Letters*, 2:41.

81. William Godwin to Mary Shelley, 27 October 1818, in Lady Jane Shelley, *Shelley and Mary*, 338 A. Also printed in PBS *Letters*, 2:41 n. 2.

82. Percy Shelley to Leigh Hunt, 15 August 1819, PBS *Letters*, 2:109.

83. William Godwin to Mary Shelley, 9 September 1819, in Lady Jane Shelley, *Shelley and Mary*, 410 A-B. Portions printed in Paul, *William Godwin*, 2:269. The bracketed portions of the letter ({ }) are omitted from *Shelley and Mary* but may be located in the Abinger papers at the Bodleian Library (Dep C 524) and in Duke University's microfilm copy of the Abinger papers, reel 4. The words in square brackets ([ ]) represent a doubtful reading, due to the illegibility of Godwin's handwriting in the Abinger papers. I am grateful to Lord Abinger for permission to quote this material. In fairness to Godwin one must note, as William St. Clair does, that Godwin's cold-hearted attitude to the deaths of children had some basis in both his philosophy and in the facts of his early life (*The Godwins and the Shelleys*, 460–62).

84. Percy Shelley to John and Maria Gisborne, 30 June 1820, PBS *Letters*, 2:206.

85. Percy Shelley to John and Maria Gisborne, 30 June 1820, in ibid.

86. Percy Shelley to William Godwin, 7 August 1820, in ibid., 228.

87. William Godwin to Mary Shelley, 19 April 1822, in Lady Jane Shelley, *Shelley and Mary*, 798A. Also printed in PBS *Letters*, 2:423.

88. Lady Jane Shelley, *Shelley and Mary*, 844. The bracketed lines in the letter were excised from the printed version; they may be located in the Abinger papers at the Bodleian Library (Dep C 524) and in Duke University's microfilm copy of the Abinger papers, reel 4.

89. William Godwin to Mary Shelley, 6 August 1822, PBS *Letters*, 2:460.

90. Sunstein, *Mary Shelley: Romance and Reality*, 295.

91. William Godwin to Mary Shelley, 6 May 1823, in Lady Jane Shelley, *Shelley and Mary*, 940.

92. Boose, "The Father's House," 41.

93. William Godwin to Mary Shelley, 9 October 1827, in Lady Jane Shelley, *Shelley and Mary*, 1106E.

94. Sunstein, *Mary Shelley: Romance and Reality*, 265.

95. Lady Jane Shelley, *Shelley and Mary*, 1172 A.

96. Ibid., 1161–62.

97. Perhaps not surprisingly, a second and very different theme also echoes in the relationship between Mary Shelley and William Godwin during his last years: their sense of literary comradeship. Although Godwin relied on his daughter for emotional and financial support, he also saw her as a literary colleague, and he gave her the encouragement and advice an older author might offer a younger writer. Even though Godwin primarily saw his daughter as a source of continuing maternal support, he also saw her as his literary heir and equal—a bifocal vision that culminated a lifetime of shifting, ambiguous responses to his daughter. Godwin had summed up his respect for his daughter's gifts in 1823 when, having just lost Shelley, she was afraid she lacked the talent to support herself by her pen. As Godwin wrote:

> Do not, I entreat you, be cast down about your worldly circumstances. You certainly contain within yourself the means of your subsistence. Your talents are truly extraordinary. "Frankenstein" is universally known; and, though it can never be a book for vulgar reading, is everywhere respected. It is the most wonderful work to have been written at twenty years of age that I ever heard of. You are now five-and-twenty, and, most fortunately, you have pursued a course of reading, and cultivated your mind, in a manner the most admirably adapted to make you a great and successful author. If you cannot be independent, who should be? Your talents, as far as I can at present discern, are turned for the writing of fictitious adventures.
> (14–18 February 1823, in Lady Jane Shelley, *Shelley and Mary*, 915)

Godwin helped Mary reestablish her first literary contacts when she returned to England and, later, sent her long accounts of historical background to use in her novel *Perkin Warbeck*. (See Godwin's letters to Mary Shelley dated 26 September 1827 [Lady Jane Shelley, *Shelley and Mary*, 1106C–1106D]; 29 May 1829 [ibid., 1122A-1122B]; 30 May 1829 [ibid., 1122B].) He even warned her away from drama, telling her that she had inherited her father's particular literary weaknesses: "Your talent is something like mine—it cannot unfold itself without elbow-room" [ibid., 1016B]. He then went on to praise her gifts: "As to the idea that you have no literary talent, for God's sake, do not give way to such diseased imaginations. You have, fortunately, ascertained that at a very early period" [ibid., 1016C]. Godwin's sense of literary comradeship with his daughter—his sense that she resembled him and was his literary heir—stands, of course, as the culmination of his lifetime of literary hopes for her. Ironically, it was the development of just this literary talent that allowed Mary Shelley to be both son and daughter to her father in his last years—that is, to offer him devoted support, but to achieve this support by wielding the pen he had taught her to take up as his literary heir.

Chapter 2. *Frankenstein*

1. Godwin, *The Elopement*, 16.

2. Ellen Moers, "Female Gothic," in *The Endurance of Frankenstein*, ed. George Levine and U. C. Knoepflmacher (Berkeley: University of California Press, 1979), 79.

3. Alan Bewell writes about Mary Shelley's use of eighteenth-century obstetrical theory, with its emphasis on the power of the female imagination to mark or deform a fetus growing in the woman's womb (Alan Bewell, "An Issue of Monstrous Desire: *Frankenstein* and Obstetrics," *Yale Journal of Criticism and Interpretation in the Humanities* 2, no. 1 [Fall 1988]: 105–28). Other discussions of *Frankenstein*, birth, and babies can be found in Gordon Hirsch, "The Monster was a Lady: On the Psychology of Mary Shelley's *Frankenstein*," *Hartford Studies in Literature* 7 (1975): 116–53; Barbara Waxman, "Victor Frankenstein's Romantic Fate: The Tragedy of the Promethean Overreacher as Woman," *Papers on Language and Literature* 23, no. 1 (Winter 1987): 14–26; James B. Twitchell, "*Frankenstein* and the Anatomy of Horror," *Georgia Review* 37 (1983): 41-78; and others. Several important pieces have recently appeared that study *Frankenstein* as a search for identity with the lost mother. Marc Rubenstein's is still the best ("My Accursed Origin: The Search for the Mother in *Frankenstein*," *Studies in Romanticism* 15 [Spring 1976]: 165–94; see also J. M. Hill, "*Frankenstein* and the Physiognomy of Desire," *American Imago* 32 (1975): 335–58. Janet Todd writes persuasively of the many connections between *Frankenstein*'s monster and Jemima, the warder and fallen woman in Mary Wollstonecraft's *Maria, or the Wrongs of Woman* (Janet M. Todd, "Frankenstein's Daughter: Mary Shelley and Mary Wollstonecraft," *Women and Literature* 4 [1976]: 18–27).

4. See Morton Kaplan and Robert Kloss, "Fantasy of Paternity and the Doppelgänger: Mary Shelley's *Frankenstein*," in *The Unspoken Motive: A Guide to Psychoanalytic Criticism* (New York: Free Press, 1973), 119–45; Rosemary Jackson, "Narcissism and Beyond: A Psychoanalytic Reading of *Frankenstein* and Fantasies of the Double," in *Aspects of Fantasy: Selected Essays from the Second International Conference on the Fantastic in Literature and Film*, ed. William Coyle (Westport, Conn.: Greenwood Press, 1986), 43–53; Gerhard Joseph, "Frankenstein's Dream: The Child as Father of the Monster," *Hartford Studies in Literature* 7 (1975): 97–115; Gordon Hirsch, "The Monster Was a Lady," 128; James Twitchell, "*Frankenstein* and the Antomy of Horror," 53; J. M. Hill, "*Frankenstein* and the Physiognomy of Desire," 335–58. William Veeder, particularly in "The Negative Oedipus: Father, *Frankenstein* and the Shelleys," *Critical Inquiry* 12, no. 2 (Winter 1986): 365–90, reverses the equation, but still uses a psychoanalytic model. Other works that examine incest in *Frankenstein*, though not necessarily using a psychoanalytic model are Anca Vlasapolos, "*Frankenstein*'s Hidden Skeleton: The Psycho-Politics of Oppression," *Science Fiction Studies* 10, no. 2 (July

1983): 125–36; Mary Patterson Thornburg, "The Monster in the Mirror: Gender and the Sentimental/Gothic Myth in *Frankenstein*," *Studies in Speculative Fiction* 14 (Ann Arbor, Mich.: University Microfilms International Research Press, 1987); George Levine, "*Frankenstein* and the Tradition of Realism," *Novel* 7 (1973): 14–30; Sandra Gilbert and Susan Gubar, *The Madwoman in the Attic* (New Haven: Yale University Press, 1979); David Ketterer, *Frankenstein's Creation: The Book, The Monster and the Human Reality*, ELS Monograph series no. 16 (Victoria, B.C., 1979); Christopher Small, *Mary Shelley's Frankenstein: Tracing the Myth* (Pittsburgh: University of Pittsburgh Press, 1973). As Paul Sherwin points out, the psychoanalytic critics manage to lay bare the source of much of the sexual tension in *Frankenstein*, but fail to account for two very important aspects of the novel: the monster's interiority and the vast sympathy he calls forth from the reader (Paul Sherwin, "*Frankenstein:* Creation as Catastrophe," *Publications of the Modern Language Association* 96, no. 5 [October 1981], 891).

5. See in particular Gilbert and Gubar (in *Madwoman in the Attic*), U. C. Knoepflmacher, James P. Carson, Douglas Bond, and Marc Rubenstein. Knoepflmacher's essay is a particularly acute study of some of the psychological dynamics underpinning Mary Shelley's creation of her monster ("Thoughts on the Aggression of Daughters").

6. Mary Wollstonecraft Shelley, *Frankenstein; or, The Modern Prometheus: The 1818 Text*, ed. James Rieger (Chicago: University of Chicago Press, 1974). This discussion of *Frankenstein* uses the first edition, published in 1818. Mary Shelley offered revisions to the 1818 edition on two significant occasions. In 1823, she wrote variants into a published copy of *Frankenstein* and presented the copy to Mrs. Thomas; in 1831, she revised the novel in a more thorough fashion for its inclusion in Colburn and Bentley's "Standard Novels" series. As the following discussion will indicate, the 1831 version of *Frankenstein* is a very different novel from the one that first appeared in 1818. Shelley's 1831 revisions sentimentalize the female characters in *Frankenstein* and adopt a whole series of other literary techniques that look forward to Shelley's particular storytelling strategies in *Falkner*. These were not the same strategies Mary Shelley employed when she originally conceived and wrote *Frankenstein*. This discussion, therefore, uses the 1818 text, and all subsequent references to it will be cited parenthetically. Any references to the 1831 edition will be specifically indicated; the 1831 variants are conveniently collated at the back of Rieger's edition of *Frankenstein*.

7. In her 1831 revisions, Shelley makes Elizabeth Lavenza an Italian foundling rather than a blood relation. And the 1831 revisions accentuate even more the possessive, protective, paternal character of Victor Frankenstein's attachment to her. As Victor puts it: "On the evening previous to her [Elizabeth] being brought to my home, my mother had said playfully,—'I have a pretty present for my Victor—to-morrow he shall have it.' And when, on the morrow, she presented Elizabeth to me as her promised gift, I, with childish seriousness, interpreted her words literally, and looked upon Elizabeth as mine—mine to protect, love, and cherish. All praises bestowed on her, I received as made to a possession of my own" (235–36).

8. Here again, the 1831 revisions emphasize the paternal character of Victor's relationships yet more specifically. In the 1831 text, for example, Elizabeth writes to Victor and describes Victor's two brothers, Ernest and William, as "our dear children" (243). Such a characterization casts Victor in a paternal role; it also emphasizes the incestuous currents of the relationship between Elizabeth and Victor, a point to be taken up in due course.

9. Small, *Mary Shelley's Frankenstein*, 108.

10. Many critics have discussed the resemblances between Percy Bysshe Shelley and

Victor Frankenstein. Two of the most thorough discussions may be found in Christopher Small's *Mary Shelley's Frankenstein: Tracing the Myth* and William Veeder's *Mary Shelley and Frankenstein: The Fate of Androgyny*. Among other helpful sources are P. D. Fleck, "Mary Shelley's Notes to Shelley's Poems and *Frankenstein*," *Studies in Romanticism* 6 (1967): 226–54; William H. Hildebrand, "On Three Prometheuses: Shelley's Two and Mary's One," *Serif* 1, no. 2 (1974): 3–11; Richard Holmes, *Shelley: The Pursuit* (New York: Dutton, 1975); Mary Graham Lund, "Shelley as Frankenstein," *Forum* 4, no. 2 (1963): 28–31; Peter Dale Scott, "Vital Artifice: Mary, Percy, and the Psychopolitical Integrity of Frankenstein," in *The Endurance of Frankenstein*, ed. George Levine and U. C. Knoepflmacher (Berkeley: University of California Press, 1979), 172–202; Ketterer, *Frankenstein's Creation*, 100–102.

11.   Numerous critics have discussed William Godwin's life and works as a source for *Frankenstein*. See Pollin, "Philosophical and Literary Sources of *Frankenstein*," 99; Clifford, "*Caleb Williams* and *Frankenstein*," 601–17; Harvey, "*Frankenstein* and *Caleb Williams*," 21–27; Knoepflmacher, "Thoughts on the Aggression of Daughters," 88–110; Small, *Mary Shelley's Frankenstein*, 68–99; May, "Publish and Perish," 489–512; and Powers, *The Influence of William Godwin on the Novels of Mary Shelley*. Powers's is the most extended study to date: it traces the reappearance in Mary Shelley's work of Godwin's ideas about education, benevolence, justice, and reason. Although useful, Powers's study treats the problem of "influence" in a facile manner. Powers does not sufficiently take into account the powerful psychic currents at work when a daughter comes to grips with the varieties of a father's influence, or the various strategies a daughter might employ to rewrite her father. Knoepflmacher's "Thoughts" is the best piece available on William Godwin and Mary Shelley to date.

12.   Mary Shelley's subsequent additions to the text of *Frankenstein* make Victor Frankenstein's work yet more sexually suggestive. In the Thomas copy (1823), Frankenstein's work leaves him "exalted to a kind of transport" (46); he is afflicted with "trembling hands" and an "alternate tremor and passionate ardour" (51). Likewise, in 1831, Shelley describes Frankenstein's "fervent longing to penetrate the secrets of nature" (238). Devon Hodges makes a similar point about the sexual suggestiveness—and menacing power—of Frankenstein's posture as he hovers over his creature: "Frankenstein's desire for domination and his expectation of submission are captured in the pose he takes before his inanimate creature: Frankenstein stands erect above its prone body, a position that has been called the classical spectacle of male power and female powerlessness in patriarchal society" (Devon Hodges, "*Frankenstein* and the Feminine Subversion of the Novel," *Tulsa Studies in Woman's Literature* 2, no. 2 (Fall 1983): 159.

13.   In the 1818 edition of *Frankenstein*, Victor Frankenstein's desire to reanimate the dead serves as the central, if masked, motivation in his creation of the "monster"; in the 1831 revisions to the novel Shelley stresses different themes. Specifically, she accentuates Frankenstein's thirst for knowledge and glory and emphasizes the role of fate in determining what Frankenstein attempts and suffers. Poovey (*The Proper Lady*, 133ff.) and Mellor (*Mary Shelley*, 170ff.) each provide excellent discussions of the significance of the 1831 revisions. It is worth making an additional point about them: When Shelley's 1831 revisions accentuate an additional motivation for Frankenstein's creation of his monster, they deflect the reader's attention away from his desire to reanimate his mother, and, thus, away from the incest theme. This strategy of deflection is consistent with other aspects of Shelley's last two novels, *Lodore* and *Falkner*, the first of which Shelley began shortly after she revised *Frankenstein*.

14.   In the Thomas copy (1823), the sexually suggestive convulsions that bring the

creature to life continue to the end of this physical description of the "monster." In the Thomas copy, this description concludes with the sentence: "And the contortions that ever and anon convulsed & deformed his un-human features" (52).

15.   The 1818 text is inconsistent in naming the exact period of time over which Frankenstein works to make his creature. Frankenstein at one point remarks that he had "worked hard for nearly two years" (52). At another point, he says his creation has taken roughly nine months: "Winter, spring, and summer, passed away during my labours" (51).

16.   In a tantalizing suggestion, Ellen Moers argues that Frankenstein's creature, with its jaundiced, wrinkled skin and weak eyes, is ugly in precisely the way newborn babies are. See Moers, "Female Gothic," 81.

17.   I am grateful to Gilbert Tippy's essay "Feminine Rage in Mary Shelley" (Greenvale, N.Y.: C.W. Post Center, Long Island University, 1991) for this observation.

18.   Gilbert and Gubar, *Madwoman in the Attic*, 240.

19.   Ibid., 19.

20.   Shelley's 1831 revision makes Elizabeth even more of "an orphan and a beggar," and thus more closely allies her to the wretched, rejected, penniless "monster." In the 1831 version, Elizabeth is not Frankenstein's cousin, but the daughter of an Italian nobleman and a mother who died at her birth. Her father abandons her while he goes to fight for Italy against Austria; Elizabeth lives in the cottage of some poor Italian peasants until she is discovered by Caroline Frankenstein, who rescues her and takes her home. In the 1831 version, Shelley specifically refers to Elizabeth as "an orphan and a beggar" (235).

21.   Note, too, that Frankenstein's creature receives an education intended for a daughter when he hides in his hut next to the Delacey house—he overhears the lessons intended for Safie. See also Knoepflmacher's excellent discussion of the similarities between Frankenstein's creature and Agatha, DeLacey's daughter ("Thoughts on the Aggression of Daughters," 101–3).

22.   Marc Rubenstein suggests that the creature's fascination with a written account of his "accursed origin" (126) parallels Mary Shelley's own. Shelley has the creature describe how he finds and reads Frankenstein's journal of "the four months that preceded my creation" (126). In this journal, Frankenstein describes every step of the progress of his work, mingled with accounts of "domestic occurrences." As Rubenstein points out, Frankenstein's diary echoes the contents of the correspondence between William Godwin and Mary Wollstonecraft as their affair began and Mary Wollstonecraft Shelley was conceived. Rubenstein suggests that the creature looks at the written account of his origin with precisely the same horror and fascination that Mary Shelley looked at hers (Rubenstein, "My Accursed Origin," 168–72).

23.   Knoepflmacher, "Thoughts on the Aggression of Daughters," 89.

24.   While Janet Todd has noted that Mary Shelley cast her monster as male because "creator and creature should be of the same sex to avoid sexual implications" (Todd, "Frankenstein's Daughter," 27 n. 7), one can argue Todd's point from a slightly different, and for our purposes more revealing, angle: that Mary Shelley made her monster male as part of an evasionary tactic that repressed the sexual overtones of much of what she was writing. What happens, in short, if we read the relationship between Victor Frankenstein and his creature as the relationship between a father and a daughter? Reading the "monster" as a daughter does emphasize the sexual suggestiveness of several scenes in Frankenstein, such as the animation scene and the closing scene of the novel, in which the creature hangs, loverlike, over Frankenstein's coffin. Shelley may have made her "monster" male to cloak, or deflect,

some of the sexual suggestiveness of a tale in which a father figure rejects his creature because of his incestuous guilt. Other authors who read the creature as female in some sense, or as a daughter, are Gilbert and Gubar, in *Madwoman in the Attic;* U. C. Knoepflmacher, in "Thoughts on the Aggression of Daughters"; Gordon Hirsch, in "The Monster Was a Lady"; Marc Rubenstein, in "My Accursed Origin"; James P. Carson, in "Bringing the Author Forward: *Frankenstein* Through Mary Shelley's Letters," *Criticism* 30, no. 4 (Fall 1988): 431–53; and Douglas Bond, in "The Bride of Frankenstein," *Psychiatric Annals* (December 1973): 10-22.

25. William Godwin, *Caleb Williams,* edited and with an introduction by David McCracken (London: Oxford University Press, 1970), 103–5. Subsequent references to *Caleb Williams* will be taken from this edition, and indicated parenthetically.

26. Shelley borrows from Godwin for other elements of Justine's situation, too. In the stories of both Hawkins and Justine, a crucial element in the jury's vote to convict is the apparent ingratitude of the accused toward a benefactor. In Hawkins's case, "the compassion of the public was in great measure shut against him, as they thought it a piece of barbarous and unpardonable selfishness, that he . . . [suffered] . . . Mr. Falkland . . . who had been so desirous of doing him good, to be exposed to the risk of being tried for a murder that [Hawkins] had committed" (*Caleb Williams,* 104). In this context, Hawkins's apparent ingratitude to Falkland sets the jury against him, and seals Hawkins's fate. Similarly, in Justine's case, Elizabeth's impassioned defense of Justine only makes the jury marvel at Justine's ingratitude toward the Frankenstein family, and thus seals her conviction: "A murmur of approbation was heard; but it was excited by [Elizabeth's] generous interference, and not in favour of poor Justine, on whom the public indignation was turned with renewed violence, charging her with the blackest ingratitude" (*Frankenstein,* 80).

And other, more minor contours of Victor Frankenstein's situation are also borrowed from *Caleb Williams.* Both Falkland and Frankenstein are doomed by a fatal flaw in their educations: Falkland's fondness for Italian romances leads him to murder Tyrrel (*Caleb Williams,* 97); Frankenstein's affection for the occult sciences provides an early impetus for his scientific experiments. And both Falkland and Frankenstein listen passively as an innocent character is unjustly condemned for murder—murders for which Falkland and Frankenstein are actually responsible. Falkland and Frankenstein are then both haunted by the guilt of allowing an innocent to be executed in their place

27. See especially A. D. Harvey, "*Frankenstein* and *Caleb Williams,*" 24–25, and Locke, *Fantasy of Reason,* 279–80. For other discussions of similarities between *Caleb Williams* and *Frankenstein,* see Sylvia Bowerbank, "The Social Order vs. the Wretch: Mary Shelley's Contradictory-Mindedness in *Frankenstein,*" *English Literary History* 46 (1979): 418–31; Clifford, "*Caleb Williams* and *Frankenstein,*" 601–17; Pollin, "Philosophical and Literary Sources of *Frankenstein,*" 99; Small, *Mary Shelley's Frankenstein,* 76–99; Powers, *The Influence of William Godwin on the Novels of Mary Shelley.*

28. Gilbert and Gubar, *Madwoman in the Attic,* 240.

29. Herman, *Father-Daughter Incest,* 117; Boose, "The Father's House," 36.

30. Boose, "The Father's House," 35-36.

31. See especially Poovey, *The Proper Lady,* 137–42 and Rubenstein, "My Accursed Origin," 178–85. Poovey and Rubenstein both argue, essentially, that when Shelley places the origins of *Frankenstein* in a "waking dream," she expresses a deep need to "hide her own originality within someone else's imagination" ("My Accursed Origin," 182)—specifically,

a male imagination. They further suggest that Shelley accepts the notion of the female as being passively creative, and therefore strives to disclaim any role for her own imagination in the creative act that spawned the novel. Bewell, on the other hand, reads the 1831 introduction, with its discussion of Shelley's "waking dream," as Shelley's ambiguous assertion of her own imaginative authority ("Issue of Monstrous Desire," 124).

32. A great many commentators discuss the various ways in which Frankenstein and his creature are "doubles," often basing the discussion on psychoanalytic patterns of "projection" and "otherness." Some examples are Kaplan and Koss, "Fantasy of Paternity," 131–45; Thornburg, *The Monster in the Mirror*, 79–92; Ketterer, *Frankenstein's Creation*, 56–65; Jackson, "Narcissism and Beyond," 43–51; Hirsch, "The Monster Was a Lady," 130–39; Joseph, "Frankenstein's Dream," 100–112; and Sherwin, "Creation as Catastrophe," 886–87.

33. Knoepflmacher, "Thoughts on the Aggression of Daughters," 100–103.

34. As we have seen, Knoepflmacher argues that when the creature murders William, he gains revenge against a father (since he mistakes William for Victor Frankenstein's son) and commits fratricide (since William is named after Shelley's half-brother, William Godwin, Jr., for whom she felt hostility and by whom she felt displaced). For additional discussion of the name "William," see Knoepflmacher, "Thoughts on the Aggression of Daughters," 93.

35. The 1818 edition implies this difference in age; the 1831 edition makes it specific: "There was a considerable difference between the ages of my parents, but this circumstance seemed to unite them only closer in bonds of devoted affection" (1831 text, 233).

36. Shelley stresses and elaborates upon this tendency, too, in her 1831 revisions: "He strove to shelter her, as a fair exotic is sheltered by the gardener, from every rougher wind, and to surround her with all that could tend to excite pleasurable emotion in her soft and benevolent mind" (1831 text, 233–34).

37. See, for example, Gerhard Joseph, "Frankenstein's Dream," 109.

38. As Rieger notes, the 1818 edition gives the honeymoon destination as Cologny, Byron's residence in 1816 (xxiii), near where Shelley had the nightmarish dream that resulted in *Frankenstein*. Her use of Cologny as the honeymoon destination links Frankenstein's union with Elizabeth and the generation of the "monster" in yet one more way. In the 1831 edition, Shelley changed the honeymoon destination to a villa on the shores of Lake Como.

39. See especially Poovey, *The Proper Lady*, 134, and Mellor, *Mary Shelley*, 175–76.

40. But see Kate Ellis's "'Subversive Surfaces" for a very different opinion. Ellis views the sentimentality of Shelley's later work as a deliberate artistic strategy.

41. These are the page numbers of the 1818 and 1831 variants on Elizabeth, all collected in the Rieger edition: pp. 29–32 (1818), variant pp. 233–37; pp. 33–34 (1818), variant p. 238; p. 37 (1818), variant p. 239; pp. 38–39 (1818), variant p. 240; pp. 58–62 (1818), variant pp. 242–43; p.75 (1818), variant p. 245; pp. 82–83 (1818), variant p. 246; p. 88 (1818), variant p. 247; p. 89 (1818), variant pp. 247–48.

42. I cannot agree with Veeder's contention that the most important death in the novel is that of Alphonse Frankenstein. The idea of "father" is certainly central to the relationship between Frankenstein and his creature, but in a very different sense from Veeder's discussion. Veeder's analysis is based on Freud's concept of the "negative Oedipus"—a concept that is not particularly useful for discussing women's developmental psychology, the relations between a father and his daughter, or the ways in which a woman portrays parent/child relationships in a novel such as *Frankenstein*. Veeder is, I think, too intent upon reading

Mary Shelley through the lens of Percy Shelley and his influence. See Veeder, "The Negative Oedipus," 385–86.

43. For other discussions of this point, see Rosemary Jackson, "Narcissism and Beyond," 49; James Twitchell, "Frankenstein and the Anatomy of Horror," 52–54; and Gerhard Joseph, "Frankenstein's Dream," 109.

44. Gilbert and Gubar, *Madwoman in the Attic*, 243.

45. Herman, *Father-Daughter Incest*, 45, 77.

46. Rubenstein provides an excellent discussion of the centrality of the mother figure to *Frankenstein*, and of the emotions of desire and dread she inspires in both Victor Frankenstein and his creature.

47. Gary Kelly, in his introduction to *The Wrongs of Woman*, notes that Wollstonecraft was also inspired by the way in which Godwin used the fictional elements of *Caleb Williams* to illustrate the political ideas he enunciated in *Political Justice*. As Kelly puts it: "Godwin's *Things As They Are; or, The Adventures of Caleb Williams* had presented a fictive version of his *Enquiry Concerning Political Justice*, and now *The Wrongs of Woman; or, Maria* was to fictionalize the arguments of *A Vindication of the Rights of Woman*" (Gary Kelly, introduction to *Mary, A Fiction* and *The Wrongs of Woman*, by Mary Wollstonecraft [Oxford: Oxford University Press, 1976], xvi). All subsequent references to *The Wrongs of Woman* will be taken from this edition, and indicated parenthetically.

48. Janet Todd provides an excellent reading of *Frankenstein* and its relation to *The Wrongs of Woman*. Specifically, Todd argues that the creature's fate in *Frankenstein*, like that of Jemima in *Wrongs of Woman*, is the fate of the fallen woman who is excluded from both family and the dominant male society because of the ghastly aspects of her physicality.

49. There are also other suggestive parallels between Maria and Frankenstein's monster. Like the creature, Maria sees herself as a "wretch," and reads Milton's *Paradise Lost* to distract herself from the sorrows of her imprisonment (*Wrongs*, 85). Maria also comments on the ways in which society makes monsters of the female sex: "By allowing women but one way of rising in the world, the fostering the libertinism of men, society makes monsters of them, and then their ignoble vices are brought forward as a proof of inferiority of intellect" (137).

50. Wollstonecraft died before she finished writing *The Wrongs of Woman*, but left notes for several different endings. In one of them, Maria's daughter is found alive and reunited with Maria at the story's end. See *Wrongs*, 201–4.

51. William Godwin edited and published *The Wrongs of Woman* shortly after Wollstonecraft's death. He notes in his appendix to *Wrongs* that Wollstonecraft intended her novel to be composed of three parts, and that chapters 1 through 14 constituted the first of those three parts (*Wrongs*, 186).

52. Rubenstein also argues that the story of Safie's dead mother lies at the emotional center of *Frankenstein*, though he reads Safie's mother as a cartoon for Mary Wollstonecraft herself ("My Accursed Origin," 169–70; 189–90).

53. Mary Shelley, *Mathilda*, in *The Mary Shelley Reader*, ed. Betty T. Bennett and Charles E. Robinson (New York: Oxford University Press, 1990), 71–72. All subsequent references to *Mathilda* will be taken from this edition, with page numbers cited parenthetically.

54. See Bette London's "Mary Shelley, Frankenstein, and the Spectacle of Masculinity," *Publications of the Modern Language Association* 108, no. 2 (March 1993): 255 for a very different reading of the iconography of Frankenstein's death scene.

Chapter 3. *Mathilda*

1. *Mathilda* was first published in 1959, in an edition prepared by Elizabeth Nitchie as a special number of *Studies in Philology*. *Mathilda* has recently been republished in *The Mary Shelley Reader*, ed. Betty Bennett and Charles Robinson (Oxford: Oxford University Press, 1990). Shelley's diary indicates that she began writing *Mathilda* in early August 1819, had finished writing and copying the work by 12 September, and did some revision of the work on 8 November of the same year. Shelley dated the manuscript of *Mathilda* 9 November 1819, three days before the birth of her son, Percy Florence. The following discussion uses the Bennett and Robinson edition of *Mathilda*.

2. Nitchie, introduction to *Mathilda*, xii–xiii.

3. William Veeder, *Mary Shelley and Frankenstein: The Fate of Androgyny* (Chicago: University of Chicago Press, 1986), 217.

4. Knoepflmacher, "Thoughts on the Aggression of Daughters," 115. Other discussions of *Mathilda* may be found in Ellis, "Subversive Surfaces," 227–28; Locke, *Fantasy of Reason*, 298–99; Macpherson, *The Spirit of Solitude*, 92–96; Peter Marshall, *William Godwin*, 331; Mellor, *Mary Shelley*, 191–201; Palacio, *Mary Shelley dans son oeuvre*, 39–48; Scott, *Vital Artifice*, 183–86; Small, *Mary Shelley's Frankenstein*, 182–87; and Walling, *Mary Shelley*, 109–13. Macpherson analyzes the theme of narcissism in *Mathilda* and relates Mathilda to "Alastor" (Jay Macpherson, *The Spirit of Solitude* [New Haven: Yale University Press, 1982], 92-96). Walling also discusses *Mathilda* in the context of "Alastor," suggesting that incest in *Mathilda* is a metaphor for all the forms of behavior society most abhors. (William Walling, *Mary Shelley*, Twayne's English Author Series 128 [New York: Twayne, 1972], 109–13). Small discusses the incestuous love in *Mathilda* as part of an analysis of the themes of guilt and innocence in Shelley's work, and concludes that the intensity of Mathilda's love for her father is an expression of the intensity of Mary Shelley's love for Percy Shelley (182–87). Palacio (*Mary Shelley dans son oeuvre*, 39–48) discusses *Mathilda* in the context of Shelley's indebtedness to Dante for her portrayal of her major female characters; Locke *(Fantasy of Reason*, 298–99) and Peter Marshall *(William Godwin*, 331) both mention *Mathilda* as part of William Godwin's biography, in the context of Mary Shelley's passionate attachment to her father. Mellor analyzes the treatment of incest in *Mathilda* as part of Shelley's critique of the ideology of the bourgeois family (*Mary Shelley*, 191–201). Scott (*Vital Artifice*, 183–86) reads *Mathilda* as an analogue of Shelley's feelings for Percy, analyzing the way she polarizes her characters into creatures who are either angelic or monstrous.

5. Percy Shelley composed *The Cenci* just before Mary Shelley began *Mathilda*. He began *The Cenci* in May of 1819 and sent the completed manuscript to Peacock in July 1819 (PBS *Letters*, 2:101–3). In May of the previous year, Mary Shelley had copied the Cenci family story from an old Italian manuscript given to the Shelleys by the Gisbornes (MWS *Journals*, 1:211). She probably also provided Shelley with the English translation of the Cenci manuscript that he enclosed in his letter to Peacock. The point is that Mary Shelley was thoroughly familiar with the Cenci story, having recopied it in Italian and translated it into English. With Percy Shelley's version of the tale off in the mail to Peacock, Mary Shelley began her own tale about father-daughter incest in early August of 1819. For an excellent discussion of Mary Shelley's translation of the Cenci tale, see Betty T. Bennett's introduction to "Relation of the Death of the Family of the Cenci, Bodleian MS Shelley adds. e.13," trans. Mary Wollstonecraft Shelley, in *The Bodleian Shelley Manuscripts*, vol. 10 (New York: Garland, 1992), 161–70.

6. Herman, *Father-Daughter Incest*, 96–108.

7. See also the imagery of Mathilda's lament for the few months of happiness she spent with her father: "I lament now, I must ever lament, those few short months of Paradisaical bliss; I disobeyed no command, I ate no apple, and yet I was ruthlessly driven from it. Alas! my companion did, and I was precipitated in his fall" (*Mathilda*, 189).

8. Herman, *Father-Daughter Incest*, 109–10; 125.

9. Ibid., 117; Boose, "The Father's House," 36.

10. Elizabeth Nitchie, *Mary Shelley* (New Brunswick, N.J.: Rutgers University Press, 1953), 90–91.

11. Percy Shelley to William Godwin, 3 January 1812, PBS *Letters*, 1:220. Shelley does alter the portrait of Mathilda's father in one significant way: unlike Godwin, Mathilda's father is quite a young man. Since Mathilda's father marries Diana before his twentieth birthday, has a child fifteen months later, and returns to Mathilda when she is sixteen, the father can't be more than thirty-seven years old. Shelley's decision to make the father so young certainly satisfies an aesthetic need. Many years later, in a reference to Alfieri's *Myrrha*, she wrote that to make an incest tale more believable, father and daughter must be made closer in age: "To shed any interest over such an attachment, the dramatist ought to adorn the father with such youthful attributes as would be by no means contrary to probability" (Mary Shelley, *Lives of the Most Eminent Literary and Scientific Men of Italy, Spain, and Portugal*, 3 vols., nos. 63, 71, and 96 of the Rev. Dionysius Lardner's *Cabinet Cyclopaedia* [London: Longman, Rees, 1835–37], 2:291–92).

12. The date Mary Shelley gives to the *Mathilda* fair copy manuscript—9 November 1819—was, incidentally, the very day that Mary Shelley received from her father the news that his lawsuit had been decided against him. She was devastated by the outcome of the case. She feared for her father's safety; she also feared for her husband's life, since Shelley might have to travel to London to raise £1500 for Godwin, and that journey "is next door to death for him." On 9 November 1819, Mary Shelley, like Mathilda, could "see nothing but despair.... while I have life, I expect nothing but misery" (Mary Shelley to Maria Gisborne, MWS *Letters*, 1:112).

13. Carolyn Heilbrun, *Writing a Woman's Life* (New York: W. W. Norton, 1988), 33; 96–97.

14. Herman, *Father-Daughter Incest*, 117.

15. Susan Gubar, "Mother, Maiden and the Marriage of Death: Women Writers and an Ancient Myth," in *Women and Men: The Consequences of Power*, ed. Dana Hiller and Robin Sheets (Cincinnati: University of Cincinnati, Office of Women's Studies, 1976), 386–97.

16. The 1820 version of *Proserpine* was published in 1922 in *Proserpine & Midas: Two Unpublished Mythological Dramas by Mary Shelley*, ed. A. Koszul (London: Humphrey Milford, 1922). The definitive text of the 1820 version has recently been transcribed and edited by Charles Robinson as "Mythological Dramas: *Proserpine* and *Midas*, Bodleian MS Shelley d.2," in *The Bodleian Shelley Manuscripts*, vol. 10 (New York: Garland, 1992). Subsequent references to *Proserpine* will use the Robinson edition and will be cited parenthetically.

17. Gubar, "Mother, Maiden and the Marriage of Death," 388.

18. Alan Richardson, "*Proserpine* and *Midas:* Gender, Genre, and Mythic Revisionism in Mary Shelley's Dramas," in *The Other Mary Shelley*, ed. Audrey Fisch, Anne K. Mellor and Esther H. Schor (New York: Oxford University Press, 1993), 126–30.

19. As Alan Richardson observes, Phyllis Chesler also reads the Proserpine myth as a

fable of father-daughter incest (ibid., 128). See also Charles Robinson's introduction to *Proserpine*, 9–21. Robinson's introduction makes the important point that the play was originally intended for a juvenile audience and was probably written under the influence of Lady Mount Cashell (10). Robinson also notes that when Shelley revised *Proserpine* for the 1832 *Winter's Wreath*, she turned it "into a more adult narrative that places more blame on the parent Ceres than on the child Proserpine, in effect making the drama into something more than a vehicle for preaching obedience to an audience of children or adolescents" (13–14).

20. See MWS *Journals*, 1:183–84.

21. Shelley seems to have begun translating Vittorio Alfieri's *Myrrha* in 1818. See MWS *Journals*, 1:226 and n. 4; see also PBS *Letters*, 2:39. Palacio also discusses Shelley's indebtedness to *Myrrha*. See Palacio, *Mary Shelley dans son oeuvre*, 133–37.

22. Elizabeth Nitchie points out that, at key points, the condition of the *Mathilda* manuscript betrays "Mary's emotional disturbance" at committing her material to paper. As Nitchie says, the pages of the manuscript "look more like the rough draft than the fair copy. There are numerous slips of the pen, corrections in phrasing and sentence structure, dashes instead of other marks of punctuation, a large blot of ink . . . [and] one major deletion" (Nitchie, notes to edition of *Mathilda*, 83 n. 26). Significantly, the manuscript shows Shelley's "emotional disturbance" as she begins to write about the father's unexpected rejection. It continues as Shelley suggests the sexuality of Mathilda's tie to her father, and through the scene in which Mathilda forces her father to confess his passionate love for her.

23. See also Nitchie's note (*Mathilda*, 81 n.4) for additional similarities in the two tales.

24. Robinson discusses *Mathilda* in terms of Shelley's interest in tragedy as a genre. See introduction to *Proserpine*, 10.

25. Gilbert and Gubar, *Madwoman in the Attic*, 150, 316–17, 473.

26. For an intriguing discussion of the theme of father/daughter incest in the Book of Genesis, see Boose, "The Father's House," 51–57. Boose argues persuasively that father-daughter incest is the real "original sin" in Genesis—that is, the sin that lies behind and prior to the act of rebellion and hunger for knowledge inaugurated in Eve's desire for the forbidden fruit.

27. Revealingly, this same imagery from *Mathilda* reappears in two of Mary Shelley's letters, where it refers to Mary's relationship to her husband rather than to a daughter's relationship to a father figure. In a letter to Maria Gisborne of 15 August 1822 in which Shelley describes her husband's death and the way she and Jane Williams traveled, in despair, for news of their husbands, she says: "It must have been fearful to see us—two poor, wild, aghast creatures—driving (like Matilda) towards the *sea* to learn if we were to be for ever doomed to misery" (MWS *Letters*, 1:247). In *Mathilda*, the heroine pushes frantically to the edge of the sea to save her father from death; in the passage from Shelley's letter, Mary pushes frantically toward the sea for news of her husband. The same transformation occurs in a letter Shelley wrote Maria Gisborne the following spring. Shelley says, writing of Percy Shelley's death and her own intense grief afterward: "But it seems to me that in what I have hitherto written I have done nothing but prophecy what has arrived to. Matilda fortells even many small circumstances most truly—& the whole of it is a monument of what now is—" (MWS *Letters*, 1:336). In this second passage, Shelley again conflates husband and father—Mathilda's loss of her father and her lonely longing to be reunited with him in death become synonymous with Mary Shelley's loss of her husband, Percy, and her desire to die to avoid being separated from him. Shelley's use of imagery from *Mathilda* in her letters accentuates yet

again the extent to which the figure of the father and the figure of the lover overlapped in her imagination.

28. Herman, *Father-Daughter Incest,* 44-49; 77-81.

29. This is what Herman says: "It has frequently been observed that the mother in incestuous families is ill, incapacitated, or for some reason emotionally unavailable to her husband and children. The families adapt to this stressful situation by reassigning many of the mother's traditional obligations to the oldest daughter. The family may come to rely on this daughter for a large part of the housework and child care and for emotional support and comfort. For the daughter, the duty to fulfill her father's sexual demands may evolve almost as an extension of her role as 'little mother' in the family" (ibid., 45).

30. See also Nitchie's note on the manuscript of *Mathilda* and this allusion: Nitchie points out that Shelley has written "little Arthur" above the name "Constance" in the manuscript. *Mathilda,* 85 n. 47.

31. Herman, *Father-Daughter Incest,* 87.

32. See Lynda Boose's discussion of father-daughter incest and the daughter's maternal behavior in "The Father's House," 41.

33. Shelley describes Mathilda's crippling depression after her father's death in a revealing turn of phrase. After indicating that her life is idle and useless, yet choosing initially not to commit suicide, Mathilda says: "Let me not be reproached with inutility" (221). William Godwin had, of course, specifically and bitterly reproached Mary Shelley for inutility in his letter to her of 9 September 1819, which reached her as she was finishing *Mathilda.* (See chapter 1.) As Nitchie notes in her edition of *Mathilda,* the manuscript of the novel is heavily corrected at precisely this point, indicating that "it is another passage that Mary seems to have written in some agitation of spirit" (Nitchie, ed., *Mathilda,* 85-86 n. 50). Mathilda's language may be Shelley's very specific reproach to Godwin's angry denunciation of her grief at this time.

34. Mathilda's self-annihilating fantasy of a reunion with her father in a realm beyond the complications of sex is important in one other respect: it points to another of the novel's literary antecedents and suggests why Shelley names her heroine "Mathilda." The daydream that leads to Mathilda's death is structured upon the events of cantos twenty-eight through thirty of Dante's *Purgatorio.* In these cantos, Matilda leads Dante in triumph into the earthly paradise, where Beatrice appears in a car of light to take Dante to his final purification and heaven. Shelley fashions her heroine's dangerous fantasy around the events of *Purgatorio* in a very self-conscious way. Shelley's Mathilda envisions herself gathering flowers along the banks of a river, just as Dante's Matilda does; Shelley's Mathilda quotes the lines from *Purgatorio* that herald the appearance of Dante's Matilda; Shelley's Mathilda sees her beloved descend in a car of light, just as Dante's Beatrice descends. The use of the *Purgatorio* parallel thus forecasts what Mathilda's dream accomplishes: the entry of hero and heroine into a spiritual realm beyond sex. But Shelley uses the *Purgatorio* parallel in one other way. Before Dante ascends to heaven, after all, Matilda first returns him to the garden of Eden. Shelley's Mathilda does precisely the same thing. Shelley's Mathilda repeats to herself, "all that lovely passage that relates the entrance of Dante into the terrestrial Paradise" (74)—a passage in which Dante both experiences the bliss of reentering the garden of Eden and curses Eve's fatal recklessness (Canto 29). Throughout *Mathilda,* Shelley has characterized her heroine as a reincarnation of Eve; at the close of the novel, Shelley suggests that Mathilda is also something quite different. Shelley names her heroine "Mathilda" because she does precisely what Dante's heroine does: she returns the hero to the lost garden of asexual

innocence and thus in some sense repairs the damage done by her predecessor Eve. In this evocation of the name "Mathilda," Shelley's heroine personifies the sexless and saintly daughter who ennobles, elevates, and purifies the men connected to her.

35. Sunstein, *Mary Shelley: Romance and Reality*, 175.

36. Gisborne, *Maria Gisborne & Edward E. Williams: Their Journals and Letters*, 43-44.

Chapter 4. *Lodore*

1. All references to Shelley's short stories use Robinson's *Collected Tales and Stories*. Pages numbers will be indicated parenthetically.

2. For a very different reading of the extent to which Clarice is a parricide, see Ellis, "Subversive Surfaces," 229–30.

3. PBS *Letters*, 2:428. Shelley began writing *Valperga* on 6 April 1820; she finished writing the last volume in late July 1821 and copied and corrected the work from August 1821 until 25 January 1822 (MWS *Journal*, 25 January 1822, 1:392). In February 1822, Shelley sent the manuscript of *Valperga* to William Godwin (MWS *Letters*, 1:218), with the instruction that he revise and publish the work in whatever way suited his financial needs. Sunstein does an admirable job of placing *Valperga* in the context of Godwin's money difficulties and Shelley's attempts to support him financially (Sunstein, *Mary Shelley: Romance and Reality*, 178ff.): Godwin insisted that Percy Shelley had promised him an additional £400; when the money was not forthcoming from Percy, Mary hoped to provide her father the same £400 through the sale of *Valperga*. Godwin did not attempt to sell *Valperga* immediately (see PBS *Letters*, 2:428). He feared that publishers, aware of his dire financial situation, would give him too low a price, and he thought the manuscript needed editing. Godwin cut the manuscript and reworked parts of it, changed the title from *Castruccio* to *Valperga*, and arranged for the novel to be published in February 1823.

On 15 November 1822, Godwin wrote Shelley this opinion of *Castruccio*, as it was then called: "Perhaps it may be of some use to you if I give you my opinion of 'Castruccio.' I think there are parts of high genius and that your two females are exceedingly interesting; but I am not satisfied. 'Frankenstein' was a fine thing; it was compressed, muscular and firm; nothing relaxed and weak; no proud flesh. 'Castruccio' is a work of more genius; but it appears, in reading, that the first rule you prescribed to yourself was, I will let it be long. It contains the quantity of four volumes of 'Waverley.' No hard blow was ever hit with a woolsack!" (Lady Jane Shelley, *Shelley and Mary*, 904 B–904 C).

On 14 February 1823, Godwin wrote Shelley the following about the way he edited *Valperga*: "Your novel is now fully printed, & ready for publication. I shall send you a copy either by Peacock's parcel or John Hunt's. I have taken great liberties with it, & I fear your *amour propre* will be proportionably shocked. I need not tell you that all the merit of the book is exclusively your own. The whole of what I have done is nearly confined to the taking away things that must have prevented its success. I scarcely ever saw anything more unfortunately out of taste, than the long details of battles & campaigning, after the death of Beatrice, & when the reader is impatient for the conclusion. Beatrice is the jewel of the book; not but that I greatly admire Euthanasia; & I think the characters of Pepi, Binda & the Witch, decisive efforts of original genius. I am promised a character of the work in the Morning Chronicle & the Herald, & was in hopes to have sent you the one or the other by this time: I also sent a copy of the book to the Examiner for the same purpose" (Abinger papers, Bodleian Library

[Dep C524] and in Duke microfilm, reel 4; also printed, with deletions, in Lady Jane Shelley, *Shelley and Mary*, 915). Given what Godwin describes as his extensive revisions to *Valperga*, commentators must exercise caution in interpreting the work until more is known about the exact nature and extent of his cuts and emendations. But the characterizations and imagery of *Valperga* are entirely consonant with Shelley's other works.

4. Mary Shelley, *Valperga; or, the Life and Adventures of Castruccio, Prince of Lucca*, 3 vols. (London: G. and W. B. Whittaker, 1823), 2:265. All subsequent references to *Valperga* will be taken from this edition and cited parenthetically.

5. Gilbert and Gubar, *Madwoman in the Attic*, 210ff. *Madwoman in the Attic* provides a wide ranging exploration of the theme of paternal blindness and its counterpointed theme, daughterly insight. See also 214–15; 219–21; 578–79.

6. Mary Shelley, *Lodore* (Brussels: Ad. Wahlen, 1835), 272. Subsequent references to *Lodore* will be taken from this edition, with page numbers cited parenthetically.

7. That is to say, Wilhelmina sees herself as a female Christ figure, as the Daughter, rather than the Son, of God. Like Christ, Wilhelmina was born after an angelic annunciation; like Christ, Wilhelmina is the Word Incarnate (*Valperga*, 2:26). Wilhelmina's stature as a female incarnation of the Word gives her characterization particular resonance. For a different perspective on Wilhelmina, see also Joseph Lew's excellent discussion of the female cult leaders who preached during Shelley's youth, especially Joanna Southcott, whose story lies behind that of Beatrice and her mother. Joseph Lew, "God's Sister: History and Ideology in *Valperga*," in *The Other Mary Shelley*, ed. Audrey Fisch, Anne K. Mellor, and Esther H. Schor (New York: Oxford University Press, 1993), 159–81.

8. See also Lew's discussion of other aspects of Shelley's identification with Beatrice ("God's Sister," 172–73).

9. *Valperga* offers a dark portrait of Imagination, that human faculty so prized by the male romantic poets. After Beatrice gives herself to Castruccio, the narrator remarks: "Poor Beatrice! She had inherited from her mother the most ardent imagination that ever animated a human soul. Its images were as vivid as reality, and were so overpowering, that they appeared to her, when she compared them to the calm sensations of others, as something superhuman; and she followed that as a guide, which she ought to have bound with fetters, and to have curbed and crushed by every effort of reason" (*Valperga*, 2:86–87). Toward the end of the novel, Euthanasia gives Beatrice a long description of the inner recesses of the human mind, which she describes as the home of "Poetry and Imagination," but also as the home of "owls, and bats, and vipers, and scorpions, and other deadly reptiles. This recess receives no light from outward day; nor has Conscience any authority here. Sometimes it is lighted by an inborn light; and then the birds of night retreat, and the reptiles creep not from their holes. But, if this light do not exist, oh! then let those beware who would explore this cave. It is hence that bad men receive those excuses for their crimes, which take the whip from the hand of Conscience, and blunt his sharp crown; it is hence that the daring heretic learns strange secrets. This is the habitation of the madman, when all the powers desert the vestibule, and he, finding no light, makes darkling, fantastic combinations, and lives among them. From thence there is a short path to hell, and the evil spirits pass and repass unreproved, devising their temptations" (3:101–2). Not surprisingly, Euthanasia's words drive Beatrice to retort: "Talk no more in this strain. . . . No content of mind exists for me . . . and, if imagination live, it is as a tyrant, armed with fire, and venomed darts, to drive me to despair" (2:102). Anne K. Mellor has noted that female Romantic authors tend to forswear "the concern of their male peers with the capacities of the creative imagination" (*Romanticism and*

Gender [New York: Routledge, 1993], 2). In Mary Shelley's case, the imagination is a faculty that often produces as much harm as it does beauty.

10. Percy Shelley recognized the shock value inherent in Beatrice's behavior and fate. He wrote Mary Jane Godwin, for William Godwin's benefit, that "I am sure that Mary would be delighted to amend any thing that her father thought imperfect in it; though I confess that if his objections relate to the character of Beatrice, I shall lament the deference which would be shewn by the sacrifize of any portion of it to feelings & ideas which are but for a day" (PBS *Letters*, 2:428). As we have seen, Godwin thought that Beatrice was the "jewel of the book."

11. Boose, "The Father's House," 31ff. Boose's discussion is also important for what it suggests about the role of the father's incestuous desire for his daughter in Western marriage rituals: "For fathers compelled by cultural dictates to lose their daughters, the rationale of 'gift-giving' in order to acquire kin-group benefits might better be understood as being not necessarily the *cause* for such an exchange but an invaluable psychic defense *against* its necessity. Such a rationale would serve as a powerful way by which the loss of a daughter through marriage could be psychologically reconstrued as an investment. For losing one's daughter through a transaction that the father controls circumvents her ability ever to choose another man over him, thus allowing him to retain vestiges of his primary claim. And patriarchal history may have hung on to father bestowal so stubbornly not only because it reified society's male dominance . . . but also because giving daughters such as Ophelia primary rights in themselves would threaten a psychic defense valuable to the father. The bestowal design places the daughter's departure from the father's house and her sexual union with another male into a text defined by obedience to her father—not preference for another male. . . . Within this fiction, daughters do not abandon or displace their father, nor do fathers reexperience the Oedipal defeat once felt at the hands of their own fathers. Daughters leave their father's house because their fathers decree and then enact this severance by giving them away" ("The Father's House," 31–32).

12. Lew, "God's Sister," 160.

13. Shelley had plans for another novel, which proved to be *The Last Man*, by February 1824, when she wrote Leigh Hunt that "I am going to plunge into a novel, and hope that its clear water will wash off the . . . mud of the magazines" (MWS *Letters*, 1:412). By 14 May 1824, she knew her novel would focus on the fate of "the last man" (MWS *Journal*, 2:476-77); *The Last Man* was published by Henry Colburn in February 1826.

14. Mary Shelley, *The Last Man*, ed. Hugh J. Luke, Jr. (Lincoln: University of Nebraska Press, 1965), 18. All subsequent references to *The Last Man* will be taken from this edition, with page numbers indicated parenthetically.

15. Mary Shelley's journals also reflect her need to idealize her dead husband during this period of her life. From the time of Percy Shelley's death in 1822 until the end of 1826, Shelley filled her diaries with passages that yearned for his presence and elevated him to the status of a near divinity. A typical entry occurs on 17 September 1825, on the occasion of Shelley receiving Percy's portrait, painted by Amelia Curran: "Thy picture is come, my only One!—thine—those speaking eyes—that mild yet animated look—Unlike aught earthly wert thou ever & art now! . . . Thou art near to guard & save me, Angelic one; thy divine glance will be my protection & defence. I was not worthy of thee & thou hast left me—Yet that dear look assures me that thou wert mine—& recalls & narrates to my backward-looking mind a long tale of love & happiness" (MWS *Journals*, 2:496-97).

16. Like Caleb Williams, Verney also suffers a prison term that breeds hatred rather

than spiritual reform: "I was sent for a month to the county jail. I came out, my morals unimproved, my hatred to my oppressors encreased tenfold. Bread and water did not tame my blood, nor solitary confinement inspire me with gentle thoughts. I was angry, impatient, miserable; my only happy hours were those during which I devised schemes of revenge" (11).

17. Ellis, "Subversive Surfaces," 225–27.

18. Gilbert and Gubar, *Madwoman in the Attic,* 246.

19. Shelley wrote to Charles Ollier, saying she planned to begin writing *Lodore* in January or February 1831 (MWS *Letters,* 2:125). Shelley had nearly completed *Lodore* by 31 January 1833 (MWS *Letters,* 2:185), was correcting the first of the proofs by 18 March 1834 (MWS *Letters,* 2:199), and then had to rewrite large stretches of the novel's closing sections when her manuscript was lost in the mail (MWS *Letters,* 2:206). *Lodore* was published in 1835 and was so successful that Ollier immediately asked Shelley for another novel.

20. Since Shelley did not have access to all the historical books she needed to write *Perkin Warbeck,* she corresponded frequently about the novel with Godwin, who provided her with background information taken from his own library. See the following letters from Godwin to Shelley in Lady Jane Shelley, *Shelley and Mary:* 26 September 1827; 29 May 1829; 30 May 1829. See also Godwin's letter of 13 August 1828, Abinger papers, Bodleian Library, Dep C 524.

21. With the recent exceptions of Poovey, Mellor and Veeder (in *Mary Shelley and Frankenstein*), discussions of *Lodore* have tended to read the novel solely from a biographical point of view, looking for correspondences between the actions of characters and the lives of Shelley's friends and family. Some sixty-six years ago, Sylva Norman described *Lodore* as "a competition ground" for biographical interpretations (*On Shelley,* 72). More recently, Veeder has examined the way in which Shelley's "bifurcation" exhibits itself in *Lodore* (*Mary Shelley and Frankenstein,* 67–68), and Poovey has cited *Lodore* as an illustration of Shelley's increasing conservatism (*The Proper Lady,* 116, 160). Mellor's discussion of *Lodore* focuses on the importance of Fanny Derham and on the family ideology Shelley illustrates through the novel (*Mary Shelley,* 206–8; 186–91).

22. See MWS *Letters,* 2:147, where Shelley asks Hogg for legal information concerning entailment, background material she probably needed for "The Elder Son." All parenthetical references to "The Elder Son" are taken from Robinson's edition of Shelley's *Collected Tales and Stories.*

23. Mary Wollstonecraft, *Vindication,* 29, 48.

24. Shelley wrote *Lodore,* in fact, largely to earn money to give William Godwin. As she wrote Maria Gisborne on 16 January 1833: "My Father's Novel [*Deloraine*] is printed & I suppose will come out soon. Poor dear fellow! It is hard work for him—I am in all tremor of fearing what I shall get for [*Lodore*], which is nearly finished—His & my Comfort depend on it." (MWS *Letters,* 2:183).

25. The narrator tells us that the two men have very different temperaments—that the "abstracted, wounded, yet lofty spirit of Lodore was totally dissimilar to the airy brightness of Villiers' disposition" (134). Yet both men revere the values of "society" and sacrifice the daughter's concerns in favor of society's codes of honor and decorum. Lodore, for example, challenges a man to a duel over a twelve-year-old insult. When Lodore dies in the duel, Ethel is prostrate with grief and robbed of the paternal protection she has come to rely upon. Similarly, Edward decides at one point to break off his engagement to Ethel, since he has no money and cannot support her in a style he thinks appropriate to his social rank. Ethel is

again distraught at being thus "orphaned" (193) but agrees to Edward's stipulations. In each case, Lodore and Edward conclude that matters of honor and worldly appearance are more important than the suffering imposed, in their name, on a female figure.

26. Edward Villiers, for his part, largely behaves toward Ethel in as paternal and cloistering a way as Lodore did. Villiers sees Ethel as a tiny bird in need of his protection and guidance; Shelley repeatedly uses bird imagery to describe Villiers's attitude toward her. In one instance, Villiers is "overjoyed to have her safe at Richmond—secure from Lady Lodore—shut up apart from all things, except nature—her unsophisticated aunt, and his own admiration—a bird of beauty, brooding in its own fair nest, unendangered by the fowler" (176). Much later in the novel, Villiers "grew more desirous than Mrs. Derham to feed his poor famished bird, whose eyes, in spite of the joy that shone in them, began to look languid" (249). Ethel herself participates in this imagery of birdlike dependence on Villiers. When their engagement is ensured, she likens her feelings to those of a bird returning to its nest, and the protective care of its parent: "She felt it rather like a return to a natural state of things, after unnatural deprivation. As if, a young nestling, she had been driven from her mother's side, and was now restored to the dear fosterage of her care" (201). This pattern of imagery serves to underscore the paternal nature of Villiers's relation to Ethel and her dependence on him.

27. Poovey, *Proper Lady*, 168.

28. *Lodore* abounds with similar sentimental passages that associate female acts of sacrifice and submission with religious veneration. See also 248–50, 291, 293, and 316-317. But on at least one occasion, in a telling disjunction of tone, Shelley punctures her own sentimentality by referring to Ethel and Edward's celestial happiness as a "fairy land": "they, nestling close to each other, were so engrossed by the gladness of re-union, that had Cinderella's godmother transmuted their crazy vehicle for a golden coach, redolent of the perfumes of fairy land, they had scarcely been aware of the change. Their own hearts formed a more real fairy land, which accompanied them whithersoever they went, and could as easily spread its enchantments over the shattered machine in which they now jumbled along, as amidst the cloth of gold and marbles of an eastern palace" (284–85).

29. In this sense, Lodore is spiritually present, and an abiding influence, throughout the novel that bears his name. The actions and personality of the titular character inform the novel to its very end, though Lodore himself dies before the novel is half over. This point has been missed by many critics who criticize the apparently overelastic plot Shelley uses to reveal the struggles of her daughter figures. One example is William Walling, who puts it this way: "Unhappily for him [Lodore], and for the aptness of Mary's title, he is killed in New York in a duel; and the novel is left to make its way along (with increasing triviality) for two more volumes without the presence of its titular hero" (Walling, *Mary Shelley*, 105). But Walling's criticism misses one of Shelley's major points in the design of *Lodore:* fathers—and especially fathers of motherless girls—shape their daughters in ways that determine whether the daughters are questing or submissive, "intellectual" or feeling, proud or humble; this paternal influence continues long after a father's death. A father's training also shapes a daughter's response to her sexuality and her choices about marriage and work. In short, a father's training and behavior toward his daughter, especially if her mother is absent, largely determine whether she is "feminine" in a conventional or an unconventional sense. If Mary Shelley had called her novel "Ethel" or "Fanny" or "Cornelia," she would have missed an opportunity to underline this central theme in her novel. Further, the plot of the last two

volumes of *Lodore* can hardly be called "trivial," since the actions of both Ethel and Cornelia grow directly out of their response to Lodore's influence. Lodore is, in fact, a continuing presence throughout the novel, and he is powerful in his continuing impact on two very different women: his actual daughter and the wife he tries to make into a daughter.

30. Veeder, *Mary Shelley and Frankenstein*, 83.

31. Mary Wollstonecraft, *Vindication*, 7–11.

32. I cannot agree with Paul Youngquist's speculation that "Shelley's autonomy as a creator, as much as Victor Frankenstein's, depends upon the elision of motherhood from the creative enterprise" ("Frankenstein: The Mother, The Daughter, and the Monster," *Philological Quarterly* 70, no. 3 [Spring 1991]: 353). This observation may hold true for *Frankenstein* and *Mathilda*, but certainly not for *Lodore* and *Falkner*, where Shelley's portrayal and exploration of maternal power becomes a weapon against male domination.

33. Veeder, *Mary Shelley and Frankenstein*, 12.

34. As Anne Mellor puts it in her discussion of the role of nature in *Frankenstein*, "As an ecological system of interdependent organisms, Nature requires the submission of the individual ego to the welfare of the family and the larger community" ("Possessing Nature," 229).

35. The lines are from Sir Walter Scott's *Lochinvar* and prefigure Cornelia's metamorphosis from a social butterfly to a devoted, self-sacrificing mother:

> O Woman! in our hours of ease,
> Uncertain, coy, and hard to please,
> And variable as the shade
> By the light quivering aspen made;
> When pain and anguish wring the brow,
> A ministering angel thou!

Chapter 5. *Falkner*

1. Review of *Lodore*, by Mary Shelley, *Fraser's Magazine for Town and Country*, 11 May 1835, 600–605. Quoted in W.H. Lyles, *Mary Shelley: An Annotated Bibliography* (New York: Garland, 1975), 179.

2. Review of *Falkner*, by Mary Shelley, *Monthly Repository* 124 (April 1837): 228-236. Quoted in ibid., 182.

3. Review of *Falkner*, by Mary Shelley, *Monthly Repository* 124 (April 1837): 228–36. Quoted in ibid.

4. William Godwin, *Deloraine*, 3 vols. (London: Richard Bentley, 1933), 1:125 Subsequent references to *Deloraine* will be taken from this edition with page numbers indicated parenthetically.

5. 13 April 1832, in Lady Jane Shelley, *Shelley and Mary*, 1161–62. In the opening pages of *Deloraine*, Godwin employs imagery strikingly similar to the imagery Mary Shelley attaches to her two daughters made monstrous by the incestuous overtones of the father-daughter relationship. Like Mathilda, Deloraine himself bears the mark of Cain on his forehead; like Frankenstein's creature and Mathilda, Deloraine sees all men shrink from him as a result: "Like Cain, I have a mark trenched in my forehead, that all men should shrink from me. I sit alone; for no one will come near me, no one will endure me" (3). Deloraine also inhabits a symbolically solitary and walled-in landscape, much as Frankenstein's creature

and Mathilda do: "My situation in life was like that of the obscure and sequestered valley" (5).

6. Boose, "The Father's House," 41

7. Sunstein, *Mary Shelley: Romance and Reality,* 334.

8. Mary Shelley, *Falkner,* 3 vols. (London: Saunders and Otley, 1837), 2:182 Subsequent references to *Falkner* will be taken from this edition with page numbers cited parenthetically.

9. As in the case of *Lodore,* criticism of *Falkner* has been largely biographical until the last few years. The best recent criticism of *Falkner* is by Poovey and Mellor.

10. For a discussion of Satan, Eve, and incest in *Paradise Lost,* and its importance for *Frankenstein,* see Gilbert and Gubar, *Madwoman in the Attic,* 213–47. For a discussion of the theme of father/ daughter incest in Genesis, specifically in the story of Eve, Satan, and God the Father, see Boose, "The Father's House," 51–57.

11. With the exception of Poovey and Mellor, critics have uniformly dismissed *Falkner.* Walling's discussion of the work is a typical example (*Mary Shelley,* 106–9).

12. Lynda Zwinger, *Daughters, Fathers, and the Novel: The Sentimental Romance of Heterosexuality* (Madison: University of Wisconsin Press, 1991), 5. Zwinger also argues that our culture's conception of heterosexual love is grounded in the sexual desire existing between father and daughter.

13. See also 1:173; 1:199; 3:145-47; and others.

14. Poovey, *The Proper Lady,* 168.

15. Ibid., 164–65.

16. Chodorow, *The Reproduction of Mothering,* 89-90.

17. Freud "Female Sexuality," *The Standard Edition of the Complete Psychological Works of Sigmund Freud,* 24 vols., translated and edited by James Strachey et al. (London: Hogarth and The Institute for Psychoanalysis, 1953–74), 21:226. For an excellent essay on fathers and daughters in Freudian theory—and, implicitly, the mother who lies behind all object-relations—see David Willbern, "*Filia Oedipi:* Father and Daughter in Freudian Theory," in *Daughters and Fathers,* ed. Lynda Boose and Betty Flowers (Baltimore: Johns Hopkins University Press, 1989), 75-96.

18. See Sandra Gilbert, "Life's Empty Pack: Notes Toward a Literary Daughteronomy," in *Daughters and Fathers,* ed. Lynda Boose and Betty Flowers (Baltimore: Johns Hopkins University Press, 1989), 265, 271.

19. See Gilbert, "Life's Empty Pack," 276. Gilbert reads the mother's buried story as a terrible warning to her daughter.

20. Poovey, *The Proper Lady,* 163–65.

21. Boose, "The Father's House," 43.

22. I cannot agree with Veeder's interpretation of the triangular relationship that closes *Falkner* ("The Negative Oedipus," 371–72). Veeder contends that the triangular relationship between Elizabeth, Neville, and Rupert Falkner is important because it is a symbol of the bond cemented between Neville, the son figure, and Rupert, the symbolic father. Veeder's interpretation ignores the fact that Elizabeth, not either of the men, is positioned at the emotional center of the triangular relationship.

23. Boose, "The Father's House," 43.

24. For another reading of this same phenomenon, see Robert Seidenberg and Evangelos Papathomopoulos, "Daughters Who Tend Their Fathers: A Literary Survey," *Psychoanalytic Study of Society* 2 (1962): 135-60.

Conclusion

1. Shelley eventually died of a brain tumor. But Sunstein argues that from 1837 (shortly after Godwin's death) until 1848, Shelley's major debilitating difficulty was a psychological illness that manifested itself in extreme physical symptoms, turning the sufferer into a near invalid. Today's medicine would term this illness a somaticization disorder (Sunstein, *Mary Shelley: Romance and Reality,* 54 n. 15). As Sunstein points out, it was the same disease that afflicted Elizabeth Barrett Browning, who finally "arose from the sofa on which she had spent twenty-five years with a weak back and under her father's domination, married Robert Browning and went to Italy." It is tempting to speculate on the causes of such a disorder. Perhaps Shelley, as Sunstein argues, broke "the back of her protest; or, like a Prometheus, drove the vulture away by agreeing to make her bed on the rock" (373–37). Perhaps the beginnings of Shelley's illness were related to the death of Godwin, whom she had battled and adored for her entire life. See MWS *Letters,* 3:389 (appendix 1) for a different opinion on Shelley's last illnesses.

2. Trelawny asked Shelley to write a pamphlet on women's rights for the Philosophic Radicals in 1838, and she refused. When Trelawny subsequently accused Shelley of being politically conservative and in love with the opinions of "society," Shelley wrote a long apologia in her journal, observing, among other things, that "If I have never written to vindicate the Rights of women, I have ever befriended women when oppressed—at every risk I have defended & supported victims to the social system—But I do not make a boast . . . for in truth it is simple justice I perform—and so I am still reviled for being worldly" (MWS *Journal,* 2:557). Though some commentators still conclude that "Mary Shelley was no feminist" (Lucy Newlyn, review of *Mary Shelley: Her Life, Her Fiction, Her Monsters,* by Anne K. Mellor, *Times Literary Supplement,* 17 February 1989, 171), recent critics, following the lead of Poovey and Mellor, think otherwise. Among others, see Ellis's "Subversive Surfaces" and Youngquist, "*Frankenstein:* The Mother, the Daughter, and the Monster."

Works Cited

The following list cites the original publication of works by Shelley, Godwin, and Mary Wollstonecraft. Whenever possible and appropriate, first editions have been consulted. If the first edition has not been used, the second bibliographic citation indicates what edition has been used.

WORKS BY MARY WOLLSTONECRAFT SHELLEY

Collected Tales and Stories. Edited by Charles E. Robinson. Baltimore and London: Johns Hopkins University Press, 1976.

Falkner: A Novel. 3 vols. London: Saunders and Otley, 1837.

The Fortunes of Perkin Warbeck, a Romance. 3 vols. London: Henry Colburn and Richard Bentley, 1830.

Frankenstein; or, The Modern Prometheus. 3 vols. London: Lackington, Hughes, Harding, Mavor, & Jones, 1818. Reprinted as *Frankenstein; or, The Modern Prometheus: The 1818 Text.* Edited by James Rieger. Chicago: University of Chicago Press, 1982.

Frankenstein, or the Modern Prometheus. London: Henry Colburn and Richard Bentley, 1831. Reprint edited by M. K. Joseph. Oxford: Oxford University Press, 1969.

The Journals of Mary Shelley. Edited by Paula R. Feldman and Diana Scott-Kilvert. 2 vols. Oxford: Oxford University Press, 1987.

The Last Man. 3 vols. London: Henry Colburn, 1826. Reprint edited by Hugh J. Luke, Jr. Lincoln: University of Nebraska Press, 1965.

The Letters of Mary Wollstonecraft Shelley. 3 vols. Edited by Betty T. Bennett. Baltimore: Johns Hopkins University Press, 1980–88.

Lives of the Most Eminent Literary and Scientific Men of Italy, Spain, and Portugal. 3 vols. Nos. 63, 71 and 96 of the Rev. Dionysius Lardner's *Cabinet Cyclopaedia.* London, 1835–37.

Lodore. London: Richard Bentley, 1835. Brussels: Ad. Wahlen, 1835.

Mathilda. Written 1819–20. First publication edited by Elizabeth Nitchie. *Studies in Philology*, extra series 3. Chapel Hill: University of North Carolina Press, 1959. Collected in *The Mary Shelley Reader*, edited by Betty T. Bennett and Charles E. Robinson, 173–246. New York: Oxford University Press, 1990.

Proserpine: A Mythological Drama in Two Acts. Completed 1820; revised by Shelley for publication in *The Winter's Wreath* for 1832 (1831), pp. 1-20. Unrevised version first

233

published in *Proserpine & Midas: Two Unpublished Mythological Dramas by Mary Shelley*. Edited by A. Koszul. London: Humphrey Milford, 1922. Definitive text of unrevised version published as "Mythological Dramas: *Proserpine* and *Midas:* Bodleian MS. Shelley d.2." Edited by Charles E. Robinson. In *The Bodleian Shelley Manuscripts*, vol. 10. New York: Garland Publishing, 1992.

Relation of the Death of the Family of the Cenci. Translated from the Italian by Mary Wollstonecraft Shelley. Edited by Betty T. Bennett. In *The Bodleian Shelley Manuscripts*, vol. 10. New York: Garland Publishing, 1992.

Unfinished memoir of William Godwin. Portions printed in C. Kegan Paul, *William Godwin: His Friends and Contemporaries*, 1:25–26, 36-37, 47, 64, 73–74, 76, 78-83, 120-21, 123-25, 129-35, 161-62, 231-32, 238-39, 332-33. Original MS. in the Abinger MSS., Bodleian Library, Oxford.

Valperga; or, The Life and Adventures of Castruccio, Prince of Lucca. 3 vols. London: G. and W. B. Whittaker, 1823. (Heavily edited and revised by Godwin.)

SELECTED WORKS BY WILLIAM GODWIN

Caleb Williams. 3 vols. London: B. Crosby, 1794. Edited and with an introduction by David McCracken. London: Oxford University Press, 1970.

Cloudesley: A Tale. 3 vols. London: H. Colburn & R. Bentley, 1830.

Deloraine. 3 vols. London: Richard Bentley, 1833.

The Elopement of Percy Bysshe Shelley and Mary Wollstonecraft Godwin. As Narrated by William Godwin. With commentary by H. Buxton Forman. London: Privately printed, 1911.

Enquiry Concerning Political Justice and Its Influence on Morals and Happiness. 1793. 3 Vols. Edited by F. E. L. Priestley. Toronto: University of Toronto Press, 1946.

Fables, Ancient and Modern, Adapted for the Use of Children. [Edward Baldwin, pseud.]. London: T. Hodgkins, 1805.

Fleetwood; or, The New Man of Feeling. 3 vols. London: R. Phillips, 1805. 2d ed., R. Bentley, 1832.

Godwin and Mary: Letters of William Godwin and Mary Wollstonecraft. Edited by Ralph M. Wardle. Lincoln: University of Nebraska Press, 1966.

The History of England, for the Use of Schools and Young Persons. [Edward Baldwin, pseud]. London: T. Hodgkins, 1806. Reprint, London: M. J. Godwin, 1812.

Mandeville: A Tale of the Seventeenth Century in England. 3 vols. London: Longman, Hurst, Rees, Orme & Brown, 1817. Philadelphia: M. Thomas, 1818.

Memoirs of the Author of a Vindication of the Rights of Woman. London: 1798. Philadelphia: James Carey, 1799.

Memoirs of Mary Wollstonecraft. Edited by W. Clark Durant. London: Constable, 1927. (This is a revised version of the *Memoirs*, containing some useful additional material.) Reprint, New York: Haskell House Publishers, Ltd., 1969.

St. Leon: A Tale of the Sixteenth Century. London, 1799. New York: Arno Press and McGrath Publishing Company, 1972.

Uncollected Writings. Edited by Jack W. Marken and Burton R. Pollin. Gainesville, Fla.: Scholars' Facsimiles & Reprints, 1968.

OTHER WORKS

Abel, Elizabeth, et al., eds. *The Voyage In: Fictions of Female Development.* Hanover, N.H.: University Press of New England, 1983.

Arens, W. *The Original Sin: Incest and Its Meaning.* New York: Oxford University Press, 1986.

Bewell, Alan. "An Issue of Monstrous Desire: *Frankenstein* and Obstetrics." *The Yale Journal of Criticism: Interpretation in the Humanities* 2, no. 1 (Fall 1988): 105–28.

Bloom, Harold. Afterword to *Frankenstein.* New York: New American Library, 1965.

———, ed. *Modern Critical Views on Mary Shelley.* New York: Chelsea House, 1985.

Bond, Douglas. "The Bride of Frankenstein." *Psychiatric Annals* (December 1973): 10–22.

Boose, Lynda, and Betty Flowers, eds. *Daughters and Fathers.* Baltimore: Johns Hopkins University Press, 1989.

Boose, Lynda. "The Father's House and the Daughter in It: The Structures of Western Culture's Daughter-Father Relationship." In *Daughters and Fathers*, edited by Lynda Boose and Betty Flowers, 19-74. Baltimore: Johns Hopkins University Press, 1989.

Bowerbank, Sylvia. "The Social Order vs. the Wretch: Mary Shelley's Contradictory-Mindedness in *Frankenstein*." *English Literary History* 46 (1979): 418–31.

Cameron, Kenneth Neill, ed. *Shelley and His Circle.* Vols.1–4; Donald H. Reiman, ed., vols. 5-8. Cambridge: Harvard University Press, 1961–86.

Carson, James P. "Bringing the Author Forward: *Frankenstein* Through Mary Shelley's Letters." *Criticism* 30, no. 4 (Fall 1988): 431–53.

Cervo, Nathan. "Shelley's *Frankenstein.*" *Explicator* 46, no. 2 (Winter 1988): 14–17.

Chodorow, Nancy. *The Reproduction of Mothering: Psychoanalysis and the Sociology of Gender.* Berkeley: University of California Press, 1978.

Clairmont, Claire. *The Journals of Claire Clairmont.* Edited by Marion Kingston Stocking. Cambridge: Harvard University Press, 1968.

Claridge, Laura P. "Parent-Child Tensions in *Frankenstein:* The Search for Communion." *Studies in the Novel* 17, no. 1 (Spring 1985): 14-26.

Clemit, Pamela. *The Godwinian Novel: The Rational Fictions of Godwin, Brockden Brown, Mary Shelley.* Oxford: Oxford University Press, 1993.

Clifford, Gay. "*Caleb Williams* and *Frankenstein:* First-Person Narrative and 'Things As They Are.'" *Genre* 10 (1977): 601-17.

Crawford, Iain. "Wading Through Slaughter: John Hampden, Thomas Gray and Mary Shelley's *Frankenstein*." *Studies in the Novel* 20, no. 3 (Fall 1988): 249–61.

Dinnerstein, Dorothy. *The Mermaid and the Minotaur.* New York: Harper and Row, 1976.

Dunn, Jane. *Moon in Eclipse: A Life of Mary Shelley.* New York: St. Martin's Press, 1978.

Dussinger, John A. "Kinship and Guilt in Mary Shelley's *Frankenstein*." *Studies in the Novel* 8 (1976): 38-55.

Ellis, Kate Ferguson. *The Contested Castle: Gothic Novels and the Subversion of Domestic Ideology*. Urbana: University of Illinois Press, 1989.

―――. "Monsters in the Garden: Mary Shelley and the Bourgeois Family." In *The Endurance of Frankenstein*, edited by George Levine and U. C. Knoepflmacher, 123–42. Berkeley: University of California Press, 1979.

―――. "Subversive Surfaces: The Limits of Domestic Affection in Mary Shelley's Later Fiction." In *The Other Mary Shelley*, edited by Audrey Fisch, Anne K. Mellor, and Esther H. Schor, 220–34. New York: Oxford University Press, 1993.

Erikson, Eric. *Identity, Youth and Crisis*. New York: Norton, 1968.

Fisch, Audrey, Anne K. Mellor, and Esther H. Schor, eds. *The Other Mary Shelley*. New York: Oxford University Press, 1993.

Fleck, P. D. "Mary Shelley's Notes to Shelley's Poems and *Frankenstein*." *Studies in Romanticism* 6 (1967): 226–54.

Frank, Ann Marie. "Factitious States: Mary Shelley and the Politics of Early-Nineteenth-Century Women's Identity and Fiction." Ph.D. diss., University of Michigan, 1989.

Frank, Frederick S. "Mary Shelley's *Frankenstein*: A Register of Research." *Bulletin of Bibliography* 40, no. 3 (September 1983): 163–88.

Freud, Sigmund. *The Standard Edition of the Complete Psychological Works of Sigmund Freud*. 24 vols. Translated and edited by James Strachey et al. London: Hogarth Press and The Institute for Psychoanalysis, 1953–74.

Gallop, Jane. *The Daughter's Seduction: Feminism and Psychoanalysis*. Ithaca: Cornell University Press, 1982.

Gilbert, Sandra. "Horror's Twin: Mary Shelley's Monstrous Eve." *Feminist Studies* 4 (1978): 48–73.

―――. "Life's Empty Pack: Notes toward a Literary Daughteronomy." In *Daughters and Fathers*, edited by Lynda Boose and Betty Flowers, 256–77. Baltimore: Johns Hopkins University Press, 1989.

Gilbert, Sandra, and Susan Gubar. *The Madwoman in the Attic*. New Haven: Yale University Press, 1979.

Gilligan, Carol. *In a Different Voice: Psychological Theory and Women's Development*. Cambridge: Harvard University Press, 1982.

Gisborne, Maria. *Maria Gisborne and Edward E. Williams, Shelley's Friends: Their Journals and Letters*. Edited by Frederick L. Jones. Norman: University of Oklahoma Press, 1951.

Grylls, R. Glynn. *Claire Clairmont, Mother of Byron's Allegra*. London: John Murray, 1939.

―――. *Mary Shelley*. Oxford: Oxford University Press, 1938.

Gubar, Susan. "Mother, Maiden, and the Marriage of Death: Women Writers and an Ancient Myth." In *Women and Men: The Consequences of Power*, edited by Dana V. Hiller and Robin Ann Sheets, 386–97. Cincinnati: Office of Women Studies, University of Cincinnati, 1977.

Hatlen, Burton. "Milton, Mary Shelley and Patriarchy." *Bucknell Review: A Scholarly Journal of Letters, Arts, and Science* 28, no. 2 (1983): 19–47.

Harvey, A. D. "*Frankenstein* and *Caleb Williams*." *Keats-Shelley Journal* 29 (1980): 21–27.

Heilbrun, Carolyn. Afterword to *Daughters and Fathers*, edited by Lynda Boose and Betty Flowers, 418–23. Baltimore: Johns Hopkins University Press, 1989.

———. *Reinventing Womanhood*. New York: Norton, 1979.

———. *Writing a Woman's Life*. New York: Norton, 1988.

Hennig, Margaret. *The Managerial Woman*. New York: Doubleday, 1977.

Herman, Judith Lewis, with Lisa Hirschman. *Father-Daughter Incest*. Cambridge: Harvard University Press, 1981.

Hildebrand, William H. "On Three Prometheuses: Shelley's Two and Mary's One." *Serif* 11, no. 2 (1974): 3-11.

Hill, John M. "*Frankenstein* and the Physiognomy of Desire." *American Imago* 32 (1975): 335-58.

Hirsch, Gordon. "The Monster Was a Lady: On the Psychology of Mary Shelley's *Frankenstein*." *Hartford Studies in Literature* 7 (1975): 116-53.

Hodges, Devon. "*Frankenstein* and the Feminine Subversion of the Novel." *Tulsa Studies in Women's Literature* 2, no. 2 (Fall 1983): 155-64.

Hogg, Thomas Jefferson. *The Life of Percy Bysshe Shelley*. With an introduction by Edward Dowden. London: Routledge, 1906.

Holmes, Richard. *Shelley: The Pursuit*. New York: Dutton, 1975.

Homans, Margaret. *Bearing the Word: Language and Female Experience in Nineteenth-Century Women's Writing*. Chicago: University of Chicago Press, 1986.

Hough, Jo, Brenda Hallenbeck, and Francis Simson. "Creator, Created, Creature: A View of Mary Shelley's *Frankenstein*." In *Women Writers and the Literary Tradition*, 22–27. Adelaide: Salisbury College of Advanced Education; SCAE Occasional Papers, 1978.

Jackson, Rosemary. "Narcissism and Beyond: A Psychoanalytic Reading of *Frankenstein* and Fantasies of the Double." In *Aspects of Fantasy: Selected Essays from the Second International Conference on the Fantastic in Literature and Film*, edited by William Coyle, 43–53. Westport, Conn.: Greenwood Press, 1986.

Jacobus, Mary. "Is There a Woman in This Text?" *New Literary History* 14, no. 1 (Autumn 1982): 117–41.

Johnson, Barbara. "My Monster/My Self." *Diacritics: A Review of Contemporary Criticism* 12, no. 2 (Summer 1982): 2–10.

Joseph, Gerhard. "Frankenstein's Dream: The Child as Father of the Monster." *Hartford Studies in Literature* 7 (1975): 97–115.

Kaplan, Morton, and Robert Kloss. "Fantasy of Paternity and the Doppelgänger: Mary Shelley's *Frankenstein*." In *The Unspoken Motive: A Guide to Psychoanalytic Literary Criticism*, 119-45. New York: The Free Press, 1973.

Ketterer, David. *Frankenstein's Creation: The Book, the Monster and the Human Reality*. ELS Monograph Series, no.16. Victoria, B.C., 1979.

Kiceluk, Stephanie. "Made in His Image: Frankenstein's Daughters." *Michigan Quarterly Review* 30:1 (Winter 1991): 110-26.

Kiely, Robert. *The Romantic Novel in England*. Cambridge: Harvard University Press, 1972.

Knoepflmacher, U. C. "On Exile and Fiction: The Leweses and Shelleys." In *Mothering the Mind: Twelve Studies of Writers and Their Silent Partners*, edited by Ruth Perry and Martine Watson Browneley, 102–21. New York: Holmes and Meier, 1984.

———. "Thoughts on the Aggression of Daughters." In *The Endurance of Frankenstein*, edited by George Levine and U. C. Knoepflmacher, 88–119. Berkeley: University of California Press, 1979.

Lamb, Charles. *Letters of Charles and Mary Lamb*. 3 vols. Edited by Edwin W. Marrs, Jr. Ithaca: Cornell University Press, 1975.

Lane, Maggie. *Literary Daughters*. London: Robert Hale, 1989.

Leonard, Marjorie. "Fathers and Daughters: The Significance of 'Fathering' in the Psychosexual Development of the Girl." *International Journal of Psychoanalysis* 47 (1966): 325–34.

Levine, George, and U. C. Knoepflmacher, eds. *The Endurance of Frankenstein*. Berkeley: University of California Press, 1979.

———. "*Frankenstein* and the Tradition of Realism." *Novel* 7 (1973): 14-30.

Lew, Joseph W. "God's Sister: History and Ideology in *Valperga*." In *The Other Mary Shelley*, edited by Audrey Fisch, Anne K. Mellor, and Esther H. Schor, 159–81. New York: Oxford University Press, 1993.

Locke, Don. *A Fantasy of Reason: The Life and Thought of William Godwin*. London: Routledge & Kegan Paul, 1980.

London, Bette. "Mary Shelley, *Frankenstein*, and the Spectacle of Masculinity." *Publications of the Modern Language Association* 108, no. 2 (March 1993): 253–67.

Lund, Mary Graham. "Mary Godwin Shelley and the Monster." *University of Kansas City Review* 28 (1962): 253-58.

———. "Shelley as Frankenstein." *Forum* 4, no. 2 (1963): 28–31.

Lyles, W. H. *Mary Shelley: An Annotated Bibliography*. New York: Garland, 1975.

McGann, Jerome. *The Romantic Ideology—A Critical Investigation*. Chicago: University of Chicago Press, 1983.

McInerney, Peter. "*Frankenstein* and the Godlike Science of Letters." *Genre* 13 (1980): 455–75.

———. "Satanic Conceits in *Frankenstein* and *Wuthering Heights*." *Milton and the Romantics* 4 (1980): 1–15.

McKinley, Virginia Susan Gallaher. "Rendering up 'The Tale of What We Are': Gothic Narrative Methods in Selected Novels of Godwin, Brown and Shelley." Ph.D. diss., Michigan State University, 1986.

Macpherson, Jay. *The Spirit of Solitude*. New Haven: Yale University Press, 1982.

Marshall, Florence A. (Mrs. Julian). *The Life and Letters of Mary Wollstonecraft Shelley*. London: Bentley, 1889.

Marshall, Peter H. *William Godwin*. New Haven: Yale University Press, 1984.

Massey, Irving. *The Gaping Pig*. Berkeley: University of California Press, 1976.

May, Marilyn. "Publish and Perish: William Godwin, Mary Shelley, and the Public Appetite for Scandal." *Papers on Language and Literature: A Journal for Scholars and Critics* 26, no. 4 (Fall 1990): 489–512.

Mellor, Anne K. *Mary Shelley: Her Life, Her Fiction, Her Monsters.* New York: Methuen, 1988.

———. "Possessing Nature: The Female in *Frankenstein.*" In *Romanticism and Feminism*, edited by Anne K. Mellor, 220–32. Bloomington: Indiana University Press, 1988.

———. *Romanticism and Gender.* New York: Routledge, 1993.

Moers, Ellen. "Female Gothic." In *The Endurance of Frankenstein*, edited by George Levine and U. C. Knoepflmacher, 77-87. Berkeley: University of California Press, 1979.

Myers, Mitzi. "Godwin's *Memoirs of Mary Wollstonecraft:* The Shaping of Self and Subject." *Studies in Romanticism* 20 (Fall 1981): 299–316.

Newlyn, Lucy. "In the Shadow of Men." Review of *Mary Shelley: Her Life, Her Fiction, Her Monsters*, by Anne K. Mellor. *Times Literary Supplement*, 17 February 1989, 171.

Newman, Beth. "Narratives of Seduction and the Seductions of Narrative: The Frame Structure of *Frankenstein.*" *English Literary History* 53, no. 1 (Spring 1986): 141–63.

Nitchie, Elizabeth. *Mary Shelley.* New Brunswick, N. J.: Rutgers University Press, 1953.

———. "Mary Shelley's *Mathilda:* An Unpublished Story and Its Biographical Significance." *Studies in Philology* 40 (July 1943): 447–62.

Nochlin, Linda. "Why Are There No Great Women Artists?" In *Women in a Sexist Society*, edited by Vivian Gornick and Barbara K. Moran, 480–510. New York: Basic Books, 1971.

Norman, Sylva. *On Shelley.* Oxford: Oxford University Press, 1938.

Oates, Joyce Carol. "Frankenstein's Fallen Angel." *Critical Inquiry* 10, no. 3 (March 1984): 543–54.

Opie, Iona, and Peter Opie, eds. *A Nursery Companion.* Oxford: Oxford University Press, 1980.

O'Sullivan, Barbara Jane. "Beatrice in *Valperga:* A New Cassandra." In *The Other Mary Shelley*, edited by Audrey Fisch, Anne K. Mellor, and Esther H. Schor, 140–58. New York: Oxford University Press, 1993.

Owen, Ursula, ed. *Fathers: Reflections by Daughters.* New York: Pantheon, 1985.

Palacio, Jean de. *Mary Shelley dans son oeuvre.* Paris: Klincksieck, 1969.

Parsons, T. *Family, Socialization and Interaction Process.* New York: The Free Press, 1955.

Patterson, Mary Katherine. "*Frankenstein* by Mary Shelley: Notes on a Divided Myth." Ph.D. diss., Ball State University, 1984.

Paul, C. Kegan. *William Godwin: His Friends and Contemporaries.* 2 vols. London: Henry S. King, 1876.

Peck, Walter E. "The Biographical Element in the Novels of Mary Wollstonecraft Shelley." *Publications of the Modern Language Association* 38 (1923): 196-219.

Pollin, Burton. "Philosophical and Literary Sources of *Frankenstein.*" *Comparative Literature* 17 (1965): 97-108.

Poovey, Mary. "Fathers and Daughters: The Trauma of Growing Up Female." *Women and Literature.* 2 (1982): 39–58.

————. "'My Hideous Progeny': Mary Shelley and the Feminization of Romanticism." *Publications of the Modern Language Association* 95 (1980): 332–47.

————. *The Proper Lady and the Woman Writer*. Chicago: University of Chicago Press, 1984.

Powers, Katherine Richardson. *The Influence of William Godwin on the Novels of Mary Shelley*. New York: Arno Press, 1980.

Randal, Fred V. "*Frankenstein*, Feminism and the Intertextuality of Mountains." *Studies in Romanticism* 23, no. 4 (Winter 1984): 515–32.

Reiman, Donald H., Michael C. Jaye, and Betty T. Bennett, eds. *The Evidence of the Imagination*. New York: New York University Press, 1978.

Richardson, Alan. "From *Emile* to *Frankenstein:* The Education of Monsters." *European Romantic Review* 1, no. 2 (Winter 1991): 147–62.

————. "*Proserpine* and *Midas:* Gender, Genre, and Mythic Revisionism in Mary Shelley's Dramas." In *The Other Mary Shelley*, edited by Audrey Fisch, Anne K. Mellor, and Esther H. Schor, 124–39. New York: Oxford University Press, 1993.

Rubenstein, Marc. "My Accursed Origin: The Search for the Mother in *Frankenstein*." *Studies in Romanticism* 15 (Spring 1976): 165–94.

St. Clair, William. *The Godwins and the Shelleys: A Biography of a Family*. Baltimore: Johns Hopkins University Press, 1989.

Scott, Peter Dale. "Vital Artifice: Mary, Percy, and the Psychopolitical Integrity of *Frankenstein*." In *The Endurance of Frankenstein*, edited by George Levine and U. C. Knoepflmacher, 172–202. Berkeley: University of California Press, 1979.

Seed, David. "Frankenstein: Parable of Spectacle?" *Criticism: A Quarterly for Literature and the Arts* 24, no. 4 (Fall 1982): 327–40.

Seidenberg, Robert, and Evangelos Papathomopoulos. "Daughters Who Tend Their Fathers: A Literary Survey." *Psychoanalytic Study of Society* 2 (1962): 135–60.

Shelley, Lady Jane, ed. *Shelley and Mary*. 4 vols. Privately printed, 1882.

Shelley, Percy Bysshe. *The Letters of Percy Bysshe Shelley*. 2 vols. Edited by Frederick L. Jones. Oxford: Oxford University Press, 1964.

————. *Shelley: Poetical Works*. Edited by Thomas Hutchinson. London: Oxford University Press, 1970.

Sherwin, Paul. "*Frankenstein:* Creation as Catastrophe." *Publications of the Modern Language Association* 96, no. 5 (October 1981): 883–903.

Showalter, Elaine. *A Literature of Their Own*. Princeton: Princeton University Press, 1977.

Simms, Karl N. "Caleb Williams' Godwin: Things as They are Written." *Studies in Romanticism* 26, no. 3 (Fall 1987): 343–63.

Small, Christopher. *Mary Shelley's Frankenstein: Tracing the Myth*. Pittsburgh: University of Pittsburgh Press, 1973.

Smith, Susan Harris. "*Frankenstein:* Mary Shelley's Psychic Divisiveness." *Women and Literature* 5 (1977): 42–53.

Southey, Robert. *The Life and Correspondence of Robert Southey*. 6 vols. Edited by C. C. Southey. London: Longman, 1850.

Spark, Muriel. *Mary Shelley: A Biography*. New York: E. P. Dutton, 1987.

Spector, Judith A. "Science Fiction and the Sex War: A Womb of One's Own." *Literature and Psychology* 31, no. 1 (1981): 21–32.

Sunstein, Emily W. *A Different Face: The Life of Mary Wollstonecraft*. New York: Harper and Row, 1975.

———. *Mary Shelley: Romance and Reality*. Boston: Little, Brown, 1989.

Thornburg, Mary K. Patterson. *The Monster in the Mirror: Gender and the Sentimental/Gothic Myth in "Frankenstein."* Studies in Speculative Fiction 14. Ann Arbor: University Microfilms International Research Press, 1987.

Tillotson, Marcia. "'A Forced Solitude': Mary Shelley and the Creation of Frankenstein's Monster." In *The Female Gothic*, edited by Julian E. Fleenor, 167–75. Montreal: Eden, 1983.

Tippy, Gilbert. "Feminine Rage in Mary Shelley." Greenvale, N.Y.: C. W. Post College, Long Island University, 1991.

Todd, Janet M. "Frankenstein's Daughter: Mary Shelley and Mary Wollstonecraft." *Women and Literature* 4 (1976): 18–27.

Tomalin, Claire. *The Life and Death of Mary Wollstonecraft*. New York: Harcourt, Brace, 1974.

Twitchell, James B. "*Frankenstein* and the Anatomy of Horror." *Georgia Review* 37 (1983): 41–78.

Veeder, William. *Mary Shelley and Frankenstein: The Fate of Androgyny*. Chicago: University of Chicago Press, 1986.

———. "The Negative Oedipus: Father, *Frankenstein* and the Shelleys." *Critical Inquiry* 12, no. 2 (Winter 1986): 365–90.

Vlasopolos, Anca. "*Frankenstein*'s Hidden Skeleton: The Psycho-Politics of Oppression." *Science Fiction Studies* 10, no. 2 (July 1983): 125-36.

Walling, William. *Mary Shelley*. Twayne's English Author Series 128. New York: Twayne, 1972.

Wardle, Ralph M., ed. *Godwin and Mary: Letters of William Godwin and Mary Wollstonecraft*. Lincoln: University of Nebraska Press, 1966.

Waxman, Barbary Frey. "Victor Frankenstein's Romantic Fate: The Tragedy of the Promethean Overreacher as Woman." *Papers on Language and Literature: A Journal for Scholars and Critics of Language and Literature* 23, no. 1 (Winter 1987): 14–26.

Wexelblatt, Robert. "The Ambivalence of *Frankenstein*." *Arizona Quarterly* 36 (1980): 101-17.

White, Newman Ivey. *Shelley*. 2 vols. New York: Alfred A. Knopf, 1947.

Willbern, David. "*Filia Oedipi:* Father and Daughter in Freudian Theory." In *Daughters and Fathers*, edited by Lynda Boose and Betty Flowers, 75–96. Baltimore: Johns Hopkins University Press, 1989.

Wollstonecraft, Mary. *Mary, A Fiction and The Wrongs of Woman*. Edited by Gary Kelly. Oxford: Oxford University Press, 1976.

———. *Thoughts on the Education of Daughters: With Reflections on Female Conduct in the More Important Duties of Life*. London: J. Johnson, 1787.

—————. *A Vindication of the Rights of Woman.* Edited by Carol H. Poston. New York: W. W. Norton, 1975.

Yaeger, Patricia, and Beth Kowalski-Wallace, eds. *Refiguring the Father: New Feminist Readings of Patriarchy.* Carbondale and Edwardsville: Southern Illinois University Press, 1989.

Youngquist, Paul. "*Frankenstein:* The Mother, the Daughter, and the Monster." *Philological Quarterly* 70, no. 3 (Summer 1991): 339-59.

Zonona, Joyce. "'They Will Prove the Truth of My Tale': Safie's Letters as the Feminist Core of Mary Shelley's *Frankenstein.*" *Journal of Narrative Technique* 21, no. 2 (Spring 1991): 170–84.

Zwinger, Lynda. *Daughters, Fathers, and the Novel: The Sentimental Romance of Heterosexuality.* Madison: University of Wisconsin Press, 1991.

Index